COERCED LIBERATION

Muslim Women in Soviet Tajikistan

In 1924, the Bolshevik regime began an unprecedented campaign to forcibly emancipate the Muslim women of Tajikistan. The emancipatory reforms included unveiling women, passing progressive family code laws, and educating women. By the 1950s, the Soviet regime largely succeeded in putting an end to veiling, child marriage, polygamy, and bride payments. Yet today there is a resurgence in these practices the Bolsheviks claimed to have eliminated. *Coerced Liberation* reveals that the Soviet regime transformed the lives of urban women within a single generation but without lasting effect.

Drawing on unique primary sources, the book examines why this occurred. It addresses questions that are pertinent to ongoing debates in the international arena: What happens when an outside force attempts to modernize a society deeply rooted in centuries of patriarchal norms and values? In what ways can a devout religious rural community respond to, survive, and adapt to such interventions? And how does a state-centred, top-down approach towards women's emancipation work?

Coerced Liberation presents critical insights for readers interested in gender dynamics within Muslim communities, the roles of women in Islam, the resurgence of Islam in former colonial territories, the effectiveness of a top-down approach towards women's movements, and more.

ZAMIRA ABMAN is an assistant professor in the Departments of History and European Studies at San Diego State University.

Coerced Liberation

Muslim Women in Soviet Tajikistan

ZAMIRA ABMAN

UNIVERSITY OF TORONTO PRESS
Toronto Buffalo London

© University of Toronto Press 2024
Toronto Buffalo London
utorontopress.com
Printed in the USA

ISBN 978-1-4875-5318-0 (paper)   ISBN 978-1-4875-5321-0 (EPUB)
ISBN 978-1-4875-5320-3 (PDF)

Library and Archives Canada Cataloguing in Publication

Title: Coerced liberation : Muslim women in Soviet Tajikistan /
   Zamira Abman.
Other titles: Muslim women in Soviet Tajikistan
Names: Abman, Zamira, author.
Description: Includes bibliographical references and index.
Identifiers: Canadiana (print) 20230587666 | Canadiana (ebook)
   20230587712 | ISBN 9781487553180 (paper) | ISBN 9781487553203 (PDF) |
   ISBN 9781487553210 (EPUB)
Subjects: LCSH: Muslim women – Tajikistan – History – 20th century. |
   LCSH: Muslim women – Government policy – Tajikistan – History –
   20th century. | LCSH: Women in Islam – Tajikistan – History –
   20th century.
Classification: LCC HQ1170 .A26 2024 | DDC 305.48/697095860904—dc23

Cover design: Liz Harasymczuk
Cover image: Photograph from Alexander Rodchenko and Varvara Stepanova,
eds. and photographers, *A Pageant of Youth* (Moscow: State Art Publishers, 1939).

We wish to acknowledge the land on which the University of Toronto
Press operates. This land is the traditional territory of the Wendat, the
Anishnaabeg, the Haudenosaunee, the Métis, and the Mississaugas of the
Credit First Nation.

University of Toronto Press acknowledges the financial support of the
Government of Canada, the Canada Council for the Arts, and the Ontario Arts
Council, an agency of the Government of Ontario, for its publishing activities.

Canada Council   Conseil des Arts
for the Arts   du Canada

ONTARIO ARTS COUNCIL
CONSEIL DES ARTS DE L'ONTARIO
an Ontario government agency
un organisme du gouvernement de l'Ontario

Funded by the   Financé par le
Government   gouvernement
of Canada   du Canada

Canadä

I dedicate this book to my husband and best friend, Ryan Abman.

Contents

Illustrations

Acknowledgments

As the first woman to leave my community to pursue a degree in the United States, I felt the need to tell the stories of women whose lives were shaped by extraordinary circumstances. I am grateful to all my interviewees for trusting me with their stories.

I fell in love with the discipline of history in the fourth grade. My history teacher, mualima Usmanova, was the source of my inspiration. During the civil war in Tajikistan from 1992 to 1997, I, like many of my peers, attended school infrequently. Yet I retained the fondest memories of being in the classroom and learning from mualima Usmanova. At the American University of Central Asia (AUCA), I learned to think critically and did my best to unlearn the Soviet memorization approach to learning. Professors who contributed to this process include Bill Hansen, Vanessa Rouget, John Heathershow, and Louis Petrich.

While pursuing a graduate degree at the University of Notre Dame, I took a course on Central Asian politics with Kathleen Collins. My lifelong friendship with Kathleen led me to stay in the United States after completing my degree. She showed me the difference a single individual can make in the lives of others. Through her support and mentorship, I was able to gain a job to provide for myself and my family in Tajikistan, which in turn showed many in my community back home that girls equipped with education can financially support themselves and their families. Today this change can be seen in the hundreds of female students from Tajikistan who are pursuing education at AUCA. When I attended AUCA in the 2000s, I was the only student from Tajikistan who was not from Pamir, in the Gorno-Badakhshan region. Students from this part of Tajikistan were generally recipients of the Agha Khan Scholarship.

While pursuing a PhD in history, I relied on my adviser, Adrienne Edgar, for mentorship. I am grateful for her dedication to her students and profession.

A number of colleagues at San Diego State University provided me with much needed advice and guidance throughout the process of writing this book. I am also very grateful to the many incredible students I got to work with. With the assistance of two anonymous reviewers, I significantly enhanced the manuscript. My editor at the University of Toronto Press, Stephen Shapiro, also played a pivotal role in the publication of this book. He expertly guided me through the publication process and provided invaluable mentorship and guidance.

This book would not have happened without my immediate family members, including my mother, Khosiyat Yusupjonova, who accompanied me to most of my interviews and worked with me at the Communist Party Archives. Despite family and neighbours telling her not to allow me to pursue education abroad, she was not afraid to break from the established gender norms. I am also grateful to my sister Zebo Nurmatova, who transcribed and, in some cases, translated my oral history interviews. It was through her social network that I was able to locate many of my interviewees. My sister Umeda Yusupova kept me informed with social news, helping me navigate my way through the many gender norms while in Tajikistan. She connected me with numerous women in the countryside who were willing to talk to me only because they knew Umeda.

My family in the United States was tremendously helpful in supporting me and my work. I am grateful to my brother-in-law Mark Abman and his wife, Mary Zost, for their continuous support with editing my writing. When I taught my first Soviet and Russian history course, my beloved sister-in-law Lauren Abman, who spent a few years in Russia studying and producing art, provided me with ideas on how to include Russian art and literature in my curriculum, further adding to my love of teaching and researching this part of the world. I am grateful to my mother-in-law, Carolyn Abman, for being a source of inspiration as a female professional, mother, friend, and more. My father-in-law, Steve Abman, whose sense of humour has always cheered me up, is another an endless source of inspiration.

Life got busier but much better with the arrival of my two daughters, Alina Carolyn Abman and Isla Lola Abman.

I dedicate this book to my best friend, my life partner, my greatest support system: my husband, Ryan Abman. This book would not have happened without him telling me that I could do it.

COERCED LIBERATION

Introduction

I was born and raised in Tajikistan.[1] I grew up listening to stories of my grandmother, who witnessed the Bolshevik takeover of the region and lived through the Soviet rule of Tajikistan (1917–90).[2] She never attended a day of school in her life and remained illiterate. At her wedding, she wore a thick veil made of horsehair that covered her entire body. In 1924, the Bolsheviks freed the women of her village from involuntary seclusion, forced them to unveil, and made primary education mandatory for boys and girls alike. My mother, after completing her secondary education, continued her studies and obtained a degree in nursing. She was married in a short, sleeveless, white, European-style dress. The lives of women in Tajikistan had completely transformed in one generation. Yet immediately after the collapse of the Soviet Union, a significant number of Tajik women took up veiling, polygamous marriages became common, the marriage age for girls steadily fell, and many families chose to homeschool their girls.

This book examines why the extraordinary interventions by the Bolshevik regime did not have a lasting effect. In doing so, it addresses questions that are pertinent to ongoing debates in the international arena: What happens when an outside force attempts to modernize a society with deeply rooted, centuries-old patriarchal norms and values? In what ways can a devout religious rural community respond to, survive, and adapt to such interventions? And how does a state-centric, top-down approach to women's emancipation work?

Women's Emancipation in the Soviet Union

The primary goal behind the Soviet emancipation campaign was the creation of a modern communist state where all citizens would receive the same education, absorb the same ideology, and identify with the

Soviet state as a whole.[3] Throughout the Soviet Union, beginning in the 1920s, the regime enacted changes in family law, provided women with education and employment, and encouraged their participation in public life.[4] In Central Asia, the Bolsheviks focused on the liberation of Muslim women by combating practices such as the wearing of the veil (*paranji* in Tajik and Uzbek). The regime regarded unveiling and progressive family and marriage reforms as a way to bring women into the public sphere and introduce them into the workforce, a prerequisite for their Sovietization and subsequent modernization.[5]

By the 1950s, the Soviet regime largely succeeded in putting an end to veiling, polygamy, child marriages, and bride payments (*kalym/kiit* in Tajik) in urban areas.[6] The Soviet regime's top-down approach to the emancipation of Muslim women in Tajikistan dramatically transformed the life experiences of urban women in a single generation. Those who benefitted from the regime's reforms became educated professionals who experienced the excitement of being pioneers.[7] However, these reforms failed to reach rural women who comprised the majority of the Muslim female population in Tajikistan. Socio-economic circumstances, cultural norms, and a residency system limited rural women's ability to migrate to urban areas.

Women and girls who remained in the rural areas of Tajikistan had the lowest level of education, the highest rate of early marriage, and the highest birth rate in the entire Soviet Union.[8] Rural girls with only primary education tended to marry earlier, which meant longer fertility periods and large families in rural Tajikistan. After marriage, rural women had to combine their responsibilities at home, including child-rearing, with full-time work, typically manual labour jobs in the agrarian sector. Unlike rural men, married women and women with children rarely pursued education or professional training after marriage, so they did not typically enjoy vertical mobility and tended to remain in the same job for extended periods. Due to a lack of government support in the form of daycare facilities and social welfare programs, rural women regularly had to rely on their daughters' help with household chores and caring for younger siblings. These responsibilities in turn often prevented rural girls from completing secondary school and continuing their education in urban areas. These circumstances trapped rural girls and women in subservient positions at work and at home, reinforcing existing patriarchal social structures in the region.

Women who did urbanize became a separate category within a predominantly agrarian population based on their dramatic transformation in appearance and education. They were commonly regarded as "Sovietized" and "Russified" (*obrusevshaia* in Russian). This label alienated them from the least Sovietized segment of the population, rural Muslim women in Tajikistan, who perceived indigenous, urban women as culturally different. Detached from their own – namely, rural women – and in competition with Slavic women for career opportunities, indigenous women professionals remained a small minority with limited authority within patriarchal political structures. Migrants from the western parts of the USSR, Russian women in particular, had an advantage over Muslim female cadres in terms of professional opportunities and advancement, since they did not have to meet the social expectations placed on Tajik women. These included notions of women's modesty and shame (*nomus/sharm* in Tajik). This was especially expected of indigenous women professionals, who were made showcases of Soviet emancipation but who also continued to symbolize the female image of their ethnic community.[9]

Based on the established social norms, Muslim women leaders had to prioritize familial responsibilities and display a more casual commitment to their careers. Because these women leaders were expected to retain their feminine qualities, they could not compete with men in the corrupt system of giving bribes to secure appointments and ensure promotions, and they were prohibited to socialize for the purpose of networking in spaces exclusively designated for men (such as Tajik tea houses).[10] These and other circumstances limited Tajik women leaders' authority in political and social arenas. Muslim men and women equally enforced these expectations on indigenous Tajik women. Yet for Muslim women leaders, ignoring established norms was not an option. Those who attempted to disregard these expectations were barred from professional opportunities. While Muslim women leaders were trapped between their overwhelming professional responsibilities and extensive social norms, many displayed unfailing loyalty to the regime.[11] The heavy professional and personal burdens borne by Tajik women leaders proved unappealing for Muslim girls. Families often prevented their daughters from following in the footsteps of Tajik women leaders.

The Soviet regime's administration of Muslim periphery was a unique social experiment because, unlike modernization campaigns around the Middle East, the Soviet campaign was launched by a multiethnic state where power was centralized in a distant capital, Moscow. It is the only campaign that gives a glimpse into the workings of similar campaigns since there have been numerous calls made to assist Muslim women around the Middle East in ending patriarchal gender norms through outside intervention.[12] Even though these calls never led to extensive outside involvement comparable to the Soviet campaign, this case study provides invaluable lessons on a top-down approach to the women's movement and state feminism in general.

Despite this relevance, Tajikistan remains one of the least understood countries in the world. This is due to the fact that the Muslim regions of the former Soviet Union remain inaccessible to most scholars. Central Asian republics are ruled by increasingly authoritarian regimes that have restricted foreign scholars' access to national archives and even to the country. Thirty-two years after the end of the Cold War and the opening of the region, there is still no established narrative of the Soviet reforms aimed at Muslim women's liberation in Tajikistan. This book addresses this shortcoming. *Coerced Liberation* is the first study to examine the Soviet campaign to liberate Muslim women in Central Asia from its inception through the post-war period. Several scholars have looked at the early stages of the Bolshevik effort to emancipate Muslim women. For instance, the works of Gregory Massell, Douglas Northrop, and Marianne Kamp focus on the Bolshevik emancipation of Muslim women campaign of the 1920s and 1930s.[13] This existing scholarship mostly focuses only on Uzbekistan. There is no literature on the post–Second World War Soviet strategy towards Central Asian women. Only by examining the campaign from its beginnings through the post-war era are we able to understand what happened and why state-enforced feminism achieved only limited success in Tajikistan.[14]

The Soviet campaign to liberate Muslim women is the only historical example of state feminism launched by a multi-ethnic state led from the capital city. For this and other reasons, some scholars including Massell and Northrop have compared the Soviet emancipatory reforms in Muslim Central Asia to Western European colonial policies in the Middle East and North Africa in the late nineteenth centuries.[15] In the 1930s, Atatürk's statist reforms, like the Bolshevik efforts in Central Asia, attempted to modernize Turkey by transforming the ethnically and religiously diverse Anatolia into a more homogenous Turkish nation.[16] Similarly, the Soviet campaign in the Muslim periphery, as Khalid explains cannot be categorized as "an encounter between 'Soviet' outsiders and an authentic, indigenous population, or even simply between 'state' and 'society.'" Tajikistan, like other Central Asian societies in this period, was divided into numerous groups and subgroups.[17]

No colonial power attempted extensive interventions aimed at women's liberation similar to the Soviet reforms in Central Asia, including women's education and legal equality.[18] But because the Soviet women's emancipation program was state-centred and happened without feminist pressures from below, there is a continuous debate regarding women's agency within it.[19] According to Shoshana Keller, in Uzbekistan, women were "trapped between state and society" in the *khujum*.[20] During an era of authoritarianism, women often felt pressure to either keep or remove their veil. Some women kept their veil due to the influence of family and community, while others removed it as a result of state-mandated campaigns. This was a time when individuals had limited ability to resist or challenge authority, whether it was official or informal.[21]

The Soviet Union sought the same transformation for all women without differentiating between metropole and periphery. Rural women in Soviet Russia equally had to undergo the emancipation campaign. The emancipation of women was part of an effort to create a uniform state where all residents would receive the same education, immerse in the same ideology, and identify as Soviet citizens.[22] This was part of a modern state-building strategy to eradicate traditional social structures based on kin and tribal ties and to replace these with a Soviet identity.[23] In this regard, the Soviet campaign to emancipate women bore resemblance to reforms in the Middle East.[24]

Women's Emancipation beyond the Soviet Union

These campaigns took place around the same time, and the modernization reforms targeted women first and foremost. These countries were ruled by different regimes: Atatürk, a charismatic war hero, presided over Turkey; in Iran and Afghanistan, modernizing monarchs ruled; and in Central Asia and the Caucasus, it was the Bolshevik regime. For the nationalists, modernizing and secularizing elites, unveiling, and marriage reforms became key symbols of modernity and a central element in an emerging national character. As a result, these regimes portrayed their authoritarian campaigns as both essential to the modernization process and liberating in nature.[25] Both elite nationalists and communists shared a common opposition to what they perceived as oppressive forces of Islam and traditional customs. Their objective was to create a new and modern perception of women who were educated, unveiled, and part of the workforce.[26]

In Turkey, similar to Soviet Central Asia, the reforms included the passing of liberal family code laws and introduction of mandatory primary education for Muslim women.[27] The Bolshevik campaign leaders also saw women's entry into paid employment as the key to their emancipation and a prerequisite for modernization.[28] The gender reforms were designed to foster socialism through rapid industrialization, universal education, vocational training, and social welfare that would include childcare, communal dining halls, and laundry rooms.

The regime focused on the liberation of Muslim women through bat-
tling Islamic traditions such as the practice of veiling, while in other
parts of the Soviet Union the state promoted fewer radical reforms. Russian peasants also had to undergo cultural transformation and faced an
attack on their religious practices.[29]

The main agenda behind the Bolshevik regime's drastic emancipatory reforms in Central Asia was the abolition of feudal practices and
traditions that oppressed Muslim women and created obstacles to the
construction of socialism in the region. Unveiling and progressive gender
reforms were a way to bring women into the public arena and introduce
them into the labour force. The regime viewed this as a prerequisite
for state modernization.[30] Muslim women's veiling became not only a
symbol of women's oppression but also clear evidence of the presence
of Islam in the region. Thus, the women's unveiling campaign was associated with a victory against Islam and the feudal past. For this reason,
the campaign is often described as a grand project.[31] The Soviet regime
aimed to introduce gender equality to all its citizens, which made the
campaign the most radical approach to achieving gender equality of
any before or since.[32]

Despite its grand aims for gender equality, the outcome of the Soviet
campaign to emancipate Muslim women more closely resembled that
of the Muslim regions in the Middle East and North Africa that had
been colonized by Western European powers. The Soviet state was a
multi-ethnic state centred in Moscow. The regime expected the emancipation of Muslim women to serve as a precursor to modernization,
yet it came into conflict with nationalism. Like Muslim women in the
Arab world, women in Central Asia considered religious marriage
ceremonies and traditional practices integral parts of their "national
identity."[33] The independent regimes in Turkey and Iran had a certain
national legitimacy that the Soviet regime simply could not create for
itself in the eyes of its Muslim citizens. The "national delimitation" of
Central Asia in 1924–5 increased this "legitimacy gap," as over time
Soviet ethnic categorization policies solidified the distinction between
"indigenous" Muslims of the titular nationality and "alien" Europeans
within each republic.[34]

Unlike the Soviet Union, the reforming states in Iran and Turkey
enjoyed greater support from local actors, including some women who
were already involved in political, intellectual, and educational activities, and shared a broad modernizing perspective. However, despite
this broader support base, the majority of women in both countries, particularly those in rural areas, did not back the reforms. In Turkey, Kemal
Atatürk made deliberate efforts to mobilize women as leadership for

its campaigns. In Iran, a new elite organization, the Kanun-i Banuvan (Ladies' Society), was created to promote women's liberation. The Iranian leadership mobilized military elites and sought support of *ulama* members, invoking Islamic modernism in its unveiling campaign.[35] In contrast to Iran, the *khujum* campaign in Soviet Central Asia played a crucial role in the regime's fight against religion and local religious authorities. The act of unveiling was seen as a significant blow to the traditional way of life, part of a continuous class war and revolutionary transformation. It was an essential part of the project to create a new Soviet woman to complement the new Soviet man.[36] In Central Asia, however, the Communist Party did little to mobilize or prepare local cadres to support or administer the emancipation of women campaign. Women's emancipation in the Muslim-majority periphery was advocated primarily by leaders in Moscow and carried out by Slavic activists within the Zhenotdel (short for *zhenskii otdel*), the Women's Department of the party's Central Committee. So, indigenous regimes in Turkey and Iran had a certain national legitimacy that the Soviet regime simply did not have and could not successfully create.[37]

Like the state feminism campaigns launched in Turkey, Tunisia, Iran, Afghanistan, and Morocco, the campaign in Tajikistan took place without much bottom-up support for change. As Kristen Ghodsee illustrates in her case study of socialist Bulgaria, women's accomplishments cannot be dismissed due to the lack of bottom-up pressures, women's affiliation with the state, or their prioritization of socialism over feminism. Bulgarian beneficiaries of the state feminism campaign were able to achieve significant progress in the spheres of education, health care, and employment for women.[38] Similarities between state-led campaigns in Soviet Tajikistan and Tunisia suggests that even if state-led "women-friendly" reforms fail to have the intended effect on legislation aimed at advancing women's rights, they can still generate a new climate for gender. In Tunisia, they contributed to the emergence of a social movement of women in the 1950s, which defended women's rights in the 1980s, and had influence over the reforms of the early 1990s.[39] Most importantly, once Tunisia became known as a women-friendly country, it became a matter of national pride and international reputation to continue on this path.[40] Conversely, the Soviet emancipatory reforms in Tajikistan did not produce comparable outcomes, namely women's movements or advocates of women's rights in post-Soviet Tajikistan. *Coerced Liberation* explains what went wrong in the Soviet campaign in Tajikistan.

Although the Soviet reforms did not produce the same cultural changes as in Tunisia and Turkey, the Bolshevik emancipation reforms in Tajikistan nonetheless changed the conditions of women. The Soviet reforms increased educational rates among Muslim girls and women from 1–2 per cent to 97 per cent.[41] Muslim women entered the labour force, obtained various legal rights, including rights to vote, to divorce, to receive inheritance, and other privileges.[42] These developments were unimaginable prior to the Bolshevik emancipatory reforms. In spite of the violent backlash resulting from the Bolshevik emancipation campaign in the 1920s, some Muslim women adopted the Soviet ideology in the 1930s. Even if in small numbers and mostly in urban areas, Tajik and Uzbek women took up leadership roles within the government. These women were a product of the Zhenotdel's activism in the country in the 1920s and the regime's nativization policy.[43] Based on this policy, known in Russian as *korenizatsiia*, the regime advanced indigenous men and women into administrative positions in the borderland territories. The role of local actors, male and female, helps counter Massell's argument that the Soviet regime did not include indigenous people in its rule of Central Asia.[44] In fact, the regime fostered local cadres and put them in positions of authority, particularly in the women's liberation campaign. This tactic was driven by the communist ideology that opposed imperialism and by the regime's belief that it would quell potential nationalistic aspirations in the borderland areas.[45] *Coerced Liberation* focuses on stories and experiences of local actors and illustrates their vital role in the progression and the outcome of the campaign.

While the 1920s and 1930s exhibited ideological change because of the Bolshevik takeover of the region, the greatest evidence of the impact on women came later. During these two decades, the Bolshevik strategy towards the women of Central Asia mostly involved rhetorical slogans and propaganda calling on Muslim women to unveil and become active members of society. The more substantial change came about from the post-1935 period. During the Second World War, Central Asian women, including the Muslim women of Tajikistan, were forced to replace men in the workforce. This led to their massive unveiling and a transition to Tajik- and European-style clothing. Only in the post-war period was the regime able to effectively put an end to practices such as polygamy, child marriages, and bride payments. A significantly higher percentage of Tajik girls entered primary school (compared to the earlier period, 1920s–30s) and completed secondary education from the 1950s to the 1980s. It was in the post-war period that some of the successes and failures of the earlier Bolshevik emancipation of Central Asian women campaign of the 1920s became apparent. To analyse the full extent and impact of these reforms, it is essential to examine the post–Second World War period.

This case study addresses the important gaps in the current scholarship and contributes to the literature on the Soviet emancipation of the Muslim women of Central Asia and Tajikistan. By doing so, this study adds to the literature on gender and colonialism, Marxist/socialist feminism, and state feminism. With sources including a previously unexplored archive (the Communist Party Archive of the Tajik Republic), oral history interviews, and Soviet propaganda, this book examines the Soviet emancipation reforms, how the regime's motivations changed over time, and how women continued practices associated with Islam even while participating in the workforce and taking pride in their Soviet identity. It is in the post-1935 era that we see women develop a new understanding of gender.[46] They actively expressed these new perceptions of their roles through hard labour in the workplace. Women came to believe in their individual contribution in their nation's economic prosperity. The Stalinist regime directed women's new understanding of gender towards collectivization of the countryside and industrialization of urban areas.[47]

Yet the Soviet regime's transformation of Muslim women was filled with contradictory approaches and outcomes. From their inception, Soviet state policies on the family fluctuated based on political and economic needs. In the 1920s, the Bolshevik regime based its approach to gender on the radical Marxist theory. The state aimed to weaken the institution of marriage and liberate women from household chores by making these chores a communal responsibility in order to achieve gender equality. During Stalin's rule, the state retreated from earlier family and marriage reforms and attempted to strengthen the institution of family in the 1930s and 1950s. One notable example is the legalization of abortion in 1920, followed by its prohibition in 1936, and its legalization again in 1955.[48] In the post-war period (from the 1950s to the1980s), the need for women's labour and the state's inability to provide adequate social welfare support forced women to combine motherhood with full participation in the workforce.[49]

To understand women's experiences, we need to consider women and gender as an integral part of the national political and economic system. Gender is manipulated for the state's domestic and international agenda, and the state, in turn, can be evaluated for its gender policies and women's experiences. Around the Middle East and Central Asia, governments have intervened in women's lives for internal and external policy objectives. Domestically, the regimes harnessed women's reproductive functions and labour contributions for their own purposes. Internationally, they utilized the female population as a means of conveying specific messages within the global arena, such as their stance on the West, religion, and veiling. This instrumentalization of women as a tool of both national and foreign policies reduced women to mere instruments of statecraft.[50]

Women from different social classes tend to react differently to state ideologies and policies. In Iran, for instance, the Shah's government prioritized the interests of urban, upper-middle-class women, who were the main beneficiaries of the state's legislative policies. However, the reforms introduced by the government had some impact on women from all social classes.[51] Somewhat comparable social and political developments took place in Tajikistan from the 1920s to the 1980s. Urban areas of Tajikistan transformed into industrial and cultural centres in extraordinary ways, while rural areas remained undeveloped. Women generally have more options in an urban setting because patriarchal family and social structures restrict choices and mobility in rural areas. Compared to rural women, urban women contributed significantly less labour input, yet rural women do not receive recognition for their own labour, or even for their children, as these belong to the patrilineal extended family. Deniz Kandiyoti's study compared the influence of the patrilineal households on the status of Turkish women in nomadic tribes, peasant villages, rural towns, and cities. In rural areas the father dominated younger men and all women. A hierarchy based on age was persistent among women in all spheres, yet less so in urban areas because of the diminished importance of male elders, specifically fathers and fathers-in-law.[52]

The Impact of Urbanization on Gender

There is growing evidence from around the world that women employed in industrial sector jobs eventually break away from patriarchal social and family structures compared to women who stay in the agriculture.[53] The state feminism campaign in Turkey challenges the notion that it was the construction of roads in the post–Second World War period that connected rural areas to cities and led to gender reforms in the countryside. Instead, it was the migration of women from villages to cities that played a significant role in improving the social status of Turkish women.[54] Based on a study of Turkish female workers, women workers' professional occupation enabled their greater participation in decision-making in the household.[55]

Based on Soviet statistics, from the 1950s to the 1980s, Tajikistan experienced a substantial urban growth rate.[56] By the 1950s, life in the large cities of Dushanbe (previously Stalinabad) and Khujand (previously Leninabad) was dramatically different than in the smaller provincial cities (such as Kuliab and Kurgan-Tiube) and there was a significant contrast between cities and rural areas. The population of these two largest cities came from all over the republic and the regions, and the Russian language was widespread.[57] By the time of the 1959 census, urbanization had risen to 33 per cent. The growth of the urban population continued for most of the post-war era. Based on population censuses, between 1959 and 1979, Tajikistan's urban population more than doubled.[58] This was a misleading statistic, as it was due in large part to the reclassification of some populated places as urban and their incorporation into existing city boundaries. This restructuring created an impression of greater urbanization in the country even though similar to neighbouring Central Asian states, Tajikistan remained predominantly agrarian, especially compared to Russia and western parts of the Soviet Union. Over 80 per cent of the indigenous population resided in rural areas during the 1980s.[59] The primary reason for the low urbanization among the indigenous population, despite rapid urban expansion, was relatively speedy rural growth. According to Jones and Grupp's studies of family structures in Soviet Central Asia, women who managed to move to urban areas and who pursued university education tended to have fewer children and were more concentrated in blue- and white-collar jobs compared to their counterparts in the countryside. In this study, equilibrium between men and women at the workplace happened to women with higher educational qualifications.[60] This is why patriarchy also needs to be understood in societal-structural and developmental terms rather than as based on religion or culture.[61] The emergence of a modern middle class tied to the capitalist economy, or the state bureaucracy, is typically accompanied by a weakening of the patriarchal order. Consequently, patriarchal structures are the strongest in Middle Eastern and Central Asian countries that are predominantly rural, such as Libya, Pakistan, Sudan, Yemen, Afghanistan, and Tajikistan. Turkey, on the other hand, serves as an example of the opposite, with more egalitarian gender and family relations due to its extensive industrialization, urbanization, and the state's implementation of women-friendly laws.[62]

Unlike some of the state feminism launched in the Middle East, socioeconomic circumstances and cultural norms limited rural women's ability to migrate to urban areas in Tajikistan. This reality did not prevent rural men and a smaller number of women from pursuing the benefits of the Soviet regime.[63] Nadia Youseff found that Muslim women in parts of the Middle East did not enter the industrial sector due to cultural restrictions, namely perception of factory jobs as involving public activity or presupposed contact with men.[64] As a result, "occupations which

in other countries became predominantly feminine from early industrialization onwards (such as the service occupations, domestic work,
factory work, retail and clerical jobs) are in the Middle East staffed by
men or foreign women."[65] In Tajikistan, industrial sector jobs in urban
areas were primarily occupied by Tajik men and female migrants from
western parts of the USSR transplanted to the periphery to introduce
industrialization. Factors that compelled Tajik women to remain in the
countryside and in manual labour jobs range beyond cultural norms.
Soviet statistics show that the majority of rural girls were caught up in
a cycle of full-time work (mostly on collective farms), household chores,
raising children, and taking care of a private plot of land. This resulted
in their lowest level of rural-to-urban migration in the Soviet Union.[66]
Married women, unlike married men, rarely pursued education, or professional training due to family obligations. Lack of education and specialization confined over 80 per cent of rural Muslim women to manual
labour jobs on collective farms.[67]

Like the state feminism launched in the Middle Eastern countries,
particularly in Iran, Turkey, Afghanistan, Tunisia, and Egypt, the Soviet
regime's emancipatory policy benefitted few Tajik women, mainly those
who were urban or managed to urbanize, were educated, and became
the professional elites.[68] Even though state emancipatory reforms, such
as public education, lead to some mobility for women of all social
classes, it is urban, educated, and employed women who traditionally promote progressive social change for their gender.[69] However, the
experience of Iranian women in administrative positions reveals that
they primarily advocated for the interests of elite men in power, rather
than promoting women's equality. They tended to distance themselves
from efforts to advance gender equality, aligned themselves with the
establishment, and supported the status quo. Additionally, they did
not prioritize seeking solidarity across class lines with other women
and often came across as elitist and arrogant to women of other classes.
As a result, even though these women were in a privileged position
to advance women's rights, they failed to do so.[70] In Soviet Tajikistan,
even the notion of affecting any gender related outcomes was beyond
Muslim women leaders' control.

Like Iranian women, urban educated Muslim women professionals in Tajikistan did not follow this projected path and failed to promote social change for their gender. Rather than being a vanguard for
further women's rights, Muslim women professionals who benefitted from the Soviet reforms because of their educational and social
transformation became a new and separate category of the population.
Rural Muslim women in Tajikistan perceived urban, Muslim women

as culturally different.[71] Alienated from rural women and in competition with Slavic women for professional opportunities, Tajik women in leadership positions remained a small minority with limited authority within patriarchal political structures.[72] Slavic women had an advantage over Muslim female candidates in terms of career opportunities because they did not have to meet restrictive social expectations placed on Muslim women.[73]

In addition to work obligations, household chores, and child-rearing, Tajik and Uzbek women in administrative jobs had to uphold established norms. While the double burden was a reality for all Soviet women, Muslim women were also expected to adhere to cultural notions of modesty and shame. The professional, personal, and social expectations Muslim women leaders faced restricted their authority in political and social arenas and limited their potential to influence gender politics. Unlike women in Turkey and Tunisia, Muslim women professionals were unable to launch cohesive movements based on gender and advocate for the rights gained under the Bolshevik regime in the post-independent Tajikistan (1991). In fact, the only women's organizations in the post-war period (1953–82), the *zhensoviety*, headed by urban Muslim and Slavic women professionals, only widened the gap between urban and rural women.[74] The *zhensoviety* within the Soviet Union were employing more bottom-up approaches, especially compared to their predecessor, the Zhenotdel. Yet in Tajikistan, the urban *zhensoviety* retained their top-down approach to rural women.[75] This centralized approach and unpopular agenda in the Tajik periphery prevented the *zhensoviety* from introducing effective change in the lives of women and from mobilizing based on gender.

During the Khrushchev government (1953–64), the state put the *zhensoviety* in charge of the renewed campaign against Islam in the periphery.[76] In the post-war period, the regime succeeded at putting an end to practices of veiling, polygamy, early marriages, and bride payments in urban areas. These practices still existed in rural areas of Tajikistan but were less common compared to the 1920s and 1930s. The Khrushchev regime viewed patriarchal practices as rooted in Islam and regarded them as the primary cause of rural women's lower educational attainment and high unemployment rate. The state subsequently launched a renewed attack against Islam and utilized the *zhensoviety* in this campaign among rural Muslim women. Analysis of the *zhensoviety*'s campaign against Islam in rural areas of Tajikistan shows that the regime maintained its ineffective approach to women's issues in the post-war period. The regime's propaganda messages and tactics suggest a lack of an understanding of the Muslim periphery.

Despite Soviet propaganda slogans that communism and religion are not compatible, the Tajikistan populace learned to seamlessly combine these identities. The central government's use of the *zhensoviety* in its unpopular agenda against practices associated with being a Muslim further challenged the women's committee's work in the countryside.

This case study of Muslim women of Soviet Tajikistan similar to Turkey affirms that "the state may be a powerful instigator of change through policies that may in some cases represent an onslaught on existing cultural practices."[77] State feminism campaigns in the Middle East and Soviet Central Asia illustrate "both the potentials and the limitations of reforms instigated by a political vanguard in the absence of a significant women's movement."[78] While local actors, women in particular, played a significant role in implementing, directing, and adjusting to orders from the central government in the post–Second World War period, orders continued to come from Moscow. The Soviet regime's approaches to all Soviet women were inconsistent, and this inconsistency had the most paradoxical outcomes on Muslim women in Central Asia. While the regime brought Muslim women into public spheres and introduced them to education, collectivization, limited modernization reforms, pro-natalist policies, and other state directives entrenched traditional social structures and kept women in the countryside. As a result, the Soviet approach to all women limited Muslim women's professional options and spatial mobility, which are commonly associated with and required for modernization, as seen in Turkey.[79] Attacks on religion tightened the association between Islam and ethnic identity, further contributing to localization of Islam in the region. Inadvertently, the Soviet regime in various ways traditionalized women's role.[80]

Sources and Methodology

During the Soviet period, Tajikistan combined a diverse set of ethnic groups including Tajiks, Uzbeks, Tatars, Russians, Ukrainians, Bukharan Jews, Chechens, Armenians, Germans, and others. Following the collapse of the Soviet Union and the civil war in Tajikistan, which took place between 1992 and 1996, many of the minority groups, including a small percentage of Tajiks, fled the country. Strong regional divisions remain. The population identifies first with their immediate community, kinship group, *mahalla* (Islamic community), or region – Pamiri, Garmi, Kuliubi, Khujandi (previously Leninabadi), and so on – and lastly with their country. In this study, references to Tajik and indigenous women encompass all Muslim women, including Uzbek women. The majority of Muslims in Tajikistan are Sunni, except for the Pamiris, who are Ismailis, a Shi'a denomination of Islam. My archival sources are based on all Tajik women regardless of their regional affiliation. In my oral history interviews, I conversed with women based on their availability from different parts of the country. While I cannot claim that this study tells the story of all women in Tajikistan equally, regardless of their ethnicity and nationality, the analysis generally applies to women who lived in Soviet Tajikistan.

Coerced Liberation integrates a variety of sources, including official government documents, Soviet periodicals, and newspapers, to analyse the role of the central and local governments. This book draws on untapped sources unavailable to earlier scholars, including previously inaccessible national archives in Tajikistan, primary sources from the Tajik Academy of Sciences, and the National Tajik Library (available only in vernacular), and interviews with Muslim women from different parts of the country. These sources reveal the role of the state, female and male elites, Islamic practices, cultural norms, and ethnic and class considerations in the attempted emancipation of Muslim women in Tajikistan. Being from the region and speaking all the regional languages, namely Tajik (a dialect of Farsi), Russian, and Uzbek, I was able to work on previously unexplored subjects.

I am the first historian to access the former Communist Party Archive of the Tajik Republic, now renamed to the Presidential Archive, to examine the Soviet emancipation of Muslim women in Tajikistan. In 2016, Tim Epkenhans wrote that the Communist Party Archive had been destroyed during a fire in the civil war in 1992.[81] I can attest that the Presidential Archive still stands. During my research, it was guarded by its then director, Perumshoev. During my first meeting with him, he told me that he is protecting the archive as his only hope for future generations, yet he strictly limited young scholars' access to the documents. My access to this archive was not easy; only after months of negotiation was I allowed to work there. This was primarily due to Perumshoev's realization that I would be researching "the woman question," which he deemed an unimportant matter. The only other person who worked at the Communist Party Archive was the part-time archivist Lola Ibragimova. Her tremendous help and support allowed me to work at the archive for extended periods and at weekends, during which she would show up during non-working hours to help me. I was given access to most, if not all, fonds with references to the Zhenotdel and *zhensoviety*. All of these are found in fond 3. Most of the folders I accessed are titled "Zhenotdel" even when the content does not pertain to the work of that organization. In the post–Second World War period, the organization was reformed into *zhensoviety*, though all women-related documents were still filed under the title of "Zhenotdel." These documents include the Zhenotdel files, government communication, public relations documents, and investigations into various cases.

I have also collected a wide range of Soviet periodicals, newspapers, and statistical data in Russian, Tajik, and Uzbek from the Tajik National Library and the Tajik Academy of Sciences library. The Soviet press was the most common transmitter of communism and the strongest ideological weapon of the party in the struggle for the construction of Soviet society, including the image of the New Soviet man and woman.[82] I spent a total of seventeen months doing research in the major archives of Tajikistan, working at the Tajik National Library and the Tajik Academy of Science, and conducting oral history interviews. I worked extensively in all three major archives of the Tajik republic, the Central State Archive, the Communist Party Archive, and the Regional State Archive of Sugd (formerly the Leninabad State Archive). These archives are the repository of documents on the activities of the Zhenotdel (1924–30) and the *zhensoviety* (1953–82) in Tajikistan. I also use archival sources to examine Soviet policies towards Muslim women as compared to women in neighbouring Uzbekistan and women in western parts of the Soviet Union.

I examined Soviet women's periodicals oriented towards Muslim women in Tajikistan, notably issues of *Zanoni Tojikiston* from the 1950s to the 1980s. I assessed similar periodicals in the Russian language, *Rabotnitsa* and *Krestianka*, and analysed the content of the major Soviet newspapers *Pravda* and *Izvestiia*. I also assessed the situation of women in Soviet Tajikistan in the post-war era through the statistical data on the agrarian sector, published in the volumes *Narodnoe khoziaistvo SSSR* and *Selskoe khoziaistvo SSSR*, which illustrate that women remained predominantly in rural areas. Annual census data on the Soviet population, contained in *Itogi vsesoiuznoi perepisi naseleniia* and *Zhenshchiny v SSSR*, the Soviet newspaper *Pravda*; and several other sources provided extensive data to compare the education levels, occupations, marriage age, and birth rate of Muslim women in Tajikistan with those of women in other parts of the Soviet Union, especially its western parts. While in Dushanbe, I worked at the National Library of Tajikistan and collected a wide range of Soviet periodicals, newspapers, and statistical data.

To fill in the gaps left by censored Soviet periodicals and the archival material, I interviewed Muslim women who personally experienced the Soviet reforms. This study heavily relies on first-hand stories of women who experienced the Soviet regime. I personally conducted all the interviews. Government control of information adds to the population's reluctance to converse about anything politics-related, and even to share individual stories about the past. I am continuously reminded by family and colleagues that today it is harder to find people who are willing to be interviewed about their past due to their fear of political repression and the consequences shared information may have for their families. I interviewed fifty-two women who were born between the 1920s and the 1950s and lived through the Soviet era. Twenty of these interviews were transcribed for inclusion in this study. My interviewees were women of different ages and social and educational backgrounds, and from different parts of the country, with the majority from various cities and several from rural areas. I conducted these interviews all over Tajikistan in Russian, Tajik, and Uzbek. I interviewed women with diverse backgrounds, ranging from those who held the highest political positions during the Soviet period to famous collective farmers and award-winning factory workers.

I asked these women to tell me about their lives, to recall their childhood and adulthood experiences. It was clear to me that many felt nostalgic about the past, when Tajikistan did not face electricity shortages, especially in the wintertime, when there was reliable supply of gas and hot and cold water, and at least one member of the family had a stable job. To break through this nostalgia, I interviewed these women at least twice whenever possible. I was fortunate to visit many of my interviewees twice or more over the course of three years. I asked open-ended questions to encourage them to pursue a range of stories and themes about their past. I contrasted these interviews with other sources, including archives, statistical data published in the Soviet Union, and the existing scholarship to make up for memory gaps and ensure that there were no discrepancies.

Most of these interviews were conducted in Tajik, though I also used Russian and Uzbek. For those interviews conducted in Uzbek, I relied on my mother, Khosiyat Yusupjonova. She is a native speaker of Uzbek, and she served as my translator and transcriber for these interviews. Being born and raised in Tajikistan, in Khujand city in the northern region of Sugd, I found it easy to engage with my interlocutors. My eagerness to learn their stories, my status as a woman, and my ability to draw on mutually shared acquaintances allowed me to engage with my interviewees for hours. My interviewees were enthusiastic to share their life stories once they learned more about me and felt at ease. Nobody asked for anonymity. I located women based on family and community networks. This provided my interviewees with some assurance that we shared intermediaries whom we all know and whom they trusted.

This is how I was introduced to Nizoramo Zaripova, chair of the Presidium of the Tajik Supreme Soviet (1982–4) – equivalent to the president today – who was also the head of the Women's Department, the republican *zhensoviet*, of Tajikistan for many years. Zaripova was our neighbour Gulruhsor kelnoya's former neighbour in Kuliab, where they had both grown up.[83] My neighbour was a little girl when Zaripova left her native village for the capital city, Dushanbe, but Zaripova remembered her and her entire family. I knew Zaripova as the most famous woman in the country, yet we quickly bonded once she recalled Gulruhsor and her entire family. It was clear to me that she was trying to show off her memory by listing the names of Gulruhsor kelnoya's brothers and sisters; I was nonetheless impressed that this former top official remembered her native community in Kuliab.

I use oral history interviews with Muslim women from Tajikistan to identify internal factors, including the roles of the Tajik male elite and the Islamic customs and practices that impacted women's choices not to pursue education and vocational training, essentially forcing them to remain in the countryside. Given the Soviet state's control over the production of documents and the relative absence of oral histories, this approach is an important part of this book. During the Soviet period, Muslim women were not able to voice their opinions openly. These interviews have enabled me to incorporate women's perspectives on the Soviet reforms and integrate these narratives within the creation of broader history of the region. By doing so, this study shows the crucial role women played in the Soviet campaign. When interviewing women who held prominent positions within the Tajik government, I was able to better analyse the archival sources. This is because women like Zaripova, Bobosadykova, Rakhimova, and a few others rose to prominent positions in the post–Second World War period and remained in the administrative role until the 1970s and 1980s. These female leaders personally knew colleagues whom I was not able to interview due to their passing away, so they helped add critical details and context to many of the specific stories I incorporated in this study.

I made it a priority to use the language my interviewees applied in telling their stories. Therefore, the use of terms like *tradition, traditional,* and *emancipation* is purposeful as they reflect how people, women in particular, understood what was happening around them. This is a unique study that applies to women's experiences in Soviet Central Asia and broadly to the borderland territories of the former Soviet Union, where women are at all times at the centre of their own stories. Given the dearth of research in this area/topic/time, I believe that this book is strongest when my source material can tell the (yet untold) story of these women. There will certainly be opportunities in future work to deconstruct how these women interpreted these terms and how they relate to our modern understanding of them, but I see this as secondary to the main contribution of this work.

I dedicate this work in part to my interviewees, some of whom have called my mother in Tajikistan to inquire if their stories were finally published. Many of these women felt proud of me for studying at a university abroad. Others offered generous blessings (*duo* in Tajik) wishing me good health and a happy marriage. I was not married at the time. I am deeply sad that I was not able to share these extraordinary accounts earlier due to the COVID-19 pandemic, which took the lives of several of my family in Tajikistan, including the matriarch of our family, my beloved aunt Lola Urunbaeva. The pandemic also slowed down this publication because my husband, Ryan Abman, and I did not have childcare for our young daughters, Alina Carolyn Abman (now six) and Isla Lola Abman (now four) while we still had to work full-time. My personal circumstances while working on this project came to intimately intertwine with some of the stories of women I introduce within these chapters.

Chapter 1, "The Attack," examines the existing literature on the Soviet campaign to liberate Muslim women of Central Asia in the 1920s. It also assesses the Zhenotdel activities in Tajikistan in the 1920s. Primary sources indicate the Women's Department's faced serious logistical, cultural, and material difficulties in its work to reach Muslim women in Tajikistan. The organization generally failed to engage Muslim women in its work and recruit them into its ranks on a massive scale. Based on the Zhenotdel's reports, the regime did not maintain its initial position regarding women's unveiling and the eradication of seclusion in Tajikistan. It changed its approach based on the situation on the ground. The Bolshevik regime acted cautiously in its attempts to eradicate patriarchal practices to instigate women's liberation. It avoided tensions against the Soviet policies to prevent aliening its primary support base, poor peasants.

Chapter 2, "The Retreat," describes the rise of ordinary Muslim women who adopted the Soviet ideology during this period. These women were a product of both the Zhenotdel's activism in the country in the 1920s and the regime's nativization policy. As a result, during Stalin's regime some Tajik and Uzbek women became active in the social and political life of Tajikistan. Contrary to the Stalinist regime's overstated claims of its great accomplishments in Muslim women's emancipation in Tajikistan, patriarchal practices of veiling, polygamy, early marriages, and bride payments continued during this period. They are most vividly reflected in the high number of rural Muslim girls dropping out of school between 1935 and 1953. Nonetheless, Stalin's regime inspired a sense of contribution to their country's economic wealth among rural and urban women. They felt empowered to have an input in their nation's fate.[84]

Chapter 3, "The Triple Burden," assesses the post-war period. During this period, it became apparent that the Soviet regime's top-down approach to the emancipation of Muslim women in Tajikistan in the 1920s and 1930s did not reach rural women. Unlike rural men, Muslim women in Tajikistan could not easily move to urban areas to pursue educational and career opportunities because of socio-economic and gender norms. Muslim women who remained in rural areas had the lowest level of education, the highest rate of early marriages, and the highest birth rate within the Soviet Union. These circumstances kept rural girls and women in Tajikistan in manual labour jobs that did not require special training or education. Rural women, even Soviet heroines of production, were rarely in positions of power to influence gender politics in the country.

Chapter 4, "The Beneficiaries," expands the discussion of the Tajik female leadership. The Soviet reforms to liberate Muslim women in Tajikistan dramatically transformed the lives of some women who were either born in urban areas or who were able to move to urban areas. These women beneficiaries of Soviet reforms often lacked the same family structure due to the loss of a central patriarchal figure, typically fathers. As a result, they faced less pressure to adhere to established social norms, and they were able to move to urban areas and pursue university education. Some girls and women also entered Soviet educational facilities because of the pressure the regime was able to put on a male family member who worked for the Communist Party to educate female family members. Therefore, the number of primary beneficiaries of the Soviet reforms remained small. Few Muslim girls' and women's lives were shaped by special circumstances that enabled them to break social norms established for their gender. Muslim women leaders and professionals were expected to combine their professional lives with strict gender norms and carry out domestic duties. These circumstances limited the authority of these women leaders even in the highest echelons of political power.

Chapter 5, "The Thaw Era," analyses women's situation during the Khrushchev regime. During this period, the state strived to return the country to the original communist and Leninist ideology, including the state's approach to the woman question. Nikita Khrushchev expanded the *zhensoviety*, the women's councils around the Soviet Union. In the post-war period through the collapse of the Soviet Union, the *zhensoviety* were the primary women's groups in charge of Muslim women's transformation in Soviet Tajikistan. The central and local regime's control over the *zhensoviety*, and its subsequent unpopular agendas contributed to these women's councils' challenge of becoming a venue for women's mobilization in Tajikistan.

Chapter 6, "'I Am Muslim and Soviet,'" focuses on the Khrushchev regime's anti-religious propaganda, primarily targeted at rural women. The regime associated patriarchal practices with Islam and regarded them as the primary reason for rural women's lower educational rates and high unemployment in Tajikistan. As a result, the state came to view eradication of these practices as requisite for women's entry into the workforce and their subsequent liberation. The Khrushchev regime renewed its attack on religion and put the *zhensoviety* in charge of this campaign in rural Tajikistan. Analysis of the *zhensoviety*'s propaganda messages as communicated from Moscow shed light to the regime's perception of the Muslim periphery, the role of religion, social structures, and more. This chapter also explores the role Islam came to play in Muslim-majority Central Asia in the post–Second World War period. Regular rituals associated with being a Muslim remained at the core of the populace's perception of their sociality and confirmed their belonging to the shared community. This chapter also confirms the recent studies, which illustrate that Muslim population of Central Asia learned to combine their Soviet identity with being a Muslim.

1 The Attack: The Soviet Campaign to "Liberate" Muslim Women of Central Asia, 1924–1935

The proletariat cannot achieve complete freedom unless it achieves complete freedom for women.

–Lenin[1]

In the 1920s, the Bolshevik regime began a campaign to forcibly emancipate the Muslim women of Central Asia. In 1924, the Soviet regime launched the *khujum* ("attack" in Tajik) campaign in the region and put the Zhenotdel in charge of this campaign.[2]

During the period 1924–9, Tajikistan was an autonomous republic within the Soviet Republic of Uzbekistan. Based on the Zhenotdel's reports, the government lacked the determination to carry out and aggressively maintain its positions with regard to women's unveiling and the eradication of seclusion in Tajikistan. The Bolshevik regime ruled cautiously in its attempts to eradicate patriarchal practices in order to instigate women's liberation. It avoided tensions with the alleged supporters of communist ideology, namely poor peasants, against the Soviet reforms. The Bolshevik regime eventually retreated from its progressive divorce laws and replaced them with more conservative regulations.[3] Also, in spite of the Zhenotdel activists and some Muslim women's requests, the regime did not make veiling illegal. This chapter examines the Bolshevik emancipation of women initially based on the Marxist theory, the Bolshevik regime's approach to the Muslims of Central Asia, the *khujum* campaign, and the roles played by some of the actors involved. The period from the 1920s to the 1930s provides an examination of some of the successes and the numerous challenges of the early campaign through Zhenotdel reports and campaigns.

While the Zhenotdel failed to engage indigenous women in its work and recruit them into its ranks on a massive scale, it nevertheless prepared the initial cohort of female candidates who rose to government positions and became active in the post–Second World War period. The Soviet regime's other successes in its campaign to emancipate Muslim women included girls' education and women's entry into the workforce. The regime also eventually put an end to the practices of veiling and polygamy, yet practices of early marriages and bride payments continued throughout the Soviet Union. This was largely due to the fact that in the post-war period, the Muslim population of Tajikistan learned to combine their new Soviet identity with their Muslim identity.[4] Although practices such as veiling and polygamy eventually disappeared, early marriages and bride payments persisted, possibly because they were more concealed from public scrutiny.

The Bolshevik Emancipation of Women

Immediately after coming to power, the Bolsheviks passed laws that made the Soviet Union the most progressive country in the world on gender issues. Under the leadership of Vladimir Lenin, Alexandra Kollontai, Nadezhda Krupskaia, Inessa Armand, and others, the Bolsheviks introduced reforms that helped to further the socialist goal of complete gender equality.[5] Lenin wrote:

> Woman continues to be a domestic slave, because petty housework crushes, strangles, stultifies and degrades her, chains her to the kitchen and to the nursery, and wastes her labor on barbarously unproductive, petty, nerve-racking, stultifying and crushing drudgery.

> Enlightenment, culture, civilization, liberty – in all capitalist, bourgeoisie republics of the world all these fine words are combined with extremely infamous, disgustingly filthy and brutally coarse laws in which woman is treated as an inferior being, laws dealing with marriage rights and divorce, with the inferior status of a child born out of wedlock as compared with that of a "legitimate" child, laws granting privileges to men, laws that are humiliating and insulting to women.[6]

Consequently, the state strived to bring women out of the prison of household chores and into public life (see figure 1.1), equipping them with equal rights.

Aleksandra Kollontai, the leading Bolshevik feminist and the founder of the Zhenotdel, declared in 1923 that the Soviet regime would "lift the burdens of motherhood from women's shoulders and transfer them to the state," and that "the family, in its bourgeois sense, will die out."[7]

Figure 1.1. Soviet propaganda poster from the mid-twentieth century. This powerful example of Soviet propaganda exemplifies the Soviet campaign for women's liberation, promoting the ideology of Soviet communism, which aimed to free women from domestic labour by communalizing these responsibilities.

In 1918, the Soviet regime introduced legal reforms in Russia giving women equal rights of inheritance, divorce, and freedom of movement.[8] The Bolshevik laws aimed to encourage the "withering away" of the family through easy divorce procedures, weakening of marriage benefits and rights, and through the provision of equal benefits to single parents. Abortion was legalized in 1920 and made available to women free of charge. The Bolsheviks believed they would achieve gender equality by destroying traditional family structures and women's established roles within it.[9]

The Bolsheviks imagined a society in which communal dining halls, daycare centres, and public laundries would gradually replace the unpaid labour of women in the home. This in turn would liberate women from domestic chores and make them equal to men.[10] The early Bolshevik emancipation reforms promoted educational programs, vocational training, work placement, and other initiatives intended at women's liberation. These policies changed throughout the Soviet period. In 1919, the government created the Zhenotdel, specifically to supervise the women's emancipation campaign.[11] The regime hoped to incentivize the greater participation of women in the party's work with the help of the Zhenotdel. For a short period, the Zhenotdel was able to successfully pursue its agenda.[12] Yet once the New Economic Policy began, the Zhenotdel's work came under scrutiny.[13] Kollontai continued with her work and believed that the regime would remain dedicated to the woman question as long as the female activists like her continued their work within the party.[14]

The Soviet Liberation Campaign in Muslim Central Asia

Initially, the Soviet reforms to emancipate women were focused on the western parts of the Soviet Union. However, in Muslim Central Asia, the campaign took on a unique approach that was specific to the region.[15] In 1927, the regime launched the *khujum* campaign, to transform Muslim women's lives and to bring them into public life through paid work, education, and membership of the party.[16] To achieve these objectives the regime focused on the abolition of religious and patriarchal practices. The campaign included eradication of veiling, child marriages, polygamy, bride payment, and other reforms.[17] The state approached Islamic traditions in Tajikistan as part and parcel of the feudal past that oppressed women and kept half of the population at home and away from workforce. This radical campaign also included the destruction of Islamic institutions and the elimination of religious authority. Nonetheless, the most controversial aspect of the campaign was the forcible unveiling of women.[18]

In colonial Turkestan (consisting of present-day Turkmenistan, Kazakhstan, Uzbekistan, Tajikistan, Kyrgyzstan, and Xinjiang), mostly urban women (Muslim and Jewish population) veiled. They covered themselves from head to toe in a robe typically made of blue and grey striped cotton in Uzbek and Tajik known as the *paranji*. It also covered the face with a veil made of woven horsehair. Women wore the *paranji* only when outside their homes. This insured women's separation from strangers while in public.[19] In Turkestan, as in other parts of the Muslim world, men predominantly led the discussion surrounding women's veiling.[20]

Local intellectuals in Uzbekistan known as Jadids deliberated women's veiling and their role in society.[21] Though a complex group, their stance on women was based on modernist discourses that were prevalent in much of the Muslim world.[22] Before the Bolshevik Revolution, the Jadids argued that for the advancement of both Islam and the nation, women needed to be educated and engaged in public life. Following the Soviet takeover, the Jadids aligned with the new regime's concerns about the position of women in society.[23] Based on Khalid's findings, "The khujum was the culmination of a decade-long effort to transform society in which both the Soviets and the Jadids had participated."[24]

As for Muslim women, a small group of proactive and educated women in Uzbekistan came to consider education as the key to ending female seclusion and inequality. These women also supported unveiling and regarded the practice as an obstacle to modernity.[25] While a small minority they were influenced by the Jadid reformers' ideas. Prior to the Soviet takeover, the local reformers established a number of teacher-training schools for women, including the Xotin-Qizlar Bilim Yurti, or Women and Girls' House of Knowledge.[26] Graduates of this school not only became teachers, but also went on to become Communist Party activists.[27] Muslim women in Uzbekistan formed their understanding of women's liberation by blending the Jadids' ideas with the Bolshevik reforms.[28]

The Zhenotdel's Work in Tajikistan

Initially, the Bolsheviks did not consider Muslim women or veiling to be significant issues. However, the unveiling campaign represented a significant policy shift.[29] The regime attacked the *paranji* to get women into productive labour and not necessarily to give them agency. The campaign did not intend to redefine gender relations or to liberate women. The land reform was more important to the party.[30] Nonetheless, due to Muslim women's distinctive situation, particularly the regime's perception of their experiences as most oppressive, Central Asian women were considered a special case and given significant priority in the work of the Women's Department.[31] The Zhenotdel staff defined women's realities in Turkestan as follows: those in "the East" were "slaves of slaves," while those in Central Asia were the most oppressed of all.[32]

The Zhenotdel activists mostly came from the western parts of the Soviet Union, Russia in particular. They were commonly single, young women in their earlier twenties, generally field organizers. Many were of Russian, Jewish, or Armenian backgrounds.[33] For these women, the geographic mobility and input in the expansion of the Soviet power in the periphery offered the greatest opportunity for realizing their own aspirations for autonomy, respect, and inclusion in the historical narratives as trailblazers.[34] In Central Asia, many of these activists dedicated their lives in the pursuit of these dreams and for the sake of the party. The Zhenotdel took up a different direction compared to the local intelligentsia in Turkestan. The organization introduced a range of initiatives similar to those it established elsewhere in the Soviet Union, including women's clubs to provide educational training, medical assistance, mobilize women locally, seek employment opportunities through labour cooperatives.[35] For European activists in the Zhenotdel their mission was "bringing women out of the lazy and inactive life they have had until now, of including them in public life and production, and thus bringing them into an active life, into the ranks of free, rights-bearing citizens."[36]

The Zhenotdel's activities were first launched in towns and cities. The first women's clubs in Tajikistan appeared in the northern part of the country, Khujand, in January 1925 and Ura-Tiube in May 1925. In the eastern part of Tajikistan, Khorog, and the capital city of Dushanbe, the Women's Division appeared in 1926. By May 1930, there were ten women's clubs, and over a three-year period this number increased to forty.[37] The Women's Department pursued a top-down approach in its work to introduce reforms aimed at liberation of Muslim women.[38] During the early years of the Zhenotdel presence in the region, it mostly engaged women in movie screenings, theatre shows, public readings of newspapers and journals, and other visual sources of propaganda.[39] The official reports declared, "The fight against veiling, *kalym* [bride payments], and underage marriage should not be forced. We need to achieve elimination of these practices based only on propaganda, through reports and lectures, to explain to women their rights and responsibilities."[40] In the late 1920s, the organization introduced other methods including group discussion in bath houses, literacy centres, women's workshops, and tea houses.[41]

Starting in 1926, massive unveiling ceremonies were organized in Soviet Central Asia, the most dramatic being that which took place in Samarkand on 8 March 1927. At this gathering, several thousand women took off their veils and burned them publicly.[42] The regime made unveiling a prerequisite for women's participation in the new literacy classes and for membership in the Communist Party. Another big part of the *khujum* was marriage reforms. Between 1926 and 1928, the Bolshevik regime replaced old legal marriage practices based on sharia law with a new Soviet civil code. Registration of all marriages with the state was made compulsory. The minimum marriage age was raised from twelve for boys and nine for girls to eighteen for both. Polygamy and *kalym* were banned. Women also obtained equal rights with men in divorce.[43]

Around Central Asia, the Zhenotdel actively disseminated information about these new Soviet laws. The organization generally strived towards "increasing the cultural level, introducing basic feelings of human pride in the female masses, awakening masses to pursue their own interests, and directing them towards the Soviet way of life."[44] The Women's Department claimed that under the Soviet regime, women have equal rights with men. The Zhenotdel set a task of educating women, so they could contribute to social and political construction of the Soviet regime. They urged women to participate and run in the elections and assisted them in learning about their rights to medical and social assistance.[45] During the early 1920s, Muslim women seldom visited women's clubs or exercised their newly acquired rights. Activists had to adopt a door-to-door approach to persuade women that the organization's activities did not pose any threat to them.[46] During the early stages of the Zhenotdel's work, its activists had to be resourceful in reaching out to indigenous women. Some even had to veil themselves to enter traditional areas of cities and visit women in their homes. While this tactic may not have been approved by the party, it proved effective in helping Slavic activists establish initial contacts with Muslim women in Central Asia.[47]

While around Central Asia the effort to transform women's lives centred on the campaign against veiling and seclusion, veiling was generally practised only in urban and sedentary agricultural areas of present-day Uzbekistan and Tajikistan. In other parts of Central Asia where the population was mostly of nomadic background, women did not veil due to differences in cultural norms and lifestyles.[48] Nomadic populations required mobility for their women during regular migration seasons, whereas sedentary groups had more permanent places of residence. Official reports even asserted that in Kyrgyzstan and Turkmenistan, women held more authority in the household. "They are commonly in charge of grain management."[49] The party consequently assumed that lack of seclusion among women in Kyrgyzstan and Turkmenistan would help the work of Zhenotdel and the task of emancipating women would be easier in these regions.[50] These reports also asserted that while nomadic people were relatively more liberal towards women, some settled nations were more cultured, specifically Tatars and Armenians.[51]

The Zhenotdel activists described the situation in Uzbekistan as complicated. "Sharia is strong in Uzbekistan. Class categorizations are greater, and the majority of women are secluded. Together, these are only some examples of difficult beginnings we face in this region," the activists emphasized. They also pointed out that "the established economic relations, and gender-based divisions in Uzbekistan provide opportunities for the Zhenotdel to work with the masses."[52] Based on the same report, Tajikistan was the most backward and difficult region in which the Women's Department operated.[53] The female party members stressed that the situation of Muslim women in Tajikistan varied based on region. They reported that in Pamir (also known as Gorno-Badakhshan, eastern Tajikistan), "women typically do not wear the *paranji* and strive towards the building of communism." "In Pendzhakent [northern Tajikistan], the emancipation campaign is difficult because of deeply entrenched patriarchal social norms. In Kurgan-Tiube [western Tajikistan], the work among women has just started, whereas in Gissar [southern Tajikistan] it has not begun."[54]

The women's organization was not able to expand its work in rural Tajikistan due to a lack of human resources.[55] According to Tsibulkina, assistant head of the Zhenotdel in Uzbekistan, it was primarily due to a lack of activists who could work with women in rural Tajikistan.[56] The Slavic activists wrote, "There is a lack of experienced and qualified workers who speak the local languages. Local cadres are not prepared for this work, and they are poorly equipped with literature in the Tajik and Uzbek languages."[57] Other difficulties in the Zhenotdel's work in Tajikistan included the size of the territory, the prevalence of illiteracy, weak government control of remote areas, and violent reaction of local men to the Zhenotdel's activities. These barriers prompted the organization to adapt methods to suit the local circumstances.[58] Activists wrote, "In 1921, our work was not easy, we carried out our activities in *hamams* [traditional saunas]. We spent hours in the heat to talk to women."[59] In the same report another Zhenotdel worker recalled a trip to rural Tajikistan, "we had to hide being part of the Zhenotdel and pretended that we were actresses who came with a show. It was the only way to talk to women."[60] Often, the most basic needs could not be met for women to take part in the Zhenotdel activities. The women's club in Ura-Tiube, for example, had visitors only during good weather. "When it rains, women do not have appropriate clothing or proper shoes, so they are not able to come to the clubs."[61]

The official reports describe other struggles women activists encountered in Tajikistan. "In Dushanbe, women do not come out to streets. They only visit tombs and watch funerals from afar.... It is difficult to approach women outside their homes." The report emphasized that "there are only two workers based in Ura-Tiube, one is Tatar and speaks fluent Uzbek but does not know any Russian. The Russian worker speaks fluent Tajik and Uzbek but does not have any experience working with women."[62] The Zhenotdel reports also claimed that "cultural backwardness in rural areas is the primary obstacle in liberating women from chains of slavery and lies of religious officials."[63]

The women's organization in Tajikistan also faced logistical difficulties. "We lack buildings not only for local women but also for Slavic activists. Ever since it became possible for the Zhenotdel to organize meetings with local women, the organization led a nomadic life, constantly moving from one place to next, which continues to the present day." The activists explained that "women gather in members' homes, but due to organizers' lack of local languages, there are no positive outcomes of their work so far."[64] On one hand, these circumstances of the Zhenotdel's work in Tajikistan suggest that the regime did not prioritize the women's emancipation campaign in its transformation of the region.

Consequently, the Zhenotdel in Tajikistan neglected to train local female cadres, which made it difficult for the organization to expand into remote parts of the country. Activists maintained that instead of establishing Zhenotdel around the country the organization needed to strengthen its presence in places where it already had a presence.[65] Despite facing significant challenges, the Women's Department persisted in spreading information about the new family laws through public and personal conversations with women, primarily in urban areas. They aimed to enhance women's awareness and understanding of their right to vote, informed them about the new laws, and educated them about the public positions they could hold.[66] Despite these efforts, few women participated in or stood for local elections. In fact, the activists openly admitted, women in rural areas were being "randomly chosen for Soviets [councils]." In some cases, local women did not even know what they are signing up for.[67]

Using diverse range of activities, the Zhenotdel established a foundation for raising political awareness among indigenous women and encouraging their participation in labour and public life.[68] As a result of these efforts, the first Muslim female activists began to emerge, primarily in urban areas.[69] Early activists became the new generation of women who took up leadership roles within the Soviet system.[70] These women also faced overwhelming harassment and discrimination within the party and in public for breaking social norms established for their gender.[71] Although local women were initially hesitant to participate in Zhenotdel activities, many ultimately benefitted from the organization's *Koshchi* ("Ploughmen's" in Uzbek) Union initiative. The Soviets established this organization in 1922 to disseminate communist teach-ings and promote the party's goals among the rural working class.[72] The work of the *Koshchi* also included rural women's mobilization and organization of their vocational training.[73] Women were trained in handicraft skills including knitting, embroidery, weaving, silk winding, silk spinning, cotton ginning, and rug making skills.[74] The economic liberation of women was closely linked to the transformation of the rural economy. The state aimed to achieve this goal by implementing measures such as establishing collective farms and designating areas within agriculture specifically for women's employment. These areas included silkworm breeding, orchard cultivation, animal husbandry, and dairy farming.[75]

The women's liberation campaign was meant to work together with other Soviet measures such as land reform. It aimed to replace the old fabric of family and community life with a modern socialist society.[76] During 1921–2, the Soviet regime implemented the land and water reform, which aimed to grant women equal rights to land by allocat-ing land plots to them on par with men.[77] The first land and water reform of 1921–2 was indeed a milestone in the process of women's economic emancipation.[78] Prishepchik, assistant head of Zhenotdel in Uzbekistan asserted that strengthening silkworm farming was increas-ing women's economical role in the agriculture and helping the wom-en's emancipation campaign.[79] Party officials believed that by helping female peasants the regime was gaining their trust and precluding them from creating obstacles to the Zhenotdel's work in the region.[80]

The impact of the Soviet campaigns to emancipate Muslim women was initially limited in rural areas as evident from the Zhenotdel reports. Based on anthropologist, Gillian Tett's interviews of rural women in Tajikistan, the campaign has left a lasting impression on the villagers' perceptions of the woman question. Most of the early Bolsheviks that the villagers encountered were Russian speakers. So, in the eyes of the rural populace, the campaign became closely associated with Russifica-tion.[81] The villagers were convinced that the communists were trying to turn virtuous Muslim women into loose Russian women, who had no respect for Islam and had no shame. As one elderly woman remem-bered: "When I was little, the communists came. The Russians – and some Tajiks too … so my father used to hide us and other girls in the hay. He said that the communists wanted to take the women away and turn us into Russian women. They told us that if we took off our scarves, they would beat us because we had no shame."[82]

Nizoramo Zaripova, chair of the Presidium of the Tajik Supreme Soviet (in office 1982–4), recollected that in her village, Pakhtakor, in the Kuliab region of southern Tajikistan, some started supporting the Bolshevik regime, but the majority sided with the Basmachi, the local opposition movement. "These were times of uncertainty. We did not know whom to believe and which side to take. But my brother served for the Bolshevik regime in the Shurabad region and was one of the few locals there. He would bring seeds for tomatoes, potatoes, and peppers from Russians."[83] According to Zaripova, there was a massive food shortage and widespread starvation in the 1920s and 1930s in her village. "We planted those seeds and had a good harvest. But nobody in the village would touch the produce. They would call it kofir's ["unbeliever" in Tajik] food. My brother would jokingly call me kofir for eating it and I would tell him to continue enjoying his dinners."[84]

The activists called for "categorically demanding that each party and Komsomol member use decrees and laws to help include their wives and sisters in Zhenotdel activities."[85] The Zhenotdel workers believed that it could help set an example to the rest of the population. Indigenous communist cadres showed public support for the campaign, but in private many continued to keep their wives veiled, some practised polygamy, and all continued the tradition of bride payments. Some indigenous party officials resisted this decree by claiming that "with the freedom the Soviet regime gave our wives, we cannot force them to do anything now."[86] Official reports make it clear that the leadership in Moscow was aware that native members of the political party endorsed the principles of women's liberation, but in private, they adhered to traditional customs.[87] As for the ordinary population of Tajikistan, initially many simply ignored the campaigns and its slogans.[88] Nonetheless, some among the clergy and wealthier segments of the indigenous population, who under the Bolshevik regime had the most to lose, openly argued that the Soviet regime was corrupting local women and advised running "to Afghanistan where the regime is still Islamic and will not interfere in your family life and touch your women."[89] Religious officials spread rumours that "the Soviet regime will take off our women's pants and send them to Moscow where they will become kofirs."[90]

Resistance also came from Muslim women who not only refused to take off their veils but also condemned those who did. They claimed that women who dared to unveil were hopeless in terms of future marriage prospects and family life.[91] Some local women openly declared to Zhenotdel workers, "The paranji is dearer to me than your party."[92] Just like in neighbouring Uzbekistan, women who unveiled in Tajikistan were considered impure. The societal norms in Central Asia held women responsible for maintaining sexual chastity, therefore any wrongdoing was attributed to them.[93] Despite opposition to the Soviet emancipatory reforms, hundreds of women in Tajikistan volunteered as translators and assistants, eventually securing administrative positions within the Zhenotdel and national government. Every year on May Day and International Women's Day (8 March), thousands of women in Soviet Central Asian territories would gather in the marketplaces and boldly remove their veils in an act of defiance.[94] For example, according to government reports, these were the total numbers of women who cast off the veil on 1 May 1927: 10,000 in Tashkent, 40,000 in Fergana, and 8,000 in Khujand.[95] Women who abandoned their veils in the initial stages of the campaign had the most to gain from the Soviet reforms. These women were typically those with the lowest status in Central Asian society, including widows, orphans, divorcees, wives of polygamists, and women of the working poor.[96] But based on the Soviet secret police (OGPU)'s assessment from 1928 on women's attitudes to unveiling, these women could be divided into three groups. The first group, the smallest one, not only rejected unveiling but also consciously opposed it. The second group, most of the female population, was for or against veiling depending on their husband's stance on the issue. The third group comprised poor women who not only unveiled but also became activists.[97]

By the late 1920s, the public reaction to the unveiling campaign was openly negative and at times violent. For instance, a Basmachi leader, Ibragim Bek, in his proclamation to the people of Turkestan declared, "The Bolsheviks are responsible for undermining the honour of women in Russian Turkestan. It is their doing that women go unveiled and are thereby converted into prostitutes."[98] The Basmachi leader called the Bolshevik regime, "treacherous and horrid.... [It] deprives its subjects of the rights to be masters of their wives and property ... and [has] robbed the populace of all its customary wedding ceremonies."[99] The Muslim women's liberation campaign in general came to be perceived as a direct attack on religious practices and Muslim men's honour.[100]

The Zhenotdel workers warned the party about the unsafe situation in the region. "We keep silent about the unveiling movement and only talk about it with the party and the Komsomol members. There is lack of work in disseminating explanation of the Supreme Soviet Congress's decree on the emancipation campaign."[101] Central Asia witnessed two hundred seventy such murders in 1929.[102] The Presidium of the Soviet Central Executive Committee, after consulting with the Zhenotdel, decided to classify such crimes as "counter-revolutionary offences."[103] The OGPU produced a report on the rise of violence in Central Asian between 1926 and 1928. The report revealed that the number of political murders had nearly doubled during that time. However, the exact number is uncertain, as neither the secret police nor local agencies kept a systematic record of "terrorist acts." The incomplete statistics provided by the OGPU for the first eleven months of 1928 showed 100 cases of "political terror" and 104 cases of assault and murder related to women's liberation campaign.[104] In most cases, women were victimized by their own or their husband's families.[105] Uzbek and Tajik men who attacked women for unveiling did so to maintain the established patriarchal social order. Women who broke away from seclusion and unveiled themselves posed a threat to the existing social system. Murders were intended to set an example to other women, making it clear to them that they should not unveil or support the Soviet regime.[106]

The opposition to the emancipation campaign resulted in its decline. Local men reacted strongly to the campaign, which led the Soviet regime to recognize its counterproductive outcomes by the end of the 1920s. The campaign not only sparked anti-Soviet sentiment among Muslim men, but also failed to achieve its goal of promoting women's liberation and altering established social structures. As attacks on unveiled women increased in 1928, many women who had abandoned the veil in 1927 resumed wearing it in 1929, indicating a setback for the women's liberation campaign.[107] The central regime in Moscow claimed that this backlash among Muslim Central Asian men was due to local party leadership and Zhenotdel activists' misunderstanding of their responsibilities and incorrect interpretation of the campaign. The regime claimed that the activists had left out the class component, mistakenly replacing it with slogans about the economic independence of women. This report served as the primary reason for resistance among some indigenous party members who refused to carry out the emancipation campaign in Tajikistan/Central Asia.[108] These difficulties in the work of the Zhenotdel also resulted in Slavic female activists quitting their jobs. Their replacement often took a long time and commonly did not happen due to a lack of trained women workers.[109]

Interestingly, no law was passed to prohibit veiling in Central Asia; only a small number of sanctions were put in place to ensure the cooperation of the indigenous population. For instance, for men, the unveiling of their wives became a condition of employment, and the veil was banned from schools and workplaces.[110] In 1927, Zhenotdel activists wrote to the Soviet government in Moscow asking to make veiling illegal. The regime refused to issue any decrees regarding veiling by insisting that it should happen on a voluntary basis.[111] In fact, the regime did not provide protection for those who took off their veils. For instance, in the village of Guliakandoz, in Tajikistan in 1927 nearly all women took off their *paranjis*. The men in the village harassed the unveiled women. The Guliakandoz women wrote to the Soviet Supreme Court and local government officials, but no measures were taken. As a result, women took up their *paranji* again.[112] The Zhenotdel activists wrote that "women in the Guliakandoz village are not alone in petitioning for legal actions against veiling."[113]

In 1928, the Soviet regime enacted the Family, Marriage, and Child Support code, which stipulated that only marriages registered in the civil registry offices (Organy zapisi aktov grazhdanskogo sostoiaoianiia, ZAGS) would be recognized, although existing marriages were still considered valid. In order to register, couples had to prove that they met the minimum age requirement and were not already married. Divorce could be granted either by mutual agreement or by court petition from one of the partners. This law applied specifically to Central Asia and intended to end the practice of unilateral male divorce that had been widely accepted.[114] The official report explained that the family situation in Central Asia, especially in Tajikistan was based on sharia law and the Koran, according to which women do not have any rights. A Zhenotdel report described the situation of Muslim women: "They are a home decoration for rich people and a labour force for poor men. Women are under their husband's whimsical will. Islam allows girls age 9–10 to enter marriage. So, from an early age girls must face a heavy burden of work around the house combined with labour in the fields." The report also explained Muslim women's early aging and higher death rate compared to men as due to of their seclusion and overwhelming responsibilities around the home.[115]

The Local Response to Soviet Rule

The report described a typical life of an ordinary girl in Tajikistan: "A poor peasant cannot afford a wife since he cannot pay *kalym*. So, he signs up to work for a young girl's father [typically when she is age five to ten] so he can marry his underage daughter." The activists asserted that "to keep his hard-earned wife, a peasant forces her into seclusion and makes her cover her body when she is outside the house. The only exception is the women in Pamir, who do not veil."[116] For this and other reasons, the Zhenotdel activists considered Muslim marriages oppressive to women. So, they tried to help as many women as possible to avoid or escape from these unions, by helping them learn about their legal rights under the Soviet regime.[117]

Examination of Turkmen men to the Soviet sponsorship of divorce shows that peasants protested and sent complaints to the provincial party committee. In 1925, local officials even warned that the large number of women filing for divorce was posing a threat of a violent backlash.[118] These officials claimed that the Soviet policy of easy divorce was primarily affecting poor and landless peasants, whose wives were leaving them to marry wealthier men. There were also claims that parents were encouraging daughters to divorce poor husbands in order marry wealthy men. Like reports from Tajikistan, Zhenotdel activists in Turkmenistan wrote that a divorced husband often had to struggle all his life to save enough money to marry the first bride who divorced them.[119] Slavic officials, more influenced by the Bolshevik rhetoric of gender equality, tended to support women's freedom to divorce without restrictions. Yet the opponents of divorce in Turkmenistan ultimately won the battle leading to strict restrictions when women elsewhere in the Soviet Union gained unprecedented freedom to end their marriages.[120]

The situation in Tajikistan resembled developments in Turkmenistan. Local officials claimed that a "poor peasant's wife strives for a better life. She does not want to starve and wants her basic needs to be met. Therefore, she is compelled to divorce her husband and to marry a rich man." According to this report since the introduction of Soviet divorce reforms, in Uzbekistan more than half of court cases were divorce cases initiated by women.[121] The report pointed to a specific event that took place in January of 1926, "On this day, in the old city of Tashkent, 250 women-initiated divorce. These women left their husbands for wealthy men and became their 2nd and 3rd wives."[122] By claiming that women's desire for divorce was harming the poor, they could pressure the regime to support "class-friendly" elements over women.[123] The effectiveness of this approach was reflected in adaptation of Turkmen authorities in 1925 and 1926 reforms that restricted divorce.[124] While it is not clear whether new restrictions on divorce applied to all Central Asian countries, it is evident that local officials in Tajikistan used techniques similar to their colleagues in Turkmenistan to manipulate Soviet officials and to achieve desired outcomes.

Local officials in Tajikistan claimed that "men are afraid to let their wives attend events organized by the Zhenotdel.... We must be careful not to instigate a massive class antagonism, which will trigger class conflict since women will be leaving their poor husbands for rich men. This might turn poor men against the state."[125] Local officials knew how to make the case against divorce in terms that Russian Bolsheviks could understand, namely by shifting the debate from gender oppression to class conflict.[126] This indicates that the local actors did play a role in influencing the Soviet laws in the region.

The payment of the bride price remained a part of marriage negotiations between families, although it was banned under the Soviet criminal code in 1924. The *kalym/kiit* was a promise that provided women some security.[127] In the case of a divorce initiated by a woman, she would have to hand the *kalym/kiit* over to her husband, but if the man initiated the divorce, then the woman would keep it in full. It was extremely difficult for a woman to obtain a divorce under Islamic law, so the *kalym/kiit* gave her some form of financial safety in case her husband proclaimed divorce. In some ways it also served to discourage divorce because a husband would be reluctant to lose it.[128] The Soviet reforms did not manage to eradicate the practice, but they did change its nature. During the Soviet period, instead of money families gave cattle, furniture, property, and other household goods as wedding presents.[129]

As for polygamy, in 1926, the Soviet regime declared that a marriage could not be registered with the Soviet state if either the bride or groom was already married to another person.[130] In the 1920s, polygamy was most practised among high-level officials, since they were the ones who could afford to support more than one wife. Consequently, an unspoken approval of the practice remained among the most privileged. Women rarely expressed opposition to polygamy, and as unhappy as some may have been in a polygamous household, the alternative was no less undesirable, which was social condemnation of unmarried women.[131] The regime failed to enforce the ban against the practice. Based on Northrop's findings, government officials found many violations of family law in Uzbekistan in the 1930s, including numerous cases of polygamy, underage marriage, widespread practices of *kalym/kiit*, and hundreds of cases of rape, murder, and abuse of women.[132]

In Soviet Central Asia, the practice of polygamy eventually ended, especially in the post–Second World War period. It was most likely due difficulties associated with hiding it from the state, especially compared to underage marriage. Marrying an underage girl could be concealed and would become irrelevant once she reached the age of 18.[133] While the regime largely succeeded in ending child marriages, the marriage of underage girls continued throughout the Soviet period. The typical marriage age for Muslim girls in Tajikistan remained between sixteen and nineteen, whereas men were of marriageable age any time beyond seventeen until their late forties.[134] The bureaucratic problems of polygamy became more complicated with time, particularly when both wives had children that needed to be registered with the state.[135] The Soviet state also eventually eradicated veiling practices in the post-war period. Few women who were born in Tajikistan after the 1920s veiled. Many covered their head with a small scarf known as *kasinka* or *qascha* (in Tajik). Yet early marriage and bride payment persisted throughout the Soviet period.

The Muslim population in Tajikistan learned to combine their Soviet identity with their Muslim one. Some scholars have argued that the official sphere was mostly dominated by the Soviet state and the private and community spheres by ethnic culture and practices associated with Islam. The boundaries between these different spheres were not always clear.[136] Based on a study of male elites in the northern region of Leninabad (now Khujand), women played an important role in safeguarding and transmitting the cultural capital that came under the Soviet regime's attack in the 1920s and 1930s.[137] Flora Roberts explains that cultural capital is transmitted in the home, and that women, who reigned in this space, therefore "played a crucial role in preserving family histories going back many generations and passing on to the next generation a code of conduct and norms considered vital to their family's identity."[138]

Despite the low attendance of girls in schools during the early 1920s, the Communist Party achieved notable success in their education over time. By the 1930s, primary education had become mandatory for both boys and girls, and co-education was widely implemented.[139] The regime encouraged Muslim girls to receive secondary education, take part in physical training, play team sports, and join performance arts, such as ballet, acting, and singing.[140] Analysis of the Zhenotdel's activities in the 1920s in Soviet Tajikistan illustrates that the regime did not prioritize Muslim women's emancipation campaign in its transformation of the region. It is especially evident in Zhenotdel's lack of resources, continuous change of tactics, and logistical difficulties. This indicates that the Bolshevik regime did not regard Muslim women as a "surrogate proletariat" in the region that lacked a true proletariat.[141] As a recent study of early Soviet rule in Tajikistan shows, the Soviet leadership generally applied "trial-and-error" strategies to administer the region. The Soviet state incorporated local actors and showed tolerance of established social structures and norms to rule the region. This approach enabled "the central power to deal with, while not solving, issues of cultural differences, the diverse context of the Soviet Union, lack of resources and, to a certain extent, the necessity of legitimacy."[142] While the Zhenotdel faced numerous challenges as it carried out the regime's trial-and-error strategies in the Muslim-majority periphery, the organization succeeded in training the initial cohort of indigenous women that eventually rose to prominent government positions in post-1935 era in Soviet Tajikistan.

2 The Retreat: The Stalinist Approach to the Muslim Woman Question, 1935–1953

In a radical campaign to liberate women during the 1920s, the Bolshevik regime denounced the family as a bourgeois institution, weakened the institution of marriage, and promised gender equality to women. In 1930, Joseph Stalin declared women's emancipation complete. This announcement coincided with the regime's closure of the Zhenotdel.[1] By the 1930s, the regime encouraged motherhood and strove to raise the birth rate. It tried to strengthen marriage by making divorce harder to obtain, banning abortion, and introducing incentives for women to have more children. The country that had launched the greatest socialist experiment to change the institution of marriage and to introduce gender equality retreated to a traditional family model and promoted an essentialized notion of women's "natural role" as mothers.[2] These developments are known in Western historiography as the "Great Retreat," which affected all Soviet women.[3] This resulted in a reversal of many of the early gains for women.[4] Nonetheless, the Second World War compelled many women in Tajikistan to replace their fathers, husbands, brothers, and sons in the fields and factories. To enter the workforce, a significant number of Muslim women threw off their veils.

A recent study based on numerous accounts shows an unusual shift in women's involvement and visibility in the mosque and in social life during Second World War. Women around the Soviet Union sent unprecedented petitions to the government requesting certain changes; hosted small and large religious gatherings; and led or attended women-only prayer groups in private homes, where they also gained instruction on how to read Arabic script.[5] These changes did not, in any way, come with significant gender reforms aimed at achieving gender equality. In fact, all aspects of life in Soviet Tajikistan remained highly gendered.[6] This chapter examines the Stalinist regime's approach to Muslim women's liberation. Specifically, it focuses on political and social developments in the lives of Muslim women in Tajikistan during this period.

There is little literature on the experiences of women in Central Asia during the Stalinist era.[7] As a result, this analysis primarily utilizes sources from the Party Archive of the Institute for Political Research of the Republic of Tajikistan for the purpose of explaining Muslim women's experiences during the Stalinist period. These sources indicate that the Soviet regime promoted more conservative propaganda messages to women in the 1930s to 1950s compared to the 1920s. These records also suggest a rise in the number of ordinary Muslim women in urban and rural areas of Tajikistan who adopted Soviet ideology under Stalin's rule. In urban areas, these women were a product of both the Zhenotdel's activism in the region in the 1920s and the regime's nativization policy.[8] Even if only in small numbers and primarily in urban areas, Muslim women became active in the social and political life of the country (see figures 2.1–2.3). They had to learn to balance their professional duties and adhere to Stalinist values, such as prioritizing their roles as mothers and wives, while also respecting community norms. However, these conflicting expectations continually limited the ability of female leaders to effect meaningful change in gender politics within the Soviet system.[9]

Contrary to the regime's exaggerated claims of its great achievements in terms of Muslim women's emancipation, the practices of veiling, polygamy, early marriage, and bride payments continued during Stalin's era. These patriarchal practices and established social structures often hindered Muslim girls' primary and university education and commonly restricted their mobility. Consequently, most Tajik and Uzbek women remained in rural areas working primarily on collective farms in jobs that did not require special training or education.[10] In spite of the widespread glorification of female collective farm workers, these heroines of production rarely held positions of power and had little opportunity to advocate for women's interests.

These circumstances did not prevent Stalin's regime from fostering urban and rural women's new understanding of gender. Women came to believe in the value of their input in their nation's economic prosperity. They actively displayed these sentiments through hard labour at the workplace, heartfelt declarations of love for their nation, and endless gratitude to Stalin. Yet the "unfixed state of gender" that Anna Krylova claims the regime facilitated did not promote women's liberation or their mobilization against patriarchal social norms.[11] The state primarily utilized women's transformed understanding of their gender roles to assist in the collectivization of rural areas and the industrialization of urban regions.[12]

Soviet literature on the woman question from the 1930s to the 1960s is scarce because many considered the matter of woman's emancipation to be solved.[13] In the West, a number of scholars have explored the change in the Stalin regime's approach to the woman question. Many contend that Stalin betrayed the early Bolshevik promises of the 1920s when he introduced policies that reinforced women's traditional roles. These developments are known as the Great Retreat in Western historiography on the Stalinist era.[14] Some historians debate whether this was a fundamental retreat or if this policy was consistent with the Bolshevik regime under Lenin.[15] Others view the Stalinist state as a radical break from the Bolshevik reforms of the 1920s. These scholars generally disagree on the motivation for this change.[16]

Several scholars have also explored the Stalinist state's endorsement of traditional family and marriage values to foster the development of obedient middle-class women. The regime supposedly wanted women to devote their attention to maintaining patriarchal families and to dedicate themselves to the upbringing of disciplined Soviet children.[17] More recent studies have shown that Soviet women, including housewife volunteers, female activists, and women who took up various professions, came to believe in their contribution to the construction of socialism.[18] The Stalinist state nurtured women's new understanding of gender and, as Krylova contends, "allowed for a construction of nonconventional female dreams, ideals, and personalities."[19] These works complement Jochen Hellbeck's collection of ordinary citizens' personal diaries during the Stalinist era. Under intense pressure from the regime, many citizens turned into lonely and self-doubting subjects. This drove many to strive for a life of social usefulness and historical purpose.[20] This longing to be part of a movement that promised stability, meaningful experiences, and fulfilment was not unique to the Soviet Union, but also spread into Europe.[21]

Women's Progress under Stalin: Successes and Limitations

In the 1920s, the campaign was more woman-centred and feminist-inspired than the state-centred initiatives of the 1930s. While the Stalinist era did bring about positive changes in gender relations, these were often side effects of the regime's new approach to women's issues. In the 1920s, women were mobilized for their own personal development, as part of a consciousness-raising movement. This was in contrast to

It is between the mountains of regenerated Tajikistan, on its fertile plains, in the collective-farm cotton fields, that these shapely sports-women work. Nobody will ever have the power to cover their happy and jolly smiles with the oppressive paranja (veil).

In the first rank marches the darling of Tajikistan: little Mamlyaket, collective farmer and physical culturist. On her breast she wears the Order of Lenin; on her wrist a little gold watch presented to her by J. V. Stalin.

Figure 2.1. Tajik women marching in a holiday parade in Moscow, 1930. Among them is the famous female collective farmer Mamlakat Nakhangova, who was selected to participate in the event for exceeding the cotton-picking quota in her region.

Source: Alexander Rodchenko and Varvara Stepanova, eds. and photographers, *A Pageant of Youth* (Moscow: Moscow State Art Publishers, 1939).

Figure 2.2. Mamlakat Nakhangova participating in the Moscow holiday parade, 1930, along with other women from Tajikistan

Notes: The women in the parade are wearing shorts (which are short even by today's standards) and displaying their bare legs, showcasing their participation in the Soviet cultural and political scene. It is worth noting that in Tajikistan, women from all ethnic groups and religions seldom wear shorts, even in urban areas. Therefore, the attire of the women in this picture stands out as a notable departure from traditional dress customs and illustrates the influence of Soviet culture on Tajikistan during this period.

Source: Alexander Rodchenko and Varvara Stepanova, eds. and photographers, *A Pageant of Youth* (Moscow: Moscow State Art Publishers, 1939).

Figure 2.3. Tajik women dancing in the Moscow holiday parade, 1930

Notes: The women in this image, who are Muslim and from the Fergana Valley region of Central Asia, are wearing trousers made from a traditional silk fabric known as atlas silk. During the period in which this photograph was taken, women in Central Asia rarely wore trousers or sleeveless tops, making this attire noteworthy. The image captures the influence of Soviet cultural and political policies in the region.

Source: Alexander Rodchenko and Varvara Stepanova, eds. and photographers, *A Pageant of Youth* (Moscow: Moscow State Art Publishers, 1939).

the women's organizations under Stalin, such as the *obshchestvennitsa* of the 1930s, which mobilized women to serve the state, particularly in its economic growth.[22] Stalin's modernization strategy emphasized rapid industrialization, which required women to mobilize and participate actively in social production. However, the state did not give priority to domestic work and childcare. As a consequence, Soviet women had to balance full-time employment outside the home with the majority of unpaid labour within it. In rural areas, women had to endure the triple burden of working on collective farms, tending individual plots, and performing household chores.[23] The USSR constitution of 1936 included a commitment to universal employment and legally enforced parental responsibility for the care of children. This reform disregarded the extra burden of women's domestic labour and made neglect of their responsibilities as mothers punishable by law.[24] Klavidiia Nikolaeva, who had directed the Zhenotdel in the mid-1920s, defined Soviet women in 1940: "In the Soviet Union woman is active in politics and government and at the same time is a mother, whom our Party and government take care of. This is a new woman."[25] In Soviet society, women were expected to give equal priority to raising children, their professional responsibilities, and retaining their public roles.[26]

Women's double and triple burdens of responsibility within the patriarchal social structures that remained strong throughout the Soviet period seriously disadvantaged the indigenous women of Tajikistan. Families, especially in rural areas, and largely due to established gender norms, commonly prevented their daughters from pursuing primary and university education before marriage, and after marriage women rarely sought these opportunities due to their double and triple burdens. A lack of education and career training chained women to rural areas and to jobs that did not require special education, like manual labour jobs on collective farms. This only increased the growing cultural, educational, and social differences between urban and rural women.

Consequences of the Mother Heroine Title

The structure of urban families underwent a dramatic transformation during the Second World War. As men went off to war, women became the temporary or permanent heads of their households. This forced many women to make decisions for themselves and their children, resulting in increased independence. As a result, urban families began to resemble those in industrialized societies, with fewer children and a preference for nuclear families rather than multigenerational extended families.[27] To address the decline in fertility in the more industrialized republics, the Soviet government promoted motherhood as a social obligation. This coincided with the social value attached to large families in a predominantly rural Central Asia.[28] Large numbers of women in Central Asia qualified for the title of Heroine Mother, awarded to those with ten or more children, and Motherhood Glory awards for mothers with seven to nine children.[29] These awards came with stipends and certain other benefits, such as early retirement and special pensions.[30] Promotion of motherhood, along with the awards and benefits that came with it, further traditionalized women's roles in Tajikistan.[31]

Large families increased women's responsibilities as mothers, which contributed to keeping them away from educational pursuits and making them eligible only for manual labour jobs in the agrarian sector. Stalin's regime ignored these circumstances of Muslim women when in 1948 it claimed that "today young Tajik women learn about the lives of their mothers from history books. They consider themselves liberated, and limitlessly grateful to the Soviet regime and their leader, Comrade Stalin."[32] The regime also declared other achievements in the region:

> Dear comrades, mothers, and sisters, we address our words to you. Russians have helped Tajikistan to skip capitalism. With the help of the revolutionary working class of the great Russian nation, Tajiks have been able to break away from the chains of feudalism and transition straight into socialism, avoiding the misery of capitalism. Women were not considered human prior to the Bolshevik victory. They had to do all the housework, labour in the cotton fields, and stay isolated from the rest of the world covered in the *paranji*. The life of Tajik women was a sad story. With the Russian Revolution, big industry appeared in Tajikistan and agriculture is completing its transition to collective farming. That is why today we are harvesting more cotton each year. The Soviet regime brought education to the masses. There are currently seven state universities, numerous vocational schools, and science institutes. Thousands of young Tajik men and women have received higher education and are now part of the Soviet intelligentsia.[33]

From the 1930s to the 1950s, the success of Soviet women's liberation and equality was measured by statistical data on women's entry into conventionally male spheres of employment.[34] The regime proudly proclaimed that socialism had for the first time freed "tens of millions of women for participation in production and social life."[35] For the first time in history, a significant number of women became doctors, engineers, and teachers, and some even saw active service during the Second World War.[36]

Women's Roles before and after the Second World War

Government sources indicate that "over one thousand women and girls from Tajikistan served in the army during the war. In 1943, 450 girls travelled to restore Stalingrad."[37] Based on these sources women from Tajikistan took care of wounded soldiers and some fought against the enemy.[38] It is not clear in what positions and how many actually fought in the war, but many (women of Tajik, Uzbek, and Slavic backgrounds) served as medical lieutenants.[39] According to official statements, for their service in the Second World War, "over eleven thousand women from Tajikistan [were] awarded the Medal of Valour."[40] As for the female population that remained at home, the government urged them to support the war effort by sending food and clothing items to soldiers. Based on government accounts, "During the first year of the war alone, the Tajik population sent five thousand coats, three thousand fur jackets, nine thousand warm blankets, seven thousand boots, thirty-two thousand gloves, eighty thousand socks and stockings, and one hundred thousand kilograms of wool."[41]

During the Second World War, indigenous female candidates were appointed to government positions. Statistics from 1945 list 10 Tajik women serving as deputies to the Supreme Soviet in Moscow and 8,784 serving as local deputies in the Supreme Soviet of Tajikistan.[42] The regime also claimed that it had educated thousands of Tajik women scientists, doctors, teachers, and government officials.[43] Among them were Mariam Bazarbaeva, minister of education; Anzurat Rakhimova, minster of social security; Habiba Gufranova, assistant minister of commerce; Ibodat Rakhimova, assistant chair of the Presidium of the Tajik Supreme Soviet; Nizoramo Zaripova, chair of the Presidium of the Tajik Supreme Soviet; Guldzhakhon Bobosadykova, first secretary of the Tajik Komsomol; and Mahfirat Karimova, chair of the Council of Ministers. Indigenous female officials in various government positions included Hamro Usmanova, Munzifat Gafarova, Saradzhon Iusupova, Munavara Kasymova, Ochaburi Muminova, Sultaimasab Mirzoeva, Muharram Saidova, Tayba Habibova, and others.[44] These new Soviet women of the 1930s–50s were not only dedicated government workers, but also good housewives and caring mothers.[45]

These Stalinist values were transmitted to girls and women in Tajikistan through various means of propaganda, including public school education. At the meeting of teachers in Stalinabad (present-day Dushanbe), Comrade Gafarova read a report on "communist moral education." She proclaimed, "We do a good job of educating our women to be engineers, doctors, teachers, and even pilots, but we poorly prepare them for family life. We need to teach [them] how to be good wives and mothers first." She emphasized that "neither the Soviet laws, nor life itself removes women from a responsibility to be mothers and wives. It is the teachers' responsibility to teach students, especially female students to have a stable approach to life and marriage."[46] At the same meeting assistant principal of Stalinabad's Girls' School #2, Comrade Geladinskie, also advocated for traditional values in girls' education. "Our Soviet women have learned to harmoniously combine their social duties to their nation, with responsibilities around the house, and childcare. Now it is our mission to educate our girls, starting from a young age, how to properly behave in public, teach them good manners, and instil in them a sense of modesty."[47] Soviet men, particularly members of the Communist Party, were also subject to these norms. In the postwar period, the party implemented policies to address social problems and instil new moral codes. Party organs used censure and expulsion to enforce these post-war communist traits.[48]

Unlike men, women were also expected to maintain a healthy and beautiful physical appearance.[49] These Stalinist standards of feminine beauty were defined in Geladinskie's report, which emphasized that "women must be beautiful and feminine and there is nothing wrong with this. But it is wrong when physical beauty hides inner beauty." She clarified that "young women need to understand that curled hair, expensive jewellery, and imitation of fashion is not good for them. It does not attract society's attention to her. It is inner beauty, proper manners, and good education that draws people's attention to her."[50] In Tajikistan, indigenous women professionals had to combine these Stalinist values with Tajik cultural norms assigned to their gender.

Muslim Women and Social Expectations

These social norms included a sense of modesty (sharm/nomus in Tajik), respect of elders (hurmat), obedient manners at home, humility while in public, and traditional (modest) clothing style.[51] Nizoramo Zaripova, chair of the Presidium of the Tajik Supreme Soviet (1982–4) and one of the most prominent female leaders in the history of Tajikistan, described her early days of professional growth. "In 1937, I was selected to go on a trip to Moscow, to the national parade. Our republic [Tajikistan] had three hundred representatives. Our leader was the first secretary of the Komsomol, Tursun Iuldzhabaev. We practised for the parade here in Dushanbe, near the Komsomol Lake." She recalled that, as representatives from Tajikistan, they had to seem Central Asian, thus have a darker skin colour. "Anzurat Rakhimova was among us. She later became the minister of social security. She had naturally darker skin tone and we would jokingly tell her, 'You do not need to get tan and fry in this heat, go rest under a tree.'" Zaripova suggested that this was because in the 1930s and 1940s, the Communist Party in Moscow, including Stalin, knew little about Tajikistan or its people, including general physical features such as their skin tone.[52]

Zaripova remembered all the details from her first trip to Moscow, defining it as one of the most memorable events in her life. "In 1937, all three hundred of us travelled to Moscow. The parade was beautiful. We wore our national cloth, representatives from each republic did the same." Based on Zaripova's recollection, after the parade, participants met with Politburo members and Stalin for dinner. "It was a lavish dinner table and a variety of food I had not seen before, but I did not touch anything," she remarked. Zaripova explained that she was a devout Muslim and was terrified of mistakenly eating pork. "I still scorned myself for not enjoying myself. Especially since in the 1930s, we barely had anything to eat in Tajikistan." Zaripova took much pride in having met Stalin in person. "He had shiny grey hair, and his face was covered in freckles. He was in his fifties then. I was honoured to see him from such a proximity. I tell everyone that if Stalin was still in power, I would be holding an important government position today," she said jokingly.[53]

Once she returned to Stalinabad (present-day Dushanbe) from Moscow Zaripova's stepfather rushed her to her native village in Kuliab (southern Tajikistan). Three days before classes at her university resumed, she had to travel to her village to address rumours that spread there about her alleged inappropriate behaviour in the city. "As I arrived in my village, my mother rushed from the gates of our house to greet me. She was crying. Instantly the villagers, about 50–60 people surrounded me. It was already nighttime." She remembered her cousin facilitating the conversation. He told her, "Nizoramo, we all came to visit you. There have been rumours going around here. Tell us where you have been, what did you see, and whom did you meet?"[54] She remembered how terrified she felt while addressing her cousin's questions. "My voice was shaking, and my brother loudly repeated what I said, so everyone could hear. I told them with whom I met, what conversations I engaged in, and what I did while in Moscow." Once everyone in her village acknowledged that she was still the same, based on her respectful manners, modest clothing style, and a sense of shame while addressing elders, the head of her village told everyone, "If you hear such rumours about her again, you need to make sure to refute it."[55] Zaripova's story is not unique, most indigenous women in administrative and public jobs experienced similar pressures. These women had to fulfil their professional duties without breaching social norms expected of Muslim women.

Women in leadership positions who were alleged to have broken the established cultural norms were highly condemned. Some of them even received anonymous letters, commonly addressed to the secretary of the Tajik Central Executive Committee (*tsentralnyi ispolnitelnyi komitet*; TsIK), criticizing their supposed inappropriate conduct. This included Mariam Bazarbaeva, secretary of the Stalinabad *obkom* (short for *oblastnoi komitet*, regional government committee). A letter was sent to Comrade Bobodzhon Gafurov, secretary of the Tajik TsIK, from people who lived on Kirov Street. It stated:

> We would like to inform you that the secretary of the Stalinabad *obkom*, Bazarbaeva, regularly takes part in activities embarrassing for the party, including the consumption of alcohol at the assistant head of the central shopping mall's [*univermag* in Russian] apartment. This is where corrupt officials bring her luxury goods and delicatessen food [during the 1930s–50s, certain goods and foods were scarce and available only through the black market]. We live on Kirova Street and know that Bazarbaeva abuses her positions and criticizes party organizations. Despite this, she has been awarded a medal and re-elected.[56]

Another anonymous letter, also addressed to Comrade Gafurov, exposed Bazarbaeva's family background:

> We as communists would like to inform you that Mariam Bazarbaeva is the daughter of a kulak.[57] In 1937, there was an article about her kulak family in the newspaper *Bahori Lenin* [Lenin's Spring]. Her uncle is currently in Afghanistan. She exchanged correspondence with him in 1938. She was not born in Tajikistan. She is Tatar by nationality, pure-blood [*chistokrovnaia* in Russian] Tatar. We think that she should not be secretary of the Stalinabad *obkom*. If you do not believe these facts, investigate her case, otherwise we will send a letter to the Central Executive Committee in Moscow.[58]

On 24 May 1948, a report was produced resolving the investigation into Bazarbaeva's family background. It was determined that she was born in Kazakhstan, in the Kyzyl-Ordinsk region. Her father, Abdumalik Bazarbaev, went through dekulakization (*raskulachivanie* in Russian) in 1930.[59] Bazarbaeva categorically denied that her uncle still resided in Afghanistan. Therefore, the allegations against her were determined to be false.[60]

The motivations behind these anonymous letters remained unclear, but some of the content suggests that Bazarbaeva was failing to meet social expectations placed on Muslim women leaders. As the first letter insinuates, Bazarbaeva was seen socializing with men who were not family members outside work and supposedly consuming alcohol. This behaviour was deemed highly unacceptable for Muslim women. The second letter was sent a few months later. This may suggest that the authors decided to use allegations that the party would take more seriously, while remaining determined to examine Bazarbaeva's conduct, namely her family's class background. These letters, along with numerous other anonymous messages sent to the Tajik Central Executive Committee about indigenous women government officials, suggest the uneasy roles these women had to undertake as the primary beneficiaries of the Soviet emancipatory reforms from the 1930s to the 1950s. They had to combine their professional duties with their roles as mothers and wives, and, most importantly, they had to meet social definitions of what constituted good Muslim women.[61]

Muslim Women Learn to "Speak Bolshevik"

Despite these burdens, these Muslim women professionals revered the Soviet regime. Some of them closely associated the image of Stalin with the father of the nation. They absorbed the ideology and idealized the regime for the opportunities it had created for ordinary Muslim women like them. They expressed their gratitude with loyalty and hard work. Zaripova, for example, stated that she

> worked in the Supreme Soviet of Tajikistan for twenty years, including as the chair in 1982–4. I never left work early. I never used excuses of household chores to avoid professional responsibilities. I never tried to escape work trips to remote rural areas to administer rural women. I managed to meet my professional responsibilities and remain a good wife and a caring mother. The Soviet regime gave us freedom and paved our way into the future. Tajik women earned an independent voice. We were finally able to say "I." Nobody predicted that we would prove ourselves the way we have, in leadership positions, the arts and sciences, and all kinds of academic jobs.[62]

As Zaripova's account suggests, female leaders faced inconceivable amount of professional, personal, and social responsibilities. These expectations continuously limited these women's authority while in positions of power and deterred their potential influence on gender politics. She noted that after the Second World War, the situation was tenser for indigenous women government officials since men expected to take their jobs back.[63] While this was not unique to Soviet Tajikistan or even to the Soviet Union, official reports disclosed this setback. "After men returned from the war, women have abandoned their jobs. Many local party organizations, having enough numbers of male candidates from among the demobilized soldiers, are reluctant to appoint women to administrative positions."[64] This explains the diminished numbers of women in government agencies, including in party TsIKs, *obkomy*, *gorkomy*, and *raikomy*.[65] Based on official statistics, in 1945 within the TsIK bureaucracy there were 760 female workers, of whom nearly half (235) were either Tajik or Uzbek. In 1948, this number decreased to 180 women, only 50 of whom were of an indigenous background. Similar decreases were recorded in the regional and district branches of the Soviet Tajik republic.[66]

Government statements assured that "while the number of Tajik women in administrative position has decreased, more educated and qualified women are being appointed to leadership positions."[67] Zaripova, then head of the Women's Department within the Tajik Central Executive Committee (1956), drew attention to the fact that among these "more educated and qualified women candidates," very few were of Tajik or Uzbek origin. According to her report, "In 1955, 86 women [mostly Slavic women] were appointed to administrative jobs and of them only 7 are Tajik women. There are 21 female school principals in the capital city [Stalinabad] and only 3 of them are Tajik."[68]

Even though the Second World War was a period of radical change in the lives of Muslim women in Tajikistan, since a significant number of them entered the workforce, most of these women entered work in the agrarian sector.[69] For example, in cotton and silkworm farming in Tajikistan, women comprised 80 per cent of the workforce.[70] This in part explains the low percentage of Muslim women in the industrial spheres. In 1955, "out of 11,668 female workers in the industrial sector, only 1,120 [were] Tajik and Uzbek, so 9.59%."[71] Local officials claimed that a high number of indigenous women were in the agrarian sector because collective farms emancipated them and made them equal to men.[72] They based this declaration on the words of Stalin, who had proclaimed, "Our women must remember the supremacy of the *kolkhoz* [collective farm]. They must know that our *kolkhoz* and *sovkolkhoz* [i.e., *sovkhoz*, "state farm"] gave them an opportunity to stand equal to men. Therefore, without collective farms there is no [gender] equality."[73]

Rural Heroines of Production

Officials duly acknowledged that the successful development of cotton in Tajikistan was due largely to the hard work of women.[74] In fact, the Soviet propaganda of the Stalinist era individually recognized and praised leading female collective farm workers, widely known as Soviet heroines. Statistically the number of these heroines around Soviet Union in general and Tajikistan was not significant, but their coverage by sources of mass media, journals, newspapers, movies, and poems, nurtured a widespread myth about these women. Choi Chatterjee explains that these women reflected the regime's social norms for their gender and their testimonies displayed and reinforced Stalinist values.[75] The Soviet heroines were often from poor families, extraordinary for their times, but not necessarily national celebrities, or experienced female party activists. They were previously disadvantaged women who had achieved wide success under the Stalinist system.[76] Kimat Tairova was one of these heroines in Tajikistan.

> Before the Bolshevik Revolution, we [Tajik women] had no rights in the Bukhara Emirates, mullahs [religious officials] and husbands deprived us of our rights and prevented us from openly walking in public. We could not start a conversation with our husbands [traditionally, women had to wait for their husbands to speak first]. Only under the sun of the Stalinist constitution [did] we became equal to men. I am an old, illiterate woman. I farm cotton and for my labour, the party awarded me with the medal of Labour and Achievements. The nation has elected me to serve as deputy to the district council [*raionyi soviet* in Russian]. Thank you to the Communist Party and personal thanks to Comrade Stalin for our happy lives.[77]

The extensive "thank you, Stalin" literature regarding political and social developments in the country, including women's issues, emerged throughout the Soviet Union in the 1930s. This literature exemplified an interconnected relationship between Stalin and the Soviet state's agricultural heroines. The women expressed gratitude towards Stalin for the remarkable progress in their social and material conditions. In return, Stalin was acknowledged as the primary proponent of women's interests and the reason for their achievements.[78]

A case study of women in Uzbekistan from the 1930s to the 1950s illustrates a massive propaganda campaign spread around the Soviet Union about a fairy-tale story of Muslim women's liberation. These stories contrasted the happy lives of Eastern women (*vostochnye zhenshini* in Russian) under the Soviet regime with oppression and dark fate they faced prior to the Bolshevik Revolution. The narratives were typically accompanied by images of young Central Asian women, looking happy, and wearing shining medals on their chests while harvesting cotton.[79] Ugulkhon Kakharova, from *kolkhoz* Dzerzhiskie in the Gissar region (southern Tajikistan), was one of these heroines. She was recognized for harvesting a previously inconceivable amount of cotton. For her achievements she was awarded the highest honour, the title of the Heroine of Socialist Labour. At the award ceremony, Kakharova professed, "It is with happiness in our hearts that we live and work. Because of the Soviet regime today we can breathe freely. We have a firm belief in tomorrow. We also know that if we work hard today, tomorrow we will have a better life. We know that our government values our work and takes care of us."[80]

These Muslim women heroines believed in their contribution to their country's prosperity, not least because the regime introduced positive changes in their lives. A woman remembered her life prior to the Soviet regime. "I used to live with my mother-in-law, who had 16 children. We lived in destitute poverty. Now I have 9 children of my own and the government supports my family [referring to the Mother Glory allowance]. Comrade Stalin takes care of us."[81] A famous milkmaid, Gulsun Tursunova from Iava region (northern Tajikistan), also expressed a deep sense of dedication to her profession and her limitless love for her nation.

> I never took days off from work. I would be officially on vacation to get my salary bonus [*otpusknye* in Russian], but I would continue to work my regular hours. When I was sick and could not make it to work, my cows would get sick too because my substitute would not know how to care for them properly. Once I was gone for eight days, to take part in the national competition of milkmaids, and when I returned my cows had swollen nipples. I did not sleep all night. I kept reciting a prayer. After this incident, I never took a single day off from work again. My country depended on me for dairy produce.... I have received numerous awards for my work and was famous for my technique to milk cows.[82]

Although these rural heroines of production achieved fame on their *kolkhozy* and beyond for their remarkable accomplishments, they rarely held positions of power to form a political movement and pursue women's interests within the Soviet system. Their claim to fame rested on the fact that they engaged in occupations traditionally reserved for men, and they saw themselves as equal to men in the workplace because they produced the same, if not better, results. For these women, this confirmed the Soviet regime's widely touted achievements in Muslim women's liberation and, most importantly, made them believe in the government's dedication to women's emancipation.[83]

Some reports described the other side of the Heroine of Socialist Labour's stories, like that of Halimakhon Suleymanova. "When I worked, I was needed, but once I got sick, nobody even wanted to look my way."[84] These reports urged local officials to personally visit homes of some of the heroines, including Rasulova, who stopped working due to arthritis. According to Rasulova, "When people came to visit me and witnessed my living conditions, I felt deeply embarrassed. I did not even have a place to sit them."[85] Officials described their visitation to Rasulova's home as appalling. "How is it possible for the Heroine of Socialist Labour to live in such destitute conditions?"[86] Ilič views stories of the Soviet heroines' abandonment as reflective of their instrumental use during the Stalin period. According to the author, women were massively drawn into the labour force in industrial and agriculture sectors, when there was a major shortage of labour. It undoubtedly provided them opportunities for self-development, education, and training, but not liberation.[87]

Although the Soviet heroines were celebrated and praised in various media outlets, they were not always welcomed at staff meetings on collective farms, behind the wheel of a tractor, or even on factory floors after the end of the war.[88] For instance, during the war the regime appointed Muslim women to leadership positions on collective farms, mostly as brigadiers. Brigadier administered a brigade by appointing tasks and deadlines for their accomplishment to individual collective farm workers. Local administrations in Tajikistan proudly claimed, "In Gissar [southern Tajikistan] alone, there are about 300 female brigades."[89] Personal accounts of Tajik and Uzbek women brigadiers reveal hardships they faced in these professions in the post-war period. A Tajik woman brigadier from *kolkhoz* Tojikstoni-Surh in the village of Dekhkan-Arikskie, disclosed that "nobody on my *kolkhoz* shows me any respect or support. Men are reluctant to accept my authority. They look at me with suspicion."[90] A similar reality is reflected in another Heroine of the Socialist Labour's daily experiences.

I wake up at 6 a.m. every day and go straight to the cotton fields. I am usually gone until 9 p.m. I rush home to breastfeed my child during lunch and run back to the field. Others on the *kolkhoz* look at me and do not want to join our collective farm. They say, look at our Heroine of the Socialist Labour's life, that's not life. My conclusion is that men do not work in the cotton fields, but they also do not want to create working conditions for us to work productively.[91]

It is evident that women were able to articulate their grievances from the 1930s to the 1950s. They frequently raised objections regarding the inadequacies in the practical implementation and overall direction of policy initiatives. Most commonly, they complained about the challenges they faced in balancing full-time work with childcare and household duties. This ability to voice their complaints may have been a result of women's opinions and objections being disregarded.[92]

According to accounts of Soviet heroines in Tajikistan, these women relied heavily on the state to maintain their authority in both the public and the private sphere. The state artificially sustained their power and it did not originate from any significant change in gender relations.[93] Some local officials recognized that "we have not helped ease women's labour." Typically, once a failure was admitted, the blame was put on a lower-level government agency. It this case, local collective farm administrations were faulted for not taking women's fragile physical build into consideration when assigning them heavy labour. "While a majority of women are doing men's work, men are occupied in jobs that do not require physical labour."[94] The proposed solution maintained that "women need to learn about their legal rights. They need to pursue and protect these rights." Interestingly, in the same report the authors also reminded readers that in capitalist countries women still do not have the rights granted to Soviet women. "In Sweden, Belgium, Greece, and Iran women are deprived of their rights. They are not even able to vote…. Women in these countries are not elected to the government."[95]

The Stalinist Regime's Exaggerated Claims of Success

While Stalin's regime widely claimed to have eradicated patriarchal practices that prevented women's social and political participation, some of these practices continued throughout the Soviet period. They remained particularly strong in the countryside and experienced resurgence in the post-war period, especially the practice of polygamy.[96] Statistical data from the 1950s suggests that polygamy was most common among collective farm administrators, most likely because only these men could financially afford to have more than one wife.[97] However, data on prosecution of the practice in the late 1940s and 1950s is surprisingly low. In 1947, only eleven men were expelled from the party for entering polygamous relationships. In 1948, this number increased to twenty-nine, but in 1950 there were only twelve men charged with polygamy.[98] Officials explained that these low numbers were due to courts and police requiring women to file a complaint against their polygamous husbands, which they rarely did.[99]

Government workers, including Shadieva, *zhen* instructor in the Kuliab *gorkom*, documented some explanations for the recurrence of polygamy after the end of the war. During her lecture on the *feudal-boy* (patriarchal) approach to women, the attending men told her, "Right now there too many single and widowed women and few men. Many of us died in the war. So, we are allowed to marry up to 4 women."[100] Another case of a polygamous family was recorded on *kolkhoz* Pushkin, where the head of the collective farm, a sixty-year-old man with two wives, married a third one. He explained it as an obligation since she was passing the acceptable marriage age and nobody was interested in her.[101] Saidov, the head of *kolkhoz* Kuybesheva in the Ordzhinikzabad region, explained having two wives as a necessity: "My first wife works on our *kolkhoz* and the second one greets guests."[102] The head of *kolkhoz* Gorkie also explained his polygamous family as a necessity: "One of my wives can make bread and the other one cannot."[103] Akramova, a *zhen* instructor in the Stalinabad *raikom*, spoke with a number of urban men in polygamous relationships, and they told her, "Our wives are illiterate and lack culture, so we are forced to attend movies with Russian women."[104]

Other enduring types of patriarchal practices included women's veiling. Officials who visited the Leninabad region in northern Tajikistan in 1950 observed that strangers mocked and harassed women and young girls who walked in public unveiled.[105] Government sources explained the resurgence of the *paranji* as forced by men who recently returned from the war. "Today a wife takes off her *paranji* and tomorrow her husband makes her to put it back on," officials observed.[106] Sources also disclose that veiling was typically associated with the countryside, even though it also existed in urban areas, including the capital city, Stalinabad.[107] There were even isolated cases of Russian women taking up the *paranji* during this period. "On *kolkhoz* Voroshilova, former Russian teacher Sorokina, after marrying a local man, took up the *paranji*."[108]

In the post-war period, Muslim women in the countryside rarely joined their husband at the dinner table and in public they walked behind them. Local government organizations also recorded numerous cases of wife beating, underage marriages, and bride payments.[109] These reports emphasized that patriarchal practices were conducted not only by ordinary men but also by government and party officials. For instance, a former assistant head of the Garm region in central

Tajikistan, Mansur Normuhamedov, married according to feudal-boy traditions and paid 1,600 rubles for his wife.[110] Lack of actions in eradicating patriarchal practices in rural areas was due in part to the regime's low prioritization of the woman question. For instance, an official source claimed that the local administrations were instructed by the central party in Moscow to strengthen women's organizations on their *kolkhozy* once they completed the task of strengthening collective farms.[111] Some reports also described a disrespectful attitude to women activists by the local party organs.[112] "At a meeting in the Leninabad *gorkom* where the woman question was being discussed, male attendees turned the conversation into jokes and mockery, until the head of the female activists intervened and imposed a more serious tone."[113] These officials knew that the regime's priorities lay elsewhere, namely with the country's economic development and not with the woman question.

As part of the campaign to relaunch the fight against patriarchal approaches to women in rural areas, local officials claimed to have disseminated information about article 109 in the constitution of the Tajik republic. The article stated, "Resistance to women's emancipation, forced marriage of underage girls, bride payment, prevention of women from attending school, entering production, or participating in the political life of the state, is punishable by law."[114] Yet most lectures organized for rural women in the 1950s were on subjects related to their labour input. The themes included "Women's participation in the spring harvest campaign," "Results of the fall harvest and women's seasonal tasks," "The development of silkworm production," "Preparation and production of crop," "Women's participation in local and the Supreme Soviet elections," and "Preparations for winter in animal farms," among others.[115]

Strong patriarchal social structures in rural Tajikistan were most vividly reflected in high dropout rates among female students in elementary and secondary schools. In 1950 the regime proudly claimed, "If before the Russian Revolution, there were 10 religious schools with 369 students, mostly sons of wealthy people who worked for the emir, today in Stalinabad alone there are 893 schools with 116,983 schoolchildren, 7 universities, and 14 vocational training facilities."[116] These statements did not acknowledge dropout rates among Tajik and Uzbek girls from the 1930s to the 1950s. Based on statistical data, in 1947–8, "three thousand Tajik and Uzbek girls dropped out of secondary schools in the Leninabad region [present-day Sugd, northern Tajikistan] alone."[117] According to the same report, "This trend is consistent in other parts of the country."[118]

A high dropout rate among indigenous female students explained the small numbers of Muslim girls who continued their education at the university level in the 1950s. For instance, "In the Stalinabad medical school, during the last graduation there were 185 students, none of them indigenous women. Currently [in 1950], there are 201 female students in the 5th year of school and only one of them is a Tajik woman."[119] Numbers of indigenous female students in the Stalinabad Nursing School and the Stalinabad Pedagogical Institute in 1951 were similar.[120] Ibragimova reluctantly admitted that "female graduates of our institute [the Stalinabad Pedagogical Institute] after graduation became housewives. These were often students who received Stalin's fellowship or Komsomol scholarships to attend university." She provided specific examples: "Dzahlalova received Stalin's stipend but after completing her studies became a housewife…. Isabaeva received a scholarship from the Komsomol and now stays at home and wears the *paranji*."[121] Reports suggest that most female students of indigenous ethnic backgrounds quit their studies due to feudal-boy practices. These girls were pressured by family members to marry early (traditionally between the ages of sixteen and nineteen) and after marriage women rarely returned to school.[122]

Officials put the blame on collective farm administrators and asserted that instead of encouraging girls to pursue education, they dissuade them from doing so.[123] This report included an example of a female student from Kanibadam region (northern Tajikistan). A Tajik girl completed the tenth grade and came to Stalinabad to continue her studies at the pedagogical institute. When the head of her *kolkhoz* was visiting the capital city, he met with her and tried to convince her to return home. He apparently told her, "Both educated and uneducated women eat the same type of bread."[124] This statement implied that she would have the same life experience with or without university education, so there was no need to continue her studies. Patriarchal social and family structures prevented rural Muslim girls from pursuing secondary and university education, which in turn locked them into manual labour jobs. Women who grew up in rural Tajikistan from the 1930s to the 1980s were unable to raise their levels of education or change their place of work. Nonetheless, the regime triggered significant changes in the lives of women in Tajikistan.

During Stalin's regime, a significant number of women from a variety of backgrounds came to believe in their ability to contribute to their country's economic development. For the first time in the history of Tajikistan, several Muslim women rose to prominent government positions during this period. Yet these female professionals rarely held strategic positions of power to affect gender issues.[125] Compelling feelings of nationalism and women's active presence within the labour force under Stalin's leadership did not significantly alter women's choices in public and private spheres. Yet changes in women's understanding of their gender roles were used by the state as part of the war effort and in the post-war restoration of the country.

3   The Triple Burden: Soviet Reforms in Post-war Rural Tajikistan, 1953–1982

It became clear in the post-war period that the Soviet regime's top-down approach to the emancipation of Muslim women in Tajikistan during the 1920s and 1930s had a significant impact on the life experiences of urban women within a single generation. Urban women enjoyed higher quality secondary education, easy access to universities and career choices in industrial and administrative spheres, prospects that remained unavailable to rural women. Women have more options in urban settings since in rural areas patriarchal family arrangements typically limit their choices and restrict their decision-making ability.[1] Rural women in Tajikistan who managed to move to urban areas and break away from the patriarchal social norms of their villages were able to benefit from the Soviet reforms. Jones and Grupp's extensive research of family structures in Soviet Central Asia have established a relationship between family size and urbanization, education, and functional specialization. Rural Central Asian women who pursued higher education in urban areas experienced greater gender equality.[2] Muslim women who managed to urbanize and pursued university education tended to have fewer children and concentrated in blue- and white-collar jobs compared to those who stayed in the countryside. Education of women, according to Jones and Grupp, is a much better forecaster of birth rate than the overall level of education in any given republic or ethnic group. Once urbanized, Muslim women could no longer rely on extended family support for childcare while preschool facilities remained of poor quality and in short supply. According to these findings, women were especially disadvantaged in Tajikistan and Turkmenistan.[3] This was primarily due to the fact that unlike rural men, Muslim women in Tajikistan could not easily move to urban areas to pursue educational and career opportunities because of socio-economic and cultural norms.

Rural Tajik women retained the lowest level of education in the union throughout the Soviet era. They also stood out for having the highest rate of early marriage and the highest birth rate. These circumstances confined rural women to subservient positions at work and at home, reinforcing the existing patriarchal social structures in the region. These are the women who were least affected by the Soviet regime's emancipatory reforms. This chapter assesses why the Soviet state's emancipatory reforms barely reached rural Tajikistan and, most importantly, why rural women remained in the countryside. In spite of the Soviet regime's promises, collectivization did not accomplish its goal of radically transforming the countryside. The persistence of patriarchal social structures and traditions linked to Islam in rural Tajikistan served to highlight perceived divisions between modern, urban Soviet society and the "backward" rural populace.[4] This was due in part to Stalin's prioritization of rapid industrialization, which required rapid expansion of the skilled labour force through education and vocational training in urban areas, where the infrastructure was already somewhat developed.[5] In Tajikistan this resulted in the industrial sector, including factories and plants; hospitals; and universities being established in urban areas, primarily in the capital city, Dushanbe, and the second-largest city, Leninabad.

Urban areas had a remarkable growth in terms of infrastructure and skilled workforce while the countryside remained overlooked. The state failed to create educational and occupational opportunities beyond collective farms for the rural population. This did not prevent rural men and some women from benefitting from the Soviet legacy of free secondary and university education and entering careers outside the agrarian sector. Yet for most rural Muslim women these prospects were inaccessible because of cultural norms. While the low quantity of secondary schools in the countryside left all rural children disadvantaged, it did not impede rural boys' secondary education. Families allowed their sons to attend schools in neighbouring villages, but they were typically reluctant to let their daughters walk long distances to get to these schools. Transportation in rural Tajikistan remained close to non-existent during the Soviet period. Girls were considered vulnerable to sexual abuse and had to stay under close parental and community watch. Without secondary education women were eligible only for manual labour jobs on collective farms.[6]

Similarly, the poor quality of secondary education, especially the quality of Russian-language instruction in the countryside, affected rural girls more than boys. Learning Russian was a strategic choice since it opened doors to good universities and eventually to white- and blue-collar jobs. Rural families typically invested in the education of their sons but not their daughters. Traditionally, sons were expected to stay and take care of parents in their old age, so it was desirable for them to have well-paid jobs. The education of daughters was not a priority, because they would eventually become part of their husband's family and leave the parental home.[7]

Other factors that explain lower educational attainment among rural women compared to rural men were gender roles assigned to girls. While all rural children were expected to help parents with work in the household's private garden and on the collective farm (most commonly in cotton fields), daughters were also expected to help mothers with household chores and caring for younger siblings. This need for child labour in the countryside kept girls away from school more than boys, thus contributing to their lower secondary education rates.[8] Rural girls with lower levels of education had fewer job options and typically remained on collective farms. They married earlier compared to peers in urban areas and consequently had a longer fertility period. This in part explains larger families in the Tajik countryside. After marriage, women would combine a full-time work with domestic duties, childcare, and responsibilities for a private plot of land and private livestock.[9] This daily routine contributed to rural Tajik women's the lowest level of rural-to-urban migration in the Soviet Union.[10] Once married women, unlike married men, rarely sought educational or vocational training due to daily obligations, including their husband and his family's objection to their engaging in activities outside work and home. Lack of specialization restricted the majority of rural Muslim women to labour-intensive jobs on collective farms.[11] These circumstances reinforced patriarchal family and social structures in the countryside.

The Soviet regime not only retreated from its initial promises to eliminate patriarchal family structures, but in fact it united workers (*dehkhon*) on collective farms (*kolkhozy* and *sovkhozy*) into brigades based on old social structures. The new structures were formed along old patriarchal familial, neighbourly, or tribal lines – that is, based on *mahalla* communal divisions.[12] The *mahalla* members, who were traditionally community elders (*myi-safed*, "elderly men"), monitored Muslim women's and girls' adherence to gender roles. These included cultural norms of women's modesty and strict sexuality (*nomus/sharm*). Girls were expected to maintain virginity until marriage, avoid romantic relationships prior to or after marriage, and behave in a manner that would not bring shame on them and their family. These social expectations required that family and the *mahalla* continually monitor Muslim girls. Parents were generally reluctant to risk the entire family's reputation for a daughter's university education away from home. This was one of the main reasons the Soviet regime failed to recruit significant number of rural Muslim girls to attend universities, which were available only in urban areas.[13]

The Soviet government provided special quotas for rural Muslim girls from remote regions of Tajikistan to enter national universities without admission exams.[14] Muslim women who were able to urbanize and pursue university education were often orphans or had a family member who was part of the communist regime and who had some education. Society strongly disapproved of those who openly defied traditional concepts and expectations associated with women. Those who did challenge the established gender norms often did so under exceptional circumstances.[15] This is why only a minority of rural Muslim women were able to migrate to urban areas and obtain university education. There were not many Muslim girls and women whose lives were shaped by such exceptional circumstances. Experiences of these rural Muslim women confirm that it was not necessarily the shortage of development or colonial nature of the Soviet regime in the rural Muslim periphery as some historians and experts in the region have argued that explain why rural women did not benefit under the Soviet system.[16] Nonetheless, the Soviet regime failed to address the social and economic obstacles that kept rural Muslim girls and women away from educational and career opportunities and impacted their prospects. Rural women who moved to urban areas, earned university degrees, and took up careers in industrial and administrative spheres were of the same ethnic and religious backgrounds. The only difference was that these women were no longer tied to the same social system and were thus able to do well under the Soviet system.

Based on the existing literature on Muslim Central Asia with references to rural Tajikistan, 80 per cent of rural Muslim women in Tajikistan were concentrated on collective farms and in manual labour jobs because of the Soviet regime's need for raw materials, cotton in particular. Historians and experts in the region have pointed to the fact that indigenous people were concentrated on collective farms while the Slavic population occupied industrial and administrative jobs to point out the colonial nature of the Soviet regime in the periphery. These experts argue that the Tajik countryside remained underdeveloped, with fewer roads, secondary schools, and daycares because it was not a priority for the regime.[17] Industrial development in Tajikistan has been closely tied to the production of cotton, including ginning, the textile industry, and related activities.[18] As a result, some scholars argue that Moscow's intentions in Tajikistan were primarily focused on extracting natural resources and raw materials to advance the development of the western regions of the USSR.[19] According to these authors, the indigenous population of Tajikistan remained in the agrarian sector to fulfil the Soviet Union's need for cotton and other raw materials.

Interviews with rural Tajik women shows that with the collectivization of agriculture, men and women were indeed chained to *kolkhozy* and *sovkhozy*, economically.[20] Collective farms did not provide material incentives for producing quality work due to a lack of opportunities for professional growth and promotion. The option of working outside collective farms did not exist, and the regime restricted migration to urban areas in search of industrial sector jobs. The passport and residency requirements, known as the *propiska* (urban registration) system, regulated rural-to-urban migration, and prevented rural people from freely moving to cities without a guaranteed educational or career placement. These controls were not intended only to keep rural workers on farms but also to address practical infrastructure concerns in urban areas.[21]

As in the rest of the USSR, a *propiska* was provided by one's employer or educational institution.[22] Urban areas throughout the Soviet Union faced a severe housing shortage from the 1950s to the 1990s, and as a result, the government regulated internal migration through passport control and the *propiska* system. Passports were typically issued to young men who were leaving to serve in the army or male students who were moving to the city to pursue education. Collective farm administrators safeguarded workers' passports, and without it, a collective farm worker could not find work elsewhere.[23] It was not easy for villagers to obtain a *propiska* unless they met all the requirements.[24] While the *propiska* system allowed the Soviet Union to avoid homeless people in urban areas, the required registration made it challenging for locals to urbanize while it seemed easily available to Russians.[25] Tajiks were at a disadvantage when it came to the distribution of apartments in urban areas. The limited housing was primarily assigned to specialists who were relocated to the region from another part of the Soviet Union. This contributed to the perception among the rural population that the cities were primarily for Russian speakers.[26] Although the passport and residency system made it more challenging for the rural population to migrate to urban areas, it did not make it impossible. Despite the restrictions, rural Muslim men in Tajikistan maintained a high rate of rural-to-urban migration.[27]

Muslim women in Tajikistan did not enter industrial sector jobs available in urban areas because of the predominantly agricultural nature of the country, and in many cases also the Muslim character of the population. Both factors created serious obstacles to the entry of indigenous women into industrial sector.[28] The existing literature on Muslim women of rural Central Asia does not extensively discuss cultural factors, namely the impact of ethnicity on women's entry into the industrial sector. Cultural constructions of femininity reinforced ethnic boundaries in predominantly agrarian, Muslim Tajikistan.[29] A significant percentage of indigenous men, in both urban and rural areas, were able to secure non-agrarian jobs and benefit from the educational opportunities provided by the Soviet Union. However, the rate of Muslim women in Tajikistan who entered non-agrarian jobs was lower compared to that of women in colonial Middle East. This was due to the perception that industrial sector work involved interaction with men.[30] In Tajikistan, women from the western parts of the USSR and a substantial proportion of Tajik men occupied factory jobs, which explains the low presence of indigenous women in the industrial sector.[31]

The Soviet collectivization of agriculture strengthened the social and cultural factors that restricted rural women's education and employment choices. The collectivization system strengthened close kin and *mahalla* relationships in the countryside as clans and specific ethnic groups in existing villages became the basis of economic organization on collective farms.[32] Soviet officials believed that they could expand cotton production while concurrently improving life and work conditions of rural populace. Yet the state's failure to mechanize labour while cotton production kept expanding necessitated more labour.[33] As a result, collective farm administration had to find ways to keep workers on the farm.[34] They offered various incentives to the rural population, such as cash rewards, construction materials, access to private land, and fertilizer. In addition, they relied on the support of *mahalla* leaders, offering them protection from persecution when practising religious traditions.[35] This reinforced gendered division of labour in the countryside, which was influenced by pre-Soviet practices.[36] The *mahalla* also encouraged the traditions of high fertility, extended family networks, and preference for sons.[27] Most importantly, these patriarchal social structures and established social norms disapproved of Muslim girls having mobility and living away from family in urban areas.[38]

Like many other cities in Central Asia, urban areas in Tajikistan did not completely shed their rural ties, so *mahalla*s also extensively existed in urban areas. In the cities due to various factors, the urban *mahalla* became less homogenously ethnic and more diverse in terms of social composition.[39] While this chapter explores rural women's experiences exclusively, some of the realities that limited women's personal and professional options also apply to urban Muslim women. Nonetheless, the case study of rural women illustrates enormity of challenges women faced to benefit from opportunities unveiled by the Soviet reforms. The Bolshevik campaign to liberate rural Muslim women in Tajikistan from the chains of patriarchal social norms through women's education, employment, and social welfare programs remained incomplete. Lack of transformation in the periphery was not simply due to undelivered promises of industrialization and development. Rather, it was a complex set of factors, including the Soviet regime's continued low prioritization of the woman question, the shortcomings of collective farms, and the failure to address the social obstacles faced by rural women in their pursuit of the benefits of Soviet reforms. As Kandiyoti explains, "Work among Muslim women were primarily geared to fulfilling economic plans rather than promoting women's liberation; from the party's perspective the two were synonymous."[40]

In the post–Second World War period, millions of rural Muslim women in Tajikistan entered the workforce, but they were typically relegated to the lowest-skilled and lowest-paying jobs on collective farms. As a result, they faced a range of challenges, including low wages, limited opportunities for advancement, harsh working conditions, and unequal division of labour within the home. Unfortunately, these problems persisted throughout the Soviet period, leaving many Tajik women trapped in low-paying, unskilled work with few prospects for improvement.[41] Tajikistan's predominantly agrarian economy meant that Muslim women were largely concentrated on collective farms. This was due in part to the country's demographic make-up. In the first Soviet census of 1926, Tajikistan was still an autonomous republic of Uzbekistan, and only 10 per cent of its population lived in urban areas. By the time of the 1959 census, urbanization had risen to 33 per cent, reflecting a significant resettlement of different ethnic groups to Central Asia, including Tajikistan. This demographic shift contributed to the country's growing urbanization, but also meant that many rural Muslim women continued to work in agriculture on collective farms. Following the Second World War, a significant number of Russians and internal political deportees from diverse ethnic backgrounds, such as Germans, Tatars, Chechens, and Koreans, migrated to Soviet Tajikistan. Many of these newcomers settled in Tajikistan's two largest cities, Dushanbe and Leninabad. These non-indigenous ethnic groups were primarily employed in expanding industrial sectors and held most of the new industrial and administrative jobs in Tajikistan. As a result, ethnic employment patterns reflected economic disparities in the country.[42]

In the post–Second World War period, the rural population in the western parts of the Soviet Union faced significant decline. Firstly, there was a significant decline in the birth rate during the Second World War. Severe shortages of daycare facilities also made it harder for women to have more than one or two children, and there was a general move towards a smaller family size around the country in the post-war period. In rural areas, the fall in the population was more evident because of the migration of young people (both men and women) to developed parts of the country. During the same period (1950s–60s), the rural population of Central Asia increased by 13.7 million. In some regions of Tajikistan, Kurgan-Tiube in particular, this was a 200 per cent increase.[43] Even when rural population growth rates in Central Asia declined by 1.8 to 2.7 per cent in the 1970s and 1980s, Tajikistan was the only exception. The rural population of Tajikistan increased by 3.4 per cent during this period.[44] In some regions of the Tajik republic, the proportion of rural inhabitants was more than twice as high when compared to the average in the rest of the Soviet Union.[45]

Large Families in Rural Tajikistan

Census data from 1970 indicates that in rural Tajikistan, 32 per cent of families had five and more children, whereas in the same year in rural Russia, 3.5 per cent families had five or more children. In neighbouring Uzbekistan, the situation was not too different. The percentage of families with five and more children in Uzbekistan was 25.9.[46] Nonetheless, the Soviet census data indicates that Tajikistan had the highest average annual rate of population growth in the Soviet Union from the 1960s to the 1980s.[47] Tajikistan experienced steady population growth in the post–Second World War period, particularly in rural areas. This growth was attributed partly to the country's political stability during this time, which had a positive impact on life expectancy and led to an increase in the number of married couples. Additionally, infant mortality rates dropped significantly due to improvements in the standard of living, access to free medical care, and other favourable conditions.[48]

In the 1970s and 1980s, surveys were conducted that shed light on the factors that discouraged many rural residents in Tajikistan from relocating to urban areas. These factors primarily revolved around the desire for large families. Children were considered crucial for taking care of younger siblings and elderly relatives, as well as providing social security for their parents in their old age. The cultural norm of extended families living together remained widespread in rural areas, allowing families to provide mutual care and support. In larger families, the cost of raising children was relatively low, leading to a higher standard of living and more spacious living conditions compared to urban areas.

Throughout the Soviet Union, rural households benefitted from income generated by private plots, lower living costs, and greater availability of housing in comparison to urban areas.[49]

In Tajikistan, a cultural preference and economic need for large families in the countryside affected rural women first and foremost. Early marriages and large families attached Muslim women to rural areas, resulting in their having the lowest rate of rural-to-urban migration in the Soviet Union.[50] The data provided in the Soviet census, the *Itogi vsesoiuznoi perepisi naseleniia*, illustrates that by 1970 in the western parts of the USSR more than a quarter of rural women were over the age of fifty-five. These republics had a low proportion of women under the age of nineteen, while in Tajikistan more than half of rural women were under nineteen.[51] While Tajikistan had the lowest number of indigenous women living in urban areas in the Soviet Union, rural Tajik men frequently moved to urban areas to pursue education and career options.[52] This often created a gender imbalance in rural areas, since some of the young men would end up staying in the city. Lower ratios of young men to young women would in turn narrow a bride-to-be's choices of future partner, commonly leading to pressure for early marriage. Since most marriages in the countryside were arranged, families feared that by not accepting a marriage proposal earlier (typically between the ages of sixteen and nineteen), a girl might face difficulties in finding a husband later. There were also many cases in which young men eventually returned to their native villages to take a wife, traditionally for their parents' sake; it was generally known that some already had families in urban areas too.[53]

Secondary Education in the Countryside

The limited availability and quality of secondary education in rural Tajikistan contributed to low levels of rural-to-urban migration among Muslim girls. Historically, education was segregated by gender in Tajikistan, and only after the 1930s, when primary education became compulsory, did co-education become more widespread.[54] In the 1970s, rural Tajikistan had the lowest number of students attending primary schools in the Soviet Union. More than half of all rural primary schools had fewer than thirty students, around 60 per cent of rural eight-year schools had fewer than two hundred students, while ten-year schools regularly attracted students, mostly male, from a 12- to 15-kilometre radius.[55] This was due to several factors, including lack of government funding, vast distances, scattered and small settlements (particularly in mountainous regions), lack of good roads and transportation, and other circumstances that created serious obstacles to the development of secondary education in the countryside. This problem was unsolved even by 1986, when Guldzhakhon Bobosadykova, the head of the Komsomol in Tajikistan, publicly acknowledged it during her presentation at the Annual Congress of Soviet Women in Tajikistan:

> One of our biggest problems in rural areas today is children's education. We still face shortage of daycares, kindergartens, and schools. As a teacher, I personally sympathize with three-shift school schedules [a system in which students attended school in three different shifts due to limited space] and rural students attending schools in neighbouring villages, which are located 3–4 kilometres away. I can only imagine how worried mothers are for their children. After all, winters in Tajikistan are long and cold. If we knew that this problem would be solved as part of the Five-Year Plan, we would not be mentioning it today. But we have made plans only for 1990, when we plan to open seven new schools for 2,208 children.[56]

While rural families sent their sons to schools in neighbouring villages, they were typically reluctant to allow their daughters walk long distances to the same schools, since transportation to schools located 15–20 kilometres away was non-existent. Girls were considered vulnerable to physical and sexual violence. This is why Hamro Kiikova, a famous collective farm worker from the Kistakoz district (the present-day Sugd region) who received several awards for exceeding production quotas for cotton picking, did not attend secondary school: "When I was a little girl [born in 1939], the closest school to our village was days of walking distance. We did not have buses back in that day. We walked everywhere. A teacher tried to recruit me to attend the closest school. She promised my father that she will be personally in charge of me, but he said no."[57]

The shortage of schools and low quality of existing ones remained problematic throughout the Soviet period. Rural schoolchildren in Soviet Tajikistan were particularly disadvantaged due to a lack of instructors and facilities in secondary schools. Lack of cultural centres and limited educational and professional prospects in the countryside did not attract well-qualified teachers and recent graduates to rural schools. As a result, few teachers had any higher education. Many instructors in rural schools also had to teach subjects outside their areas of expertise, which undermined the quality of education in the countryside. Rural schools also lacked necessary equipment, including books, science laboratories, televisions, tape recorders, and other important facilities that were available in urban schools.[58] The countryside did not have the cultural and educational facilities that the urban population enjoyed, such as public libraries, theatres, art and music schools for children, and so on. There were libraries on some *kolkhozy*, but often these buildings did not have electricity or central heating, which kept visitors away.[59]

Rural boys and girls were less advantaged than their peers in urban areas because of the lower standard of Russian-language teachers and the patchy availability of Russian textbooks. In many cases in these areas children left school without being able to speak Russian.[60] Learning Russian was often a strategic choice for indigenous populations to prepare them to become more competitive with Russians and other non-indigenous groups for high-status positions in urban areas that Russians had historically dominated.[61] Even in the 1980s, when the proportion of students in general education who used Russian as their language of instruction increased in all Central Asian republics, Tajikistan was registered for the lowest rate of fluency in Russian among rural women.[62] The Russian population in Soviet Central Asia, including Tajikistan, was concentrated in the cities. So urban Tajiks had more exposure to the Russian language and Russian-language education. Even through rural men had a higher rate of fluency in Russian compared to rural girls and women, all students, from smaller towns and rural areas arrived in Dushanbe and Khujand already at some disadvantage.[63] According to Kalinovsky, it is possible that Russian "chauvinism" may have been a factor in its being the primary language of government yet in a centrally planned economy for each republic to have its own language would be too expensive.[64] Surveys showed that even in the late 1980s only 30 per cent of Tajiks were fluent in Russian, and unlike in other Central Asia countries, few in Tajikistan spoke Russian as their primary language.[65]

In rural areas, it was common for Muslim families to have sons studying in higher educational institutions in urban Central Asia.[66] According to Tutikhon Aminova, who was raised in a village in the Kanibadam region, Muslim families prioritized their sons' education, since sons were expected to take care of their parents in their old age. It was therefore important to ensure that they had a good education and better income in the future. Daughters would become part of their husband's family and eventually leave the parental home, so there was less incentive to educate them.[67] Aminova's parents shared this sentiment: "My parents did not allow me to continue my education. They said that they had no money to send me to university, and added that even if they did, I had brothers and it was better to spend it on them."[68]

Hamro Kiikova grew up on *sovkhoz* Khamzaalieva (previously *kolkhoz* Kalinina), in the Sugd region. She explained these outcomes as due to gender roles in Muslim families. Starting from a young age, she, and not her seven brothers, had to help her mother with household chores.[69] As in Middle Eastern cultures, in Tajikistan the socialization of Muslim girls at home started with the brother-sister relationship, which assigned unequal gender roles to children. Girls were typically expected to help their parents with housework (cooking and cleaning), care for their younger siblings and grandparents, and work in the private garden and in the fields (commonly in cotton fields; see figures 3.1 and 3.2). Boys in the family were mostly expected to help parents with fieldwork during the harvest season.[70] These responsibilities tended to prevent daughters from completing secondary school and preparing for university. This reality equally affected urban and rural women. Yet all rural children were expected to help their parents in the fields. Aziza Erkaeva from the Arab village, for instance, started picking cotton at the age of thirteen. "I would go to school during the day and pick cotton in the afternoon. All girls in our *mahalla* helped their parents in the cotton fields. We worked all year long, ploughed soil, and cleared weeds."[71]

This story bears similarities to the celebrated cotton farmer Mamlakat Nakhangova's account of her children. Nakhangova was a cotton farmer who was famously featured in a picture with Stalin in 1935 (figure 3.3).[72] She gained fame after learning to pick cotton with both hands simultaneously.[73] Nakhangova was featured in numerous Soviet mass media sources, including in a children's magazine, *Koster*, in 1967:

MAMLAKAT: I do not remember when I first started in the cotton fields. There were no daycares in our region forty years ago. My parents had to bring me along to the fields. I learned to walk and play there. I started helping my parents as early as I was physically capable. We lived in the village of Shakhimansur, in a small house made of clay.

CORRESPONDENT: Who lives there now?

MAMLAKAT: Nobody. That house and the village do not exist anymore. It is part of a new town, Khimgorodok, in Diushambe *raion* [present-day Dushanbe]. That's how fast our capital city has grown. Before our capital city was covered in white cotton. We saw cotton machines only in pictures. We did everything by hand from sunrise to sunset.

CORRESPONDENT: Including the children?

MAMLAKAT: What can I tell you, in our village we had a school, nobody forced us to work, but we could not remain passive, especially during the harvest season, we had to help our parents. In 1935 there were not enough adults to harvest cotton....

CORRESPONDENT: You look really small in your famous picture where you are harvesting cotton. Was it hard to pick cotton at that age?

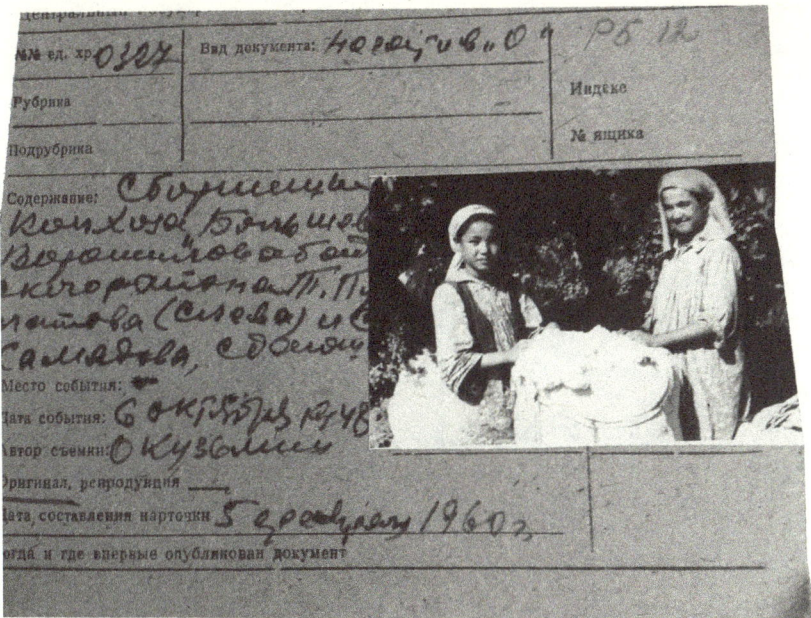

Figure 3.1. Two schoolgirls collecting cotton in the Voroshilova region, 1960

Notes: This photograph reflects the emphasis placed on agricultural production in Soviet policy and the role of education in promoting Soviet ideals. Children were often mobilized to work in the fields during harvest season, contributing to the national goal of increasing crop yields. The photograph offers a glimpse into the everyday lives of young girls in Tajikistan during the Soviet era, highlighting their participation in agricultural labour and the importance of cotton production to the national economy.

Source: Film-Photo-Audio Archive of the Republic of Tajikistan. Photograph of file taken by the author.

MAMLAKAT: No, the opposite. My height matched the cotton branches, so unlike the adults I did not have to bend down.

CORRESPONDENT: So, the secret was your height?

MAMLAKAT: No, my secret was picking cotton with two hands simultaneously....

CORRESPONDENT: How much were you able to harvest with that technique?

MAMLAKAT: I once harvested 103 kilograms of cotton a day. We made national news. An old mullah used to warn my mother, "Beware, they will steal your daughter and take her to Moscow." He was right, I visited Moscow. I was a delegate at the Soviet Union's collective farmers' congress. Michael Ivanovich Kalinin personally rewarded me with the Lenin medal – memories I will always carry with me.

CORRESPONDENT: What did you dream of becoming when you were a child, Mamlakat Akberdyevna?

Figure 3.2. Fazia Gangelieva, a cotton picker on the Stalin collective farm in the Piandzh region, holding up a new harvest of cotton, 1961

Source: Film-Photo-Audio Archive of the Republic of Tajikistan. Photograph of file taken by the author.

MAMLAKAT: When I was little, I certainly dreamed of becoming a cotton farmer.[74]

The Soviet regime justified child labour in the periphery by claiming in official reports that "in the Soviet Union children are learning practical skills not only at secondary school and university, but also through life experiences, in cotton fields. Our children are embodying the country's interests by addressing the nation's need for cotton."[75] In spite of this need for child labour on collective farms, rural boys earned secondary and university qualifications at a higher rate than girls.[76]

The Impact of Social Norms on Rural Women

Another cultural factor that contributed to this higher rate of educational attainment among rural men was the notion of modesty and

Figure 3.3. Mamlakat Nakhangova with Stalin, 4 December 1935

Notes: Mamlakat Nakhangova gained notoriety for her impressive achievements in cotton production, which led to her being selected to participate in a number of Soviet cultural events. Her close proximity to Stalin in this photograph reflects the importance of her contributions to the Soviet economy and the ways in which the regime sought to promote her as a symbol of Soviet success. The image provides insight into the political and cultural propaganda tactics of the Soviet regime and the role of women in Soviet society.

Source: Photo by Mikhail Mikhaylovich Kalashnikov. From N.A. Benediktov et al., eds., *Smotr pobed sotsialisticheskogo selskogo khoziaistva* [A Review of the Victories of Soviet Agriculture] (Moscow: Selkhozgiz, 1940), 169 via Wikimedia Commons.

strict sexual conduct attributed specifically to women. As in other Muslim societies, Tajikistan's indigenous families tied the entire family's reputation to their daughters' obedient behaviour and preservation of virginity before marriage. Women were expected to conduct themselves in a manner that would not bring shame on themselves and their families. While men's conduct could also cause shame, women were seen as the primary cause of it.[77] The central aspect of shame's definition was the sexual control of women, particularly the younger generation. Behaviour that challenged the parents' and the community's authority to oversee and regulate women's sexual conduct was deemed deeply disgraceful. For example, a Muslim girl would bring shame upon herself and her family if she rejected an arranged marriage, flirted with men, or engaged in a romantic relationship before or outside marriage. Such behaviour reflected poorly on her and her entire family, who were expected to monitor her until she was married. Consequently, female shame could also lead to male shame, as it implied that her male relatives had failed to supervise her.[78] Families were reluctant to take a chance on the entire family's reputation by sending daughters to study in the city, away from parental monitoring.[79] Subsequently, girls were discouraged and sometimes prohibited from seeking academic opportunities in urban areas.[80]

It was indeed female members of a family who would educate daughters of notions of modesty and sexuality. Mothers, grandmothers, aunts, and older sisters would teach a young girl to be obedient and observant of social norms of behaviour and instruct her on how to maintain proper conduct. After marriage and as a young wife (*kelin*), her mother-in-law would demand that she observe all the norms and rules very strictly. When a woman gave birth to children, she would start actively influencing young people, especially girls around her, demanding that they observe established norms of conduct. Similar to other Muslim societies, women typically gain more authority and influence with age, particularly post-menopause, when they are deemed as sexually safer from causing potential shame to male family members.

The *mahalla* remained strong in urban areas, but due to the smaller size of communities in rural areas, the communal monitoring was more pervasive there. Muyitabar Pochoeva, born and raised in the Bobojon Garufov district of the Sugd region, recalled of her village elders:

There were benches at the end of our street where our *mahalla* elders sat in the evening. They observed everyone who walked by. Usually these were neighbourhood people coming home from work. They would particularly observe women who walked by. The typical dialogue would go along the lines of: "Who is that woman? Sanavbar, so and so's daughter, so and so's sister, so and so's wife. Why is her head not covered?" Then they would tell men in her family about it. My father strongly reacted to such remarks. He would tell our mother to make sure that we put on our *rumols* [head-scarves] when outside. So, I always carried my headscarf in my purse. I would quickly put it on when I saw these elderly men.[81]

The *mahalla* put less pressure on rural boys.[82] If a Muslim man, for example, dressed in European clothes, failed to observe Ramadan, and engaged in conduct community members regarded as being un-Islamic, such dating before marriage, eating pork, consuming alcohol, or smoking, his conduct was deemed unfortunate but not shameful. Even when rumours about a son's misconduct (often including womanizing) reached his family and community, it was often attributed to him still being young and inexperienced. Some, women in particular, viewed it as somewhat inevitable. If however, a rural woman was caught drinking alcohol or smoking, or, even worse, was seen with a male stranger, she was deemed to have brought shame on herself and her relatives.[83] Although Soviet propaganda continuously attacked cultural norms and the strong influence of the older generation over Muslim girls and women, the central regime in Moscow took little action to change the patriarchal family and social structures in rural Tajikistan.[84] This is why the Soviet regime's attempts to recruit rural Muslim girls to universities in urban areas were largely unsuccessful because they required that Muslim girls leave parental and community supervision.

From the 1960s to the 1980s, the Soviet government made a deliberate attempt to enrol rural Muslim girls at university, even at the cost of equally or more qualified Slavic applicants. While indigenous women had gained higher education significantly in Kazakhstan and Kyrgyzstan as a whole and in urbanized parts of Uzbekistan, this was not the case in Tajikistan. According to Soviet sociological surveys, social conservatism was the main factor hindering women in Tajikistan, Turkmenistan, and rural Uzbekistan (in that order) from obtaining advanced degrees.[85] The Soviet regime's recruitment of rural Muslim girls to universities in urban areas met strong opposition in rural communities. This was due in part to cases in which rural girls studying in urban areas were reported for engaging in romantic relations with men. As the secretary of the Dangara Communist Party, S. Vakhidova, reported,

"We are sending girls to get university education in the city, and they are coming back pregnant. These circumstances make us uncomfortable about talking to parents to persuade them to allow their daughters study at university."[86]

These widely shared sentiments explain a mother's reaction to government workers' attempts to recruit her daughter: "As soon as she opened the door, instead of greeting us, she asked, did you come to take my daughter to school, if so, I will kill all of my children and myself."[87] Nizoramo Zaripova, head of the Tajik Supreme Soviet from 1982 to 1984, recalled the difficulties she encountered trying to recruit Tajik girls to attend national universities:

> Recruiting rural girls to attend university in the city was hard. Fathers, mothers, brothers, and husbands would object. The mountainous regions of Garm, Matjo, Ayni, and several others received a special quota. There were 8–10 spots for indigenous girls from these places to attend any university in the country without admission exams. We would to talk to girls and their parents to convince them to take advantage of this opportunity. But girls would insist that they did not want to attend university. I would ask, "Why do not you want to study?" They would tell me because they wanted to get married. Parents would instruct them to provide this answer.
>
> Families were afraid to send their daughters away from home because they believed that girls who leave for the city change to loose behaviour. I would tell them my personal story of being from a remote village in Kuliab. How people in my village spread rumours about my alleged inappropriate behaviour in the city and criticized my mother for allowing me to study in Dushanbe. Only thanks to my stepfather's support was I able to justify their expectations. Mothers would respond to my story by telling me, "You are a good woman, Nizoramo." Essentially, these women were saying that they do not trust their daughters and that my life story is an exception to the rule.[88]

Aziza Erkaeva, a collective farm worker from the Arab *kishlak* in the Kanibadam region, remembered her mother's words that prevented her from fulfilling her dream of becoming a teacher:

> I completed secondary school in 1963. I dreamed of becoming a teacher. But my mother was strictly against it. It is not acceptable in our culture to let an unmarried girl leave the parental home before marriage. The head of our *kolkhoz* talked me into travelling to Dushanbe and taking admission exams. I agreed. After I took the exams, and I returned home my mother greeted

me at the gate. She said, "I have been living with your father for forty years and you are destroying my family." I did not return to the city. I asked acquaintances from our *kolkhoz* to bring my documents back. Rumours would go around our village about girls' inappropriate behaviour in the city; my mother dreaded such rumours about our family and me.[89]

The majority of indigenous women professionals like Zaripova and others who managed to obtain education in urban areas were either orphans or had family members who were Communist Party members. Either these women did not have a patriarchal figure to prevent them from pursuing education in urban areas, or the regime put pressure on their family to educate them.[90] This is why only a minority of rural girls were able to urbanize and benefit from the Soviet legacy of free university education. Nonetheless, because of these isolated success stories, the regime at times put the blame on rural girls for not fighting for their rights. At the Sixth Congress of Young Women of Tajikistan, the *zhensoviety* activist Radzhabova, after describing the women's councils and the government's (at both the local and the national level) struggle to successfully recruit rural Muslim girls to attend national universities, proclaimed:

> We cannot keep blaming parents for not letting their daughters pursue education. Some girls are not exercising their rights and without objections following their parents' wishes. But we have those who refuse to put up with their parents' plans to marry them early, those who are pursuing education in the city. They are a proof that all girls need to stand up for their rights. In places where girls are not fighting for these freedoms, it is impossible for us to improve their situation.[91]

This and similar reports suggest that the Soviet government was not fully aware of social and cultural pressures rural girls faced to conform to the established social norms that limited their liberties. This is also indicative of the Soviet regime's inability to address these cultural factors due to its limited presence and authority in the Muslim periphery. During the Soviet period in Muslim Central Asia, especially in rural areas, heavy pressure was placed on unmarried girls to submit to parental authority. Parents were in charge of deciding about their daughters' education – both whether it was needed and, if so, where they would study (in the case of post-secondary education) – and typically they also chose their marriage partners. Married women were expected to follow strict rules of conduct and behave in a demure, modest, and respectful manner towards their husbands, as well as their in-laws.

The husband's parents often exerted additional pressure on the wife to conform to these expectations, making it challenging for her to assert her independence or express her own desires. In contrast, young Muslim men were generally not subject to such expectations.[92] In the 1980s, government reports more widely acknowledged that in rural Tajikistan parents prevented daughters from continuing their education, and that some of these parents were Communist Party members and occupied government jobs.[93] The practice of early marriage remained strong in Soviet Tajikistan. The Muslim families in Tajikistan like families in Middle Eastern Islamic societies, were concerned with preparing the daughter for a traditional marriage. This was one of the main factors that prevented young women from pursuing further education.[94] Early marriage made it easier for families to ensure responsibility of safeguarding their daughters' virginity and good conduct before marriage. As for men, early marriages were commonly believed to keep them from engaging in premarital romantic relationships by addressing their sexual needs early on.[95] However, marriage did not keep men away from opportunities outside their native villages, whereas married Muslim women rarely sought academic and professional opportunities outside or even within the boundaries of their native community.[96] Interestingly, Marina Tolchameva's findings illustrate that the bride price was higher for girls with lower education because they were considered to be more compliant.[97]

Early Marriages and Prolonged Fertility

A survey of Central Asian women found that Muslim girls with lower levels of education tended to be more religious and followed a traditional lifestyle that included early marriage and having large families. The survey author attributed this to the girls' age. In many rural areas, Muslim girls were commonly removed from secular education and kept at home after completing the seventh grade, when they reached puberty and became eligible for marriage.[98] At home, girls were socialized to adhere to established social norms of earlier marriages and large families. The Soviet marriage laws managed to put an end to practices of child marriages in Muslim Central Asia, yet the marriage age for girls in the region remained much lower than in the rest of the Soviet Union.

While the legal marriage age during the Soviet period for both sexes was eighteen, in Tajikistan indigenous women were considered marriageable between the ages of fifteen and nineteen. After age twenty, indigenous women experienced difficulties getting married because men their age would already be married. In 1970, a woman in rural Tajikistan was four times more likely to be married under the age of twenty than her counterpart in western parts of the Soviet Union.[99] Indigenous men were considered of marriageable age between the ages of seventeen and thirty. Even beyond the age of thirty, they did not face any obstacles marrying a younger woman or finding a spouse.[100] The Soviet regime failed to convince the Muslim population of Tajikistan to consider practices of early marriage as a crime.[101] Mostly because most of the law enforcement in the countryside was Muslim men and early marriages were rarely prosecuted and punished.

Early marriages also meant a longer fertility period. The Soviet statistics illustrate that in Tajikistan the proportion of women in their high-fertility period was twice the Soviet average. Tajik women under the age of twenty gave birth to 75 per cent of babies born in the 1980s. A relatively high proportion of women continued to have children late into their childbearing years.[102] In the USSR, women had relatively high fertility between the ages of twenty and thirty. However, in the Central Asian republics, high fertility continued until the age of forty. Muslim Central Asian women in the region had a significantly higher fertility rate, with about half of the children born to them having three or more siblings. This was in contrast to the average of 25 per cent for the entire USSR.[103] According to the 1989 census, 2 per cent of all the babies born in Tajikistan were born to women between the ages of forty and forty-four. Eighty-one per cent of those babies had been preceded by at least six other children.[104] Tajikistan retained the highest average annual rate of population growth in the Soviet Union from the 1960s to the 1980s.[105] This was largely due to early marriages and consequent longer childbearing age.

Rural Women's Triple Burden

Paradoxically, from the earlier Bolshevik regime's attempts during the 1920s to replace the oppressive institution of marriage with state-funded childcare (the Leninist theory proclaimed women's rescue from the burden of child-rearing by making these duties a communal responsibility), to the Stalinist and subsequent regimes when women had to bear responsibility for both household chores and childcare. From 1935 to 1982, the Soviet government embraced traditional family structures and emphasized the importance of motherhood. After the Bolshevik socialist experiment, the government reverted to the established family model, and incentivized motherhood by offering bonuses and medals to mothers with more than three children. The government also encouraged motherhood through promises of social welfare and extensive propaganda. However, because the government focused most of its resources on rapid industrialization, it neglected to adequately fund childcare facilities and social welfare programs that would support women in having children.[106]

The government reports acknowledged the dire situation with daycare in rural areas by putting the blame on local leaders: "On many *kolkhozy* and *sovkhozy*, local administrations are not addressing shortages of preschool facilities and the poor quality of the existing ones."[107] Another official report indicated that all preschool facilities in the country were overcrowded: "The ministry of education has received an overwhelming amount of requests from mothers who are not able to arrange their children to these facilities. In Dushanbe alone there are 7,303 unsatisfied requests. Plans for construction of new facilities get interrupted every year."[108] A shortage of daycare facilities forced rural women to rely on extended family, typically parents-in law (at least before daughters reached a certain age) to help with childcare. Based on the Jones and Grupp study, this dependence reinforced patriarchal family structures. The authors' findings illustrate that if the regime had attempted to improve women's triple burdens, in particular a need for childcare, in the long run it could have led to sharing of household responsibilities and resulted in nuclear and non-patriarchal family structures.[109] Instead, the Soviet family policy had negative consequences for women's lives and the issue of gender equality.

The emphasis on women's maternal responsibilities along with women's active participation in the workforce left them responsible for taking care of children, domestic chores, and full-time work outside the home. This triple burden of responsibilities perpetuated gender inequality in Soviet Tajikistan. Collective farm worker Zukhrokhon Negmatova recalled her triple burden of responsibilities in rural Kanibadam:

> I was in the field all day. I lived with my in-laws for two years before we built a small house and moved out. I worked all day long, seven days a week. I combined my full-time work with raising six children. After work I did not have time to take off my heavy boots, I would jump straight to milking the cow, making dinner, and feeding my children. Once the kids were asleep, I would start making dough for bread and doing laundry. I did not have a choice. My mother also worked full-time on our *kolkhoz*. When my father passed away, she only had two of her daughters arranged [married]. She was alone for her remaining six children. After I got divorced and returned to my native village, I watched my mother take care of her fourteen grandchildren, yet she felt sorry for me. She knew I

was constantly tired. Every morning I would rush to work without break-
fast. Once my daughters grew up a little, they started helping my mother
and me with household chores.[110]

The central regime in Moscow and local administrations were aware of
rural women's triple burdens. This was reflected in numerous government reports, which acknowledged that "our women in rural areas are
in a desperate situation. Besides being busy in the field all day long,
they also have to take care of household chores, children, and their private garden. There are no communal services in the countryside to ease
their burdens."[111] In spite of this awareness, the Soviet regime called on
women collective farm workers to increase production:

> We call our sisters in the agricultural sectors to move forward and increase
> our wealth with their labour, to strengthen [the] glory of cotton in our
> republic. The wealthier our nation, dear sisters, the more beautiful is life!
> We call female workers in rural areas to obtain high culture of land owner-
> ship. It is our responsibility to transform agricultural sector with exem-
> plary cultural and socialist lifestyles.[112]

Rural Tajik women heavily relied on their employment as collective
farm workers. In addition to their salary, the government allocated collective farm workers a plot of land for private use. Although this land
was not large enough to make private household farming a profitable
occupation, it played a crucial role in the diets of villagers throughout Tajikistan. According to a 1986 government study, farm workers
received nearly a quarter of their income and obtained most of their
produce from private household agriculture.[113] A family member had
to retain his or her job on the collective farm for the household to keep
their private land. Typically, men in the family would leave for seasonal work in nearby cities and women would have to stay in their
full-time job on the *kolkhoz*, which paid a minimal wage, mostly to preserve their private garden. This often came at the expense of women's
health, as Kurbonbibi Ibragimova remembered of her years on *kolkhoz*
Khizil bibi:

> Our *kolkhoz* administrators would not let us to take a single day off. Every
> morning a supervisor would come to check on us. These were the 1960s
> to the 1970s. We worked honestly back in the day. I did not miss a single
> workday. I would run home after work to make dinner and take care of
> [the] children. During the day, my in-laws would look after my children,
> and once my daughters grew up, they looked after their younger siblings

and grandparents. That's how they grew up. I sacrificed my health and time with my children to meet the production quota just so we could keep our family garden.[114]

Women's existing responsibilities diverted them from improving their qualifications, and lack of education and proper training held them back from vertical mobility. Furthermore, traditional spheres of female employment in the agrarian sector provided no incentive for women to obtain education or vocational training. For instance, in the cotton, animal, and dairy industries, workers' performance evaluations were in no way related to educational qualifications. As a result, the share of Muslim women in vocational-technical schools in Tajikistan remained the lowest in the Soviet Union in 1985. Muslim girls constituted only 15 per cent of all students admitted to vocational-technical schools in Soviet Tajikistan.[115]

Rural Women Remain in Manual Labour Jobs

An extensive survey of the major districts of Tajikistan published in *Pravda* in 1975 found that the majority of women who wanted to work outside the home and manual jobs in the agrarian sector had no vocational training or language skills.[116] Rural women would not seek career training due to family circumstances, namely, too many responsibilities around the house and lack of daycare facilities. Often husbands and mothers-in-law would prevent them from doing so anyway.[117] This explains Soviet statistics from the 1980s that indicate that Muslim women in Central Asia were more equally represented in blue- and white-collar employment, except in Tajikistan.[118] Tajikistan had the lowest number of indigenous women in white- and blue-collar jobs in the agrarian sector.[119] There were very few indigenous women on Tajik collective farms with technical and agrarian training.[120] Nonetheless, rural women's circumstances in Tajikistan were not too different from those of their peers in rural Uzbekistan and Turkmenistan.

In some regions of Tajikistan, throughout the Soviet period there were no women heads or assistant heads of collective farms, brigadiers, engineers, or technicians.[121] Agricultural machine operation required skilled workers, and as a result this field of employment was effectively closed to women.[122] This was due in part to a lack of proper training, but more importantly to cultural norms, since these prohibited Muslim women from operating vehicles and wearing trousers.[123] For example, *Pravda* reported that in Central Asia, "the officials of many farms believe that women are unable to operate machines," with one *kolkhoz* chairmen arguing, "What do I need women drivers for? The farm has 25 male machine operators. The women are just a lot of bother." The article also pointed out that in numerous areas, women had limited access to training courses. Even when they managed to receive training, moreover, they often struggled to find employment involving the use of machinery.[124]

While men were able to obtain well-paid work as operators or mechanics after attending courses or vocational training, there were few job prospects at an equivalent educational level for rural Muslim women. This is how rural women became trapped in the unskilled manual labour sector.[125] White- and blue-collar jobs remained men's areas of work in rural Tajikistan. Men on collective farms were typically concentrated in work that was already mechanized, such as clearing fields, harvesting, and transporting the harvest for sorting and processing. Rural women were engaged in the least mechanized areas of labour, which involved the heaviest physical labour. These included cotton, rice, and other types of produce that required planting, weeding, harvesting, sorting, packing, and cleaning. Women also worked on animal and dairy farms, the few arenas where they operated some machinery. As a result, much of the work that women performed on collective farms was considered unskilled and compensated accordingly.[126] Female labour remained cheap throughout the Soviet period. In 1965, the women on a Tajik kolkhoz made 150–300 rubles a year, while the men received 600–900.[127] As Keller argues, with men doing more prestigious and better-paid labour and the disincentives to mechanize the cotton harvest, picking cotton remained primarily women's work.[128]

In 1986, a government report acknowledged that women were leaving their jobs on kolkhozy and sovkhozy despite their fear of losing their private plots of land. This was due to health problems caused by poor working conditions, lack of basic hygiene, lack of mechanized labour, poor public transportation that would enable workers to get to work, and a shortage of preschool facilities.[129] Yet there were very few employment options for these women outside collective farms.[130] As famous milkmaid Safro Bokieva proclaimed at the Women's Annual Congress, "Comrades, in Isfara [present-day Sugd region], there are twelve thousand unemployed women who are currently looking for work. I call [on] the administration to build something in our region so our women can find work."[131] A report by B. Hamraeva, the assistant head of the Ministry of Culture, made a similar call: "Our women in the countryside want to work but there are no jobs. It is necessary to build factories and plants in rural areas. We have received numerous requests from women who are looking for employment outside collective farms."[132] Rural women in Tajikistan remained concentrated in manual labour jobs on collective farms during the Soviet era. Numerous social, economic, and governmental obstacles made it almost impossible for them to migrate to urban areas for educational and career opportunities for the purposes of upward mobility. These realities left rural women in Tajikistan largely unable to benefit from the Soviet gender reforms. Many of the social norms that prevented rural women from pursuing education and seeking professional opportunities outside collective farm work apply to urban women of Muslim background. Yet rural and urban women were starkly divided by the latter's access to higher education and more professional options. Institutions of higher learning and industrial sector jobs were concentrated primarily in two large cities in the country, namely Dushanbe and Khujand.

4 The Beneficiaries: Urban Women Professionals and Their Legacy, 1953–1982

Although the Soviet reforms to liberate Muslim women in Tajikistan failed to reach many in distant rural areas, these reforms dramatically transformed the lives of some women who were either born in urban areas or who were able to move there. These women, while like rural Tajik women in many ways, often lacked the same family structure due to the loss of a central patriarchal figure, typically fathers.[1] As a result, these women felt less pressured to adhere to established social norms and were therefore able to move to urban areas and receive education. Once in urban areas and educated, the state assigned these women their new identities.[2] The Soviet regime's transformation of Muslim women was characterized by contradictory approaches and results. Muslim women leaders and professionals were expected to combine their professional lives with strict culturally based gender standards while performing onerous domestic duties. The aim of this chapter is to analyse the experiences of the Tajik women professionals who benefitted most from the Soviet reforms. It provides a deeper understanding of what it took for some of the beneficiaries of the Soviet reforms to achieve professional success. This case study also illustrates the role of social expectations and established gender norms, as well as their relationship to the project of Soviet modernization.

Through *korenizatsiia*, the Soviet regime promoted indigenous men and women into leadership positions in the borderland territories. The regime adopted this tactic to suppress potential nationalistic ambitions in the periphery and to escape imperialistic approaches.[3] It put indigenous men in administrative positions, since few educated and qualified women were available in the 1920s and 1930s. This reinforced patriarchal social structures in the region. Nonetheless, the regime took active measures to educate and train Muslim women to take up leadership roles in Tajikistan. A significant number of indigenous women professionals rose to prominence from the 1940s to the 1960s. While the regime aimed to encourage Muslim women to participate in the social and political life of the country, gender equality was defined according to the male-dominated Soviet and local regimes. Soviet women did not have an independent space to pursue their interests outside the patriarchal system.[4] The regime's actions hindered the development of a comprehensive women's movement that could include the interests of women in rural areas, where the state's social engineering efforts had limited impact.[5] The divide between women able to move to urban areas and those who remained in the countryside prevented Muslim women in Tajikistan from coming together to challenge male hegemony or set their own agenda, especially in matters governed by gender.

The Tajik women who urbanized and took advantage of the Soviet regime's educational and professional opportunities became commonly known as "Russified" and "Sovietized" women. These very achievements made them a separate category and alienated them from rural Muslim women who perceived urban Tajik women as culturally different.[6] Despite the public classification of being "Russified," indigenous urban women professionals in Soviet Tajikistan did not find themselves in a closer relationship with their Russian colleagues and peers. In fact, women of Slavic and other ethnic backgrounds (Russian, Tatar, German, Ukrainian, and other ethnic groups) retained a female majority in the administrative roles of Soviet Tajikistan. Unlike Muslim women, Slavic women did not have to meet social expectations and requirements, which worked in their favour in the professional arena. Tajik women professionals were expected to embody the values of modesty that were expected of all Muslim women, but particularly of indigenous female leaders who were considered the face of their nation.[7]

Consequently, Tajik and Uzbek female leaders had to display a casual commitment to their professional responsibilities and actively communicate stronger dedication to their family and domestic chores. Not meeting these established norms was social suicide.[8] These realities limited Tajik women leaders' authority in political and social arenas, limiting their ability to make a difference for their gender. Studies indicate that society and politics in the Soviet Union remained male-dominated. Men retained control of access to political power and did not introduce significant numbers of women into positions of power.[9] As a result, they were unable to develop an autonomous identity or political consciousness besides those assigned to them by the men.[10] Experts on gender in the Soviet Union have generally agreed that in Soviet society, contrary to the regime's promises of gender equality, women remained in a subordinate position in many areas of life. All Soviet women faced a burden of doubled responsibilities and on a daily basis had to combine household chores with full-time duties at work.[11]

The existing Western scholarship on Soviet women has largely focused on education and employment as indicators of women's situation in the country. It has provided data and analyses mostly based on Russian women and to a lesser extent on other ethnic groups including Tajiks, Uzbeks, Turkmen, and others.[12] It is likely that the lack of access to the Muslim republics of the Soviet Union contributed to this phenomenon. Consequently, much of the literature on gender in the Soviet Union tends to use "Russian" and "Soviet" interchangeably. This practice has obscured the substantial differences between Soviet women of Slavic descent and Muslim women in the periphery, especially in terms of cultural expectations and established gender norms.[13] Gender norms played a significant role in shaping the experiences of Muslim women, often making it difficult for them to fulfil social and professional responsibilities. Community norms regarding sexual morality and the Muslim concept of modesty had no direct parallel in Russian society. These expectations varied widely not only between Slavic and Muslim regions, but also depending on the degree of Russification, or integration with Russian and other Slavic Soviet populations, within and across different Muslim ethnic groups.[14] In Muslim Central Asia, and Tajikistan in particular, cultural and religious norms concerning proper female behaviour intimately affected women's public and private roles.

While the Soviet regime opened previously closed opportunities for Muslim women in terms of career, education, social, and political status, Tajik women continued to play their conventional roles at home and at work. This was also expected of women in leadership positions and government jobs. The Soviet reforms introduced both positive and negative changes in women's everyday lives. The regime failed to change the most fundamental aspects of their daily experiences. Regardless of Muslim women's professional position their social status was determined primarily by their commitment to family and community.[15] This case study of Muslim women leaders in Soviet Tajikistan shows that both indigenous men and women promoted these expectations of women, albeit for different reasons. Not complying with and observing gender norms and not meeting social expectations was not an option for indigenous Muslim women leaders. Those who were seen as attempting to break with established expectations did not have a chance of survival in administrative positions. They were punished both professionally, often through elimination from positions or lack of promotion, and socially, through stigmatization and public disgrace.[16]

While the Soviets made significant changes in Muslim women's status, particularly among the educated, urban classes, in the end they failed to eliminate the patriarchal practices they had campaigned against. Tajik women found themselves confined between the state's orders, family expectations, and community mores while trying to seek their own interests in a complex world of new opportunities.[17]

Relatively few Muslim women were found among the educated and cultural elite of Tajikistan prior to the Second World War. This was in spite of the regime's determined efforts to create educational opportunities and to encourage Muslim girls and women to take advantage of them. Despite the backwardness of the region and the traditional attitudes against girls' education, the government efforts to educate a new cultural Tajik elite resulted in significant successes in the postwar era.[18] Most of the Tajik female professionals rose to prominence under *korenizatsiia*. The Soviet regime trained these indigenous cadres to become loyal to the communist regime and to replace kin and clan-based identities with the Soviet identity.[19] The newly educated female officials were appointed to administrative positions in the government. They understood the way of life, customs, and habits of the local population.[20] These women professionals were thus responsible for making the Soviet government seem indigenous rather than an external Russian, imperialistic imposition. This approach was designed to avoid the perception of the authoritarian Bolshevik regime as an empire since it promoted radical social transformation.[21] These women were expected to become a bridge between the Soviet state and the masses, particularly in rural areas and the borderland regions.

The majority of female native beneficiaries of *korenizatsiia* belonged to households where the economic dependence and reliance of women on their fathers and families had already diminished due to their life circumstances or political convictions. This trend was exacerbated during the Stalinist period of the 1930s, which was characterized by suppression, famine, and dire poverty. As a result, some Tajik families were forced to send their children to orphanages or boarding schools, which was a previously unprecedented event in this Muslim society. Women intuitively opposed this occurrence as it resulted in children being entirely disconnected from the customs of family life.[22] Many did not have other options or were pressured by relatives who were Communist Party members to send their children to boarding schools. The government utilized this opportunity to recruit indigenous girls to attend Soviet schools, which subsequently led to many of them becoming pioneering women in various fields, including government, education, and the sciences.[23]

Slavic, primarily Russian women as Zhenotdel workers in 1924–30 implemented women's emancipation in Muslim Central Asia. These activists were responsible for indigenous women's education, vocational training, and job placement.[24] By the Second World War period, an increasing number of indigenous women were employed in administrative positions. In Soviet Central Asia, Russian women continued to play a crucial role in the republic's administration but their actual power was limited. "Local nationals were required to occupy the highest hierarchical positions and all posts of representative character. Invariably, however, a local leader was either seconded by a Russian or backed by a Russian or Russians close to him in the hierarchy." Rakowska-Harmstone argues that this approach was intended for supervision purposes.[25]

Unique Trajectories of Muslim Women Leaders

In Soviet Tajikistan, Russian women officials retained their public visibility and significant presence in government and administrative jobs. Russian women played an important part in the Zhenotdel and later in its successor organization, the *zhensoviety*, in the postwar period. Nonetheless, the women's councils included more Muslim women leaders. As the regime declared, "Today we are able to appreciate the extent of Tajik women's transformation. Their physical appearance could not be more different. The Soviet regime broadened our women's world view with educational and cultural opportunities."[26] Some of these leaders who were able to dramatically transform included Mariam Bazarbaeva, minister of education (1966–73), Habiba Gufranova, assistant minister of commerce (1960–73), Ibodat Rakhimova, assistant chair of the Presidium of the Tajik Supreme Soviet (1978–82), Nizoramo Zaripova, chair of the Presidium of the Tajik Supreme Soviet (1982–4), Guldzhakhon Bobosadykova, first secretary of the Tajik Komsomol (1961–84), Mahfirat Karimova, chair of the Council of Ministers (1961–74), and others. These women became devout communists, which in turn transformed their life circumstances since they came to occupy important government positions and enjoyed an elevated social status.

Following 1945, the education levels of Muslim women increased, and urban households began to resemble families in industrialized societies, with a trend towards having fewer children. Though Muslim women did not achieve complete independence from patriarchal social structures, they did experience some economic freedom through employment opportunities that were previously unavailable to them.[27]

While rural women were mostly concentrated on collective farms, urban women ventured into the fields of politics, sciences, arts, education, and other intellectual professions. Government reports proudly proclaimed,

> If before the Russian Revolution, Tajik women could not even dream about education, today education is not just accessible, but it is of the highest quality. In our republic, there are around five thousand women working in the sphere of education in 664 different research facilities. Some of these Tajik women academics include, Sabi Khakimova, Kubri Hasanova, and Sorojon Iusupova. These women are widely known far beyond the borders of our republic. With much pride we think of our PhD candidates Kumri Tohirova, Molohat Shohobova, Munzira Gafarova, Tuhti Aminova, Mahkam Pulatova, Muharam Rasulova, Hosiiat Babaeva, and many others. There are ninety-nine women working in the Supreme Soviet of our republic, over six thousand women are deputes of local councils [soviets], twelve women are deputies of the Supreme Soviet of the SSR [Soviet Socialist Republic]. Thousands of women are actively participating in activities of the party, trade unions, the Komsomol, and other social organizations. They are making an input to the national cause.[28]

These women were regularly used to illustrate the Soviet regime's successful transformation of Muslim women. They exemplified women's enlightened lives in the post-Russian Revolution period and their bright futures under the Soviet regime. The most prominent Tajik woman leader Nizoramo Zaripova, the chair of the Tajik Supreme Soviet (equivalent to the president today) in 1982–4, was one of the Muslim women who benefitted from the Soviet reforms.

> I was born in 1923 in the Kuliab region, Vosey district, Pakhtakor village, kolkhoz Ishtimoet. I lost my father when I was five years old. My mother, Sharifamo Gafurova, raised me and my three siblings. The reason I took up my stepfather's name as my last name was because he was the only father I knew.[29] My mother was an energetic woman. She was an ordinary farmer who harvested cotton and ploughed soil to make ends meet. I started helping her with household chores as soon as I was physically capable. Another woman would have probably fallen into anguish after losing her husband and remaining with four toddlers at such a young age. My childhood coincided with the hardest years in the history of our nation. The 1930s were a period of famine. On our kolkhoz, we did not have anything to eat. We survived on herbs, grass, seeds, leftovers from cotton [zhmyt], and anything we could find growing on trees.

My stepfather was a communist. When the local administration appointed him as the chair of the regional council of workers, we moved to the Kuliab city. He worked there during 1934–5. This move opened up some opportunities for me since there was a pedagogical institute in the Kuliab city. I was too young to attend it, but my stepfather arranged for me to go there anyway. I was only eleven in 1934. In 1937, the local administration was recruiting girls to attend the women's pedagogical institute in the capital city, Dushanbe. I was selected to go, along with four other girls from remote areas of Kuliab. My mother was reluctant to give her permission. The recruiters convinced her by putting pressure on my stepfather. He could have lost his job if I did not go. On a snowy night in December, we got into a big truck and drove off. We left at 3 a.m. so my relatives could not prevent me from leaving. I still remember my mother's cries: "Bacham, bacham" [My child, my child], she cried.

My life in the city was not easy. I struggled to learn Russian. In my dorm room there were thirty-two girls, all diverse ethnic backgrounds. We were taught proper manners, how to dress, and how to carry ourselves in public. Although during this period we barely had any clothes or shoes to choose from, we wore what we had but behaved well. I studied at the Institute until 1941. I travelled home every summer. One year rumours about my alleged inappropriate behaviour in the city started spreading around our village. Everybody condemned my mother for letting me leave. In tears she wrote letters begging me to quit my studies and return home. It was hard to ignore her pleas, but I continued my studies.[30]

Zaripova's life story makes it clear that indigenous women like her did not come from a conventional background with several strong patriarchal figures in her family, including grandfather, father, and brother(s). Society rejected and condemned those who broke with traditional concepts regarding the role and position of women. Young women like Zaripova and others became exceptions due to their special circumstances. These women often had lost their parents and relatives, most commonly fathers. They did not have strong patriarchal figures to insist on their observance of established social norms.[31] In case of Zaripova, she lacked her biological father and most importantly, her stepfather, a Communist Party official, was threatened with sanctions, specifically his job, if he failed to engage his stepdaughter in the "emancipatory" activities. As an example, in 1927 a decree from the Turkmen TsIK mandated the dismissal of any Communist Party member who did not make their female family members available for literacy classes.[32]

Tajik Female Leaders as a Small Minority

This explains why indigenous women leaders remained a small minority. There were not very many Muslim girls and women whose lives fitted this pattern. Guldzhakhon Bobosadykova is another case in point. She was born in 1937 and served as the deputy to the Supreme Soviet of the Tajik SSR.

My father passed away when I was in the tenth grade. He left six children behind. My mother delivered her sixth child two months after my father's death. We lost our breadwinner. Our relatives advised my mother to marry me off immediately. At least this way there will be one less mouth to feed, they insisted. There were special quotas for Muslim girls to study in Moscow in the 1950s. My grandmother gave me all the money she had so I could travel to Moscow to take admissions exams. I was determined to pursue my dreams. Yet when my mother and I arrived in Moscow a member of the admission committee told us that even though the exams have not started yet all the spots were taken. The secretary of the Tajik *obkom* registered his two daughters for the two available spots.

Two days before the end of the admission exams in Dushanbe, I applied to the physics department and got accepted. While in school, I did not have any support from my family or relatives. I was on my own. I worked part-time jobs at the textile factory during the night shift, washed dishes in dining halls, and did all kinds of jobs before I was offered work at a secondary school. I was the head of the young pioneers [*pionervozhataia*].[33] I was hard-working, which led to my election to the Komsomol. People at the university noticed my work ethic and I was recommended for the position of secretary of the Komsomol. I was still completing my studies at this point. After graduation, the mathematics department offered me a job and I stayed at my alma mater. This enabled me to pursue a graduate degree in math with a minor in French. After I advanced to candidacy in 1961, I took a trip to Moscow to the Steklov Institute of Mathematics. I met with prominent professors there. They advised me to finish my dissertation at the Institute. But I already signed up for a position at the Komsomol, which I could not postpone.

In the fall of 1961, I was elected as first secretary of the Tajik Komsomol, a position I occupied until 1978. Starting in 1972, I also served as deputy of the Tajik Supreme Soviet. I did think about my incomplete dissertation. But I was already juggling too many responsibilities at home and at work. Graduate studies were out of the question.[34]

The educational opportunities the Soviet state created for Muslim women were unimaginable prior to the Russian Revolution. Many of these leaders were raised in Soviet schools, and some, like Zaripova, attended boarding schools. As a result, they were more detached from their community mores and the established social norms for their gender. This enabled them to internalize the Soviet ideals they learned in school. These women learned to "speak Bolshevik," and closely identified with the regime's policies.[35] This transformation was not unique to the indigenous women of Tajikistan.[36]

Sovietization under the Banner of Russification

This process of Sovietization of Muslim Tajikistan was achieved under the banner of the Russian language. Interest in Russian language and culture began under Tsarist Russia. In the post-Revolutionary period, speaking Russian became a distinguishing mark of the educated. When the nativization policy was scaled back in the late 1930s, Russian language and culture became the unifying force throughout the Soviet Union. The instruction in local schools was given from the beginning in native languages, but there were also schools with Russian as the language of instruction, and the study of Russian in local schools was compulsory between 1938 and the 1980s. Knowledge of the Russian language was critical for any Central Asian who wanted to seek upward mobility.[37]

All non-Russians, especially those at the leadership level, were required not only to learn the Russian language but also to familiarize themselves with Russian culture.[38] In the cities bilingualism became vital. Knowing Russian opened doors to jobs in the government, educational institutions, and medicine.[39] According to Dzhamilia Ismailova, the first computer engineer in the Leninabad region, Muslim officials educated in Russian were more successful professionally due to the better quality of secondary education in Russian-language schools.

I received all of my secondary and university education in Russian. [Once] it happened that the principal of my son's school, Gavkhar Dadadzhanova, asked me to substitute for a computer programming instructor for students in the Russian-language cohort. This school had both Russian- and Tajik-language-instructed groups. I instructed eleventh-grade students for six hours a week. Ninety per cent of students in this Russian-language-instructed cohort were indigenous students. Everything went fine. I also happened to substitute for a teacher in a Tajik-language-instructed cohort.

They were also eleventh-grade students. The difference was like night and day. Students in the Tajik-language-instructed group did not understand fourth-grade math.[40]

Due to the poor quality of Russian-language instruction in the Tajik countryside, the cultural gap between the Russians and rural Tajiks remained strong. In 1969, an inspection determined that most courses taught in Tajik "are thoroughly lacing in the necessary literature, and an additional difficulty arises from the lack of Russian-Tajik dictionaries for specific terminology."[41] A large percentage of the problem was exacerbated by the shortage of textbooks in Tajik.[42] The shortage of competent Russian-language instructors in primary schools was a persistent issue that exacerbated the existing educational disparity between urban and rural areas. There was a tendency for Russian-language teachers to remain in the larger cities, which contributed to this problem.[43] Soviet universities and professional-technical colleges encountered comparable obstacles as they aimed to draw in and maintain rural students. The failure to achieve this objective added to a dearth of indigenous experts in the republic, which resulted in an increasing social chasm between individuals who were able to capitalize on the upward mobility opportunities provided by the system and those who were not.[44] This divide also existed between Russians and the local elite, but it was less dramatic.[45]

Social categories often varied based on the type of education indigenous people received. People educated in either Russian or the vernacular languages could be found in administrative positions. Tajik people educated in Russian schools tended to lead a more European lifestyle. As Ismailova explained, indigenous people educated in Russian were exposed to more Slavic, particularly Russian, culture due to their active socialization with Russians and other Russian-speaking ethnic groups.[46] Bikhodzhal Rakhimova's story exemplifies how Rus sification was an integral part of receiving a good quality secondary and university education, which led to subsequent leadership roles. It also resulted in a certain detachment among Tajik female administrators from their ethnic milieu.

I was the fifth child to my parents. I was born on 27 December 1941. When I was born, my father and eldest brother were serving in the Second World War. When my father returned home in 1945, I was three years old. I clearly remember that year because we had a big wedding celebration for my brother. He married our cousin. When the music was playing my dad told me to dance. I was little so it was still socially acceptable. My brother and his new wife moved to the capital city, Dushanbe, shortly after the wedding. He took up a government job there. In 1947, I moved in with them to ease my mother's childcare responsibilities. My mother gave birth to my youngest sister later that year.

I knew some Russian because everybody on our street was either Russian or German [she was born in Khujand, the second-biggest city in Tajikistan]. So, my brother enrolled me in a Russian-language elementary school near his apartment. I struggled in the beginning, but gradually got used to the new environment and speaking only Russian. When I finished the second grade in February of 1947, my father passed away. I returned home to Khujand city. My family decided that my youngest sister, who is two years younger, should move in with my brother and his family. By then I was old enough to start helping my mother around the house. I continued my schooling in Russian at the Pushkin School, now it is called Gymnasium #1. We had strong teachers. I passed my university exams only because I had a strong secondary education in Russian.

After the war, life was still difficult. We were not hungry, but still had to wait in long lines for bread. My mother sewed cloth every day and sold it at the local market at weekends. We lived on the money she made. In 1956, I finished my secondary education and got admitted to the Polytechnic Institute Department of Energy in Dushanbe. Professor Muhammad Osimi was the rector of the Institute at that time. I clearly remember him asking me, "Are you sure you want to major in engineering? There are no girls in the department." I remember declaring to him that I would be the first one.

After graduation from the Polytechnic Institute, I was referred to the Leninabad carpet factory. I will never forget the first day at the factory. I was waiting for the director, Ishan Saidovich Akhmedov. I was in the waiting room, reading. I always had a book in my hands. The secretary directed me to Akhmedov's office when he was finally in. He opened the door and told me to come in. Without looking at me he asked, "Who issued you your referral to our factory?" I immediately responded, "Should I sit down first?" Quite surprised, he raised his head and with a puzzled face said, "Of course, sit down, are you tired?" "No, I'm not tired," I responded, "but I think I should sit down if we are going to have a proper conversation" [traditionally in Tajikistan, not being asked to sit down signifies lack of respect and is a show of dismissal of one's importance]. Our men [i.e., Tajik men] were not used to [Tajik] women using a high tone of voice and speaking with confidence. I was different because of my education in Russian schools. I was less aware of established social norms for young Muslim women.[47]

Russification was an inevitable outcome of Moscow's political control, and was also the result of objective conditions and, to a certain extent, of prevalent attitudes. According to Rakowska-Harmstone, the Western-ization of Muslim Tajikistan was inherent in the process of moderniza-tion. Under Soviet domination, this process entailed Russification in an exceptionally heavy-handed manner.[48]

The High Price of Sovietization for Muslim Women

Yet due to the poor quality of secondary education, specifically the lack of Russian-language classes, Russian was perceived as a foreign language in rural areas. This was in contrast to the widespread claims that Russian was accepted throughout the Soviet Union.[49] This factor contributed to a widening cultural, economic, and social gap between urban and rural areas.[50] Tett's study of rural women in Tajikistan shows that the rural population of Tajikistan had gradually accepted some of the Soviet reforms, such as female education and entering the work-force and working beside men. Yet members of the rural community were insistent that their female members were still good Muslim women. This was not the case for Russian women and urban, indig-enous women.[51] When asked why they wore headscarves, rural girls in Tajikistan responded, "without a headscarf a girl has no shame – she looks like a Russian." Similarly, to the questions related to arranged marriages, they would say "while the Russian girls 'had no shame' because they freely associated with men, village girls were not like that, they had 'shame.'" Tett would also hear that urban Tajik girls were not "real Tajiks" because they tended to wear Russian clothes and had often adopted a considerably more Russified lifestyle.[52] Bakhti Shaidova, the assistant secretary of the Komsomol in the Leninabad region, explained that urban indigenous women professionals were required not only to speak fluent Russian but also to wear only European-style dresses.[53] By accepting Soviet ideals, adopting the dress code, speaking fluent Rus-sian, and holding important government positions, indigenous females became a separate category of the population. They were often identi-fied as Russified women.[54]

Study of Tajik memoirs written in the Soviet era provide glimpses into the changing social lives of the intelligentsia. For instance, Khu-doinazar Asozoda's account illustrates one of many reasons why rural parents may have worried about allowing their daughters to study in the city, let alone outside the republic. Describing the transformation of the future poet Gulruhsor Safieva, he highlights that she grew up in a village before moving to the city to pursue education. Gradually, she replaced her Tajik dress with European-style clothing. She changed her hairstyle and made it more appropriate for attending and taking part in cultural events. This started getting her male attention. As the author of this article explains, "As a woman, therefore, one could join the Soviet-Tajik intellectual elite but had to be willing to shed one's "village" clothes in addition to mastering the Tajik literary language."[55] According to Asozoda, this choice to adhere to "Soviet" behaviour could have socially undesirable consequences for women such as affairs and even unplanned pregnancies. This is why young women who successfully urbanized regularly faced accusations of improper behaviour. Men, on the other hand, easily moved between the two worlds.[56] These realities contributed to Muslim women professionals becoming outsiders, detached from the rest of the indigenous population politically, economically, and socially – or, at least, that is how rural women perceived them.[57]

This social gap is commonly reflected in anonymous letters from rural women to local government administrations condemning certain indigenous women leaders. A case in point is a letter addressed to Comrade Shilkin, the head of the Stalinabad (present-day Dushanbe) *obkom*, about Mariam Bazarbaeva (1917–92), minister of education (1966–73); and Zulfiia Kadyrova, the assistant head of the Stalinabad *obkom*.

Our women [referring to Muslim women leaders] hate other women, they do not even greet us in the street.... How can such women hold important governmental positions and claim to represent us? They are immoral and should not be educating our women and girls. I wanted to go to the TsIk, *obkom*, and *gorkom* several times but my husband threatens to declare *se taloq* [a traditional declaration of divorce], that's why I am afraid to tell you my last name.... I speak for women who wear the *paranji*, please pay attention to this letter and investigate these immoral women.[58]

The anonymous letter ends with a suggestion that these women should be fired, and the author asserts, "We would much rather have Russian and Tatar women represent us."[59] This preference of Russian, Tatar, Ukrainian, and other Slavic women in administrative positions is based partly on the fact that both indigenous men and women considered women from western parts of the USSR as more qualified. This perception was rooted in the Zhenotdel's use of predominantly Russian activists. Moreover, in the early years of industrialization, Russian specialists and skilled professionals, both male and female, were relocated to the region. These candidates took up leadership positions in both the political and the economic sphere. Despite the arrival of newly trained

Tajik women by the mid- to late 1930s, the social advantage of ethnic Russians did not dissipate, and their disproportionate representation in the higher echelons of the Soviet system remained strong.[60]

Russians constituted 13 per cent of the Tajik population in 1959, and their proportion of the population of the western parts of the USSR (if the deported Germans are excluded) did not exceed 15 per cent. Nonetheless, the Slavic people in the Tajik Communist Party made up almost 40 per cent of the membership in the 1960s. Tajiks did not constitute more than 60 per cent, even though they were three-quarters of the population in Soviet Tajikistan in 1959.[61] Tajikistan had the lowest indigenous female membership in local branches of government in the Soviet Union.[62] While the government claimed that one-third of the Tajik Supreme Soviet consisted of female officials, these statements rarely acknowledged that the majority of these women officials were of diverse ethnic backgrounds and that Muslim women government officials remained a small minority.[63] Russian dominance of the strategic governmental positions in Tajikistan was due in part to a shortage of indigenous specialists and trained bureaucrats.[64]

The Impact of Ethnic Patterns on Women Professionals

A Tajik-Slavic ethnic pattern was evident in Soviet Tajikistan. The central government was concerned with the eventual mobilization of the indigenous elite, and to this end, the party included a significant number of Tajiks and members of other major nationalities in its membership. However, the regime retained control over key posts in Tajikistan primarily with Slavic, mostly Russian, officials. Based on the author's findings, similar patterns, with greater emphasis placed on Tajik representation, existed in other mass organizations.[65] The government apparatus prioritized maintaining the appearance of local participation while also maximizing efficiency in performance. As a result, the administration of affairs was primarily controlled by Slavic individuals, while symbolic positions were allocated to Tajiks. According to the data, the indigenous population was deliberately excluded from the defence apparatus.[66] This in part contributed to a perception of indigenous candidates as less qualified for government and administrative jobs. As Dzhamilia Ismailova recalled from her personal experience:

> I was the first woman computer engineer in the Leninabad region. There were barely any indigenous men who were computer programmers at that time [referring to the 1970s and 1980s]. I was called into a meeting

with the head of a construction organization. I was assigned to work on this organization's project. Nearly all the employees in the construction-planning sector used to be Russian. I got along with most of my Russian colleagues, but the head of this organization was a Tajik man. As I was leaving the meeting, I heard him tell the head of my department, "Don't you have any Russian women or men in your department to assign this project to?"

This was a common mentality of the time; Tajik women were considered incapable of mental labour. When I started working in this organization, I started at the same time as my Russian colleague, but she made more money than I did, just because she was Russian. She was regarded as more qualified. The person who determined our salaries was a Tajik man, the head of our organization. Our own people did not value cadres of the same ethnic and cultural backgrounds. That's why in the 1960s–80s, Russian men and women occupied most administrative positions in Soviet Tajikistan.[67]

Zaripova explained that Russian women had an advantage in the professional arena because they were not expected to adhere to traditional Tajik notions of modesty and appropriate behaviour for Muslim women. This was reinforced by social expectations of Muslim men as breadwinners and Tajik women as homemakers, with a less serious commitment to their career.[68]

While the Soviet state called on women professionals to participate equally in the workforce and public life, Tajik norms expected indigenous women to observe and display ethnic ideas of femininity. These included notions of female modesty, delicate manners, and strict norms of sexuality. Since indigenous female cadres were challenging existing norms for their gender as homemakers, they had to work hard to sustain the image of an ordinary Muslim woman. Zaripova recalled that, being a Muslim woman in an administrative position, she had to try even harder to prove herself a good wife and a caring mother, and thus a good Tajik woman (see figure 4.1). "Once my husband's colleague noticed his nicely ironed shirt. My husband immediately and proudly announced, 'Nizoramo irons my shirts every morning.' Our daughters usually did it. But he would tell everyone that I am an excellent cook, that I fix his clothes and take good care of his children. He had to make sure that everyone knows that I am a good wife."[69] As Browning describes, Muslim women leaders were a product of women entering the economic world, being politically conscious and socially active, while retaining those feminine qualities associated particularly with family and motherhood.[70]

Figure 4.1. Nizoramo Zaripova, chair of the Presidium of the Tajik Supreme Soviet (1982–4), reading to her children, 1985

Notes: This image showcases Zaripova's commitment to education and highlights the important role played by women in Soviet Tajikistan. Women were primarily responsible for the upbringing of their children, and the photograph captures Zaripova's dedication to her family as well as her political leadership. The image also provides a glimpse into the everyday life of a prominent female politician in the Soviet era and the complex intersection of family and professional responsibilities.

Source: Photograph provided by Nizoramo Zaripova. Reproduced with permission.

The Soviet statistics show that urban women's average time spent on housework, in addition to employment outside the home, was three hours a day on weekdays and seven hours a day at weekends. In Soviet Tajikistan women were spending even more time on household chores due to numerous traditional celebrations and frequent hosting of guests. As members of the Communist Party, women professionals were expected to participate fully in the social world of civic and political activities, as well as in trade unions and various voluntary associations. However, equal participation by men and women in the public sphere did not disrupt the unequal gender relations in the private sphere. Women were still responsible for childcare and domestic chores, especially female professionals who occupied jobs that demanded greater energy and time.[71] Prominent women were able to combine their full-time household chores with a full-time career of a women leader and motherhood mostly because of the family support, particularly that of grandmothers.[72] This included Rakhimova's family situation.

> My eldest daughter was born in 1967 and my second girl was born in 1970. I did not have other children. I simply did not have time for more. When I gave a speech at the celebration of my sixty-year career in different government jobs, I was asked whether I had any regrets. I was honest in my response, I said I wished I had more time with my children. Even after I gave birth, I did not take time off. We had fifty-six days of maternity leave back then. I was the first secretary of the Regional Committee of the Komsomol. I could not sit at home; my job needed me. It was a sense of duty; I was raised that way.
>
> As Tajik women we were expected to do all the housework on time, do laundry, iron our husband's shirts, clean the house. Even when I had to stay up late at work, my husband knew that his dinner would be ready on time and that the children were taken care of. When my youngest daughter burned herself and was put in the hospital, my mother stayed with her during the day and I went there at night, not my husband. It is a typical scenario for all Tajik women; our husbands make all the decisions, and we carry out these decisions out without relying on them for support.[73]

For Muslim women in Tajikistan to challenge existing gender relations was simply not an option.[74] Instead, many educated Tajik women in white-collar jobs resorted to having fewer children.[75] Those who dared to choose their careers over family were often publicly condemned and many kept away from professional opportunities. The experience of Zaragul Mirasanova, a member of the presidium of the *zhensoviet*, is a case in point. When she was appointed to the position of secretary of the city's *gorkom*, there were many objections. Party members were concerned about her family status, the fact that she was single. "Everyone questioned my professional abilities due to my personal status. 'How can we assume that she will be a good propaganda worker among women when she is not even married and has no children,' they objected. My family status held me back throughout my professional career, but I simply could not imagine combining my political activism with family life."[76]

Not Meeting Social Expectations

Similarly, Muslim women leaders who broke notions of what constituted a good Muslim woman were condemned and widely criticized. This included a prominent minister of industry and trade, Munavara Kasymova, about whom the city government committee received several anonymous letters. One of the letters claimed that Kasymova obtained her ministerial position through corrupt means:

> Kasymova earned her promotions by having affairs not only with high government officials, including Iuldzhabaev, Shilkin, [and] Rasulov, but also with all kinds of corrupt men. She parties with her unmarried colleagues Sabohat Kadyrova and Mumindzhanova. They are all heavy drinkers and well known as a big "P" [prostitute] in Tajikistan. This is the main reason why in Tajikistan many women still wear the *paranji*, they know that if they give it up, they will lose their reputation like her. Kasymova was sent to Moscow to train at the Party School, what's the outcome? Instead of studying, she is working there as a "P." Her lover, Iuldzhabaev, is doing her homework for her. Now she is a minister, and her husband is a director of the Party School. Kasymova is an embarrassment. Everyone is aware of her inappropriate behaviour. She is arrogant and does not care about ordinary people. She has already failed the whole organization. Before it is too late, she should be removed. She has embarrassed all the daughters of Tajikistan.[77]

An investigation into Kasymova's case by Gafurov, the secretary of the Tajik TsIK, showed that Kasymova's first husband died in the Second World War, and she remarried in 1947. Her second husband, Iuldzhabaev, was previously married.[78] Based on the content of the letter it is evident that Kasymova was being criticized for her behaviour, namely for being married twice, socializing with unmarried Tajik female colleagues, and marrying a divorced man. Stigma against second marriages remained strong in Tajikistan, even though in Kasymova's case it was due to her husband's death. The letter describes her second husband, Iuldzhabaev, as her lover, suggesting that he may have left his first wife for her. It also condemns Kasymova for her affiliation with unmarried Tajik women professionals. Single Tajik women professionals were considered a bad influence on their gender because these women were breaking the established social norms for their gender by being unmarried beyond the age of eighteen or nineteen. Moreover, the letter suggests that as an indigenous women leader she was failing to maintain and display modesty and humility. In sum, she was not embodying notions of what constituted a good Muslim woman professional. In the post–Second World War period, the party introduced new ways of championing "communist morality" to address the prevalence of absentee fathers and broken families in the post-war landscape. Party organizations used various means, such as censure and expulsion from the party, to ensure that communists fulfilled their family and parenting responsibilities.[79]

The insistence on humility and modesty are central in Bobosadykova's and Zaripova's descriptions of their career development as leaders.

Every time I was offered a promotion, I told myself that it is simply beyond my areas of expertise, and I will not be able to handle it, [but] I still did it. In all the positions I held, I worked with ordinary people. I spoke from the podium and then got off it to meet with the masses. I was nominated for the position of party secretary [comparable to a mayor] in Dushanbe. I thought a person with a background in engineering should take that position, after all it required administering the capital city with its industrial sector, government institutions, and cultural centres. When I was interviewed for this position, I was open about my sentiments, I said, "I do not think I can do it." I was told that the decision had already been made. A person grows with expanding horizons I told myself.

In December of 1979, I was appointed to the position of secretary of ideology and propaganda. Once again, I was convinced that I would not be able to handle it, but I greatly appreciated the faith entrusted in me. The job was multilayered. I had to be in communication with our intelligentsia, including our prominent academic Mirzo Tursunzoda and other high-profile intellectuals.[80] I worked in this position before I was recommended to work in Moscow in 1987. I was the first Tajik woman to work in the Soviet government at the ministerial position in Moscow.[81]

Zaripova expressed a similarly overwhelming sense of humility while describing her accomplishments as the head of the Supreme Soviet of Tajikistan and other top government positions she occupied. Both prominent Tajik women leaders consistently tried to justify why they were the ones chosen for the positions they held. In 1955–6, when news of her appointment as TsIk secretary started circulating, she remembers approaching her husband and telling him, "I am really scared; I do not think I can do it." She explained that during that period (1950s–70s), they had other educated women, especially of Slavic background. But this position required a combination of skills, the ability to find a common language with the local populace, and a personality capable of retaining influence among members of the intelligentsia – a unique set of qualifications, which few cadres possessed. "I got this position without bribing anyone and without the support of powerful relatives," Zaripova emphasized with joy in her eyes.[82]

Not all indigenous women professionals succeeded fulfilling these social and professional expectations. K.M. Mirzoalieva, a member of the republican *zhensoviet*, addressed anonymous letters condemning indigenous women in leadership positions who were being accused of being arrogant and condescending towards other women at the Women's Annual Congress.

> Some female members of our intelligentsia carry themselves arrogantly at work. They act irresponsibly towards their colleagues and their constituents. These women are not good wives or mothers and do not lead a healthy Soviet lifestyle, they take their work for granted. This is why some have wrong impressions about indigenous women in positions of power.... These women do not have proper understanding of the Leninist politics on equality between men and women.[83]

Muslim women leaders frequently faced unfounded gossip spread by their male colleagues, who did not view them as equals or competitors. These men used their authority to spread rumours about women in administrative roles, casting doubt on their behaviour and ethical conduct.[84] It was widely recognized that Muslim men who were Communist Party members publicly supported the Soviet state's stance on gender equality, while continuing to promote their traditional gender roles at home and, to some extent, in public.[85] They maintained and endorsed gender norms that limited the authority of Muslim women cadres in the political arena. Women were expected to preserve their feminine qualities, which strictly prohibited their participation in the informal male networks of securing deals through bribes, cutting deals, pursuing promotions, and so on.[86] Women who tried to take an equal part or dared to challenge the patriarchal political system did not have a chance of survival.

Despite the Soviet state's active efforts to eliminate patriarchal social norms and practices in Muslim Central Asia, both male and female professionals were equally dedicated to preserving and maintaining the existing social structures.[87] For instance, the *zhensoviety* enforced female characteristics for indigenous girls by calling for a need to instil in every single woman a sense of modesty, simplicity, respect for family, and a sense of pride in the Soviet Union.[88] In turn, Tajik women leaders placed these expectations on their female subordinates.

> I did not think much about gender differences and affiliations. Yet when Bobosadykova, the first secretary of the Komsomol was promoted to a different position, I thought I would replace her. I simply assumed that she would choose to promote my candidacy. After a while I learned that a candidate from Ayni region, Usman Ganievich, second secretary of the regional Komsomol, was appointed to replace Bobosadykova. I remember thinking to myself, well, that's stupid. He had to be trained for this position when I was readily available for it.
>
> A colleague mentioned to me that it was based on Bobosadykova's insistence on appointing a man as her replacement. I realized then that she did not like me. I used to wear fitted dresses and she even made a remark once inquiring if I am aspiring to be a ballet performer. "No, I do not have such plans," I replied. "I just know my size and like fitted dresses." I could have responded with a rude comment but choose not to. In our culture we are expected to please people in the position of authority, but I was educated differently. I did my schooling in the Russian language. I had less exposure to Tajik social norms placed on indigenous women and she wanted me to be more traditional. She would consistently tell me that she knows I have the required education and enough experience but that I am too self-confident. How can I hold a position of authority if I do not have the necessary confidence?[89]

By personally maintaining and actively promoting established characteristics assigned to Tajik women, female leaders limited their own and their female colleagues' authority within patriarchal political and social structures. These women ended up endorsing male interests in the political arena.

The challenging experiences of Tajik women leaders often made their legacy unappealing, and parents often intentionally prevented their daughters from pursuing upward mobility through higher education.

While the Soviet state opened some doors to Muslim women in Tajikistan, especially in terms of education and career opportunities, the
regime closed others. Tajik women never gained an independent space
in which to come together and frame their own identity independent of
established gender roles. Tajik women leaders, the primary beneficiaries
of the Soviet reforms, remained a small minority with limited authority,
which prevented them from creating a new climate of encouragement
and inclusivity for their gender.

5 The Thaw Era: Women's Organizations (*Zhensoviety*) in Post-war Tajikistan, 1953–1982

At the Twentieth Party Congress in 1956, Khrushchev publicly denounced Stalin and adopted welfare reforms, many of which affected women directly.[1] Most importantly, Khrushchev expanded the *zhensoviety*, the women's councils, throughout the Soviet Union. From the post–Second World War period through the collapse of the Soviet Union, the *zhensoviety* were the only women's organizations in charge of Muslim women's transformation in Central Asia. At the height of their extent in 1986, there were approximately 1,787 *zhensoviety* in Soviet Tajikistan, and they united about 31,732 female activists.[2] Each workplace, each neighbourhood, and nearly all collective farms had their own *zhensoviet*. These women's committees marked a radical change in the Soviet regime's conventional top-down approach to women's emancipation by promoting a bottom-up strategy. This made the Soviet Union the first government among regimes that enforced state feminism – whose ranks included Iran, Turkey, and Afghanistan, among others – to officially allow women to organize themselves autonomously from the state. Based on the *zhensoviety*'s organizational reports, these women's councils were more diverse in their political activities than their predecessor, the Zhenotdel (1924–30).[3] The *zhensoviety* were affiliated with the Soviet Women's Committee, which the regime reinstated in the 1980s. The new women's organizations did not have their predecessor's authority.[4] These women's committees were quite effective during the Second World War in representing urban women's rights and interests in the workplace, especially in factories and plants.

In the post-war period, Khrushchev expanded these committees to rural areas. In Tajikistan, through the women's councils, the Soviet regime aimed to transform rural women, who remained the least impacted by the state's social engineering. It intended to achieve this objective by eradicating old customs based on feudal-boy practices and religion and replacing them with new Soviet culture and practices. This chapter focuses on the *zhensoviety*'s structure, their agenda, and the Central Committee's association with their regional affiliates. It specifically assesses the women's councils' attempts to introduce Soviet culture in the Tajik countryside. The next chapter looks at the *zhensoviety*'s anti-religious campaigns in rural Tajikistan. Both agendas aimed at cultural transformation for the purposes of modernization and Sovietization of the Muslim periphery.

The Structure of the *Zhensoviety*

The majority of the *zhensoviety* leaders and urban activists were of Russian, Ukrainian, German, Armenian, Tatar, and other ethnicities. Russians in particular comprised the second-largest ethnic group in Dushanbe in the post–Second World War period.[5] The ethnic diversity of urban *zhensoviety* membership and predominantly Russian leadership made Russian the primary working language of the *zhensoviety* in Tajikistan. Most *zhensoviety* reports were written in Russian.[6] Historically, Slavic women administered Muslim women's emancipation in the 1920s and 1930s. They retained a reputation for being more educated, more Sovietized, and considerably more experienced in social activism in the post-war period.[7] This contributed to women from the western parts of the USSR constituting a significant portion of the *zhensoviety* leadership and membership. In the post-war period, the *zhensoviety* had a substantial number of urban Tajik and Uzbek women administrators and members who lived and worked the city. In the countryside, nearly all leaders and members were of Muslim background, mostly Tajik and Uzbek. The republican *zhensoviety*'s use of Russian as their primary language widened the divide between rural women and activists.[8] Rural Muslim women in Tajikistan had the lowest rate of fluency in Russian in the union during the Soviet period.[9]

While formally autonomous, the women's councils aligned women around the central regime's agenda, which consequently defined women's experience through a male culture.[10] As a result, the Soviet women were expected to take an active part in social activism of the *zhensoviety* while juggling their existing responsibilities of full-time work, household chores, and child-rearing, known as women's double burden. In rural areas women faced a triple burden since they typically also took care of their individual plot of land and livestock. These are some of the reasons the *zhensoviety* failed to mobilize Muslim women in rural Tajikistan. The cultural divide between the urban women of Slavic background and Sovietized urban women, and the even wider socio-economic divide between urban and rural women, continued throughout the Soviet period.

The councils' aims came into conflict with the realities of rural women's experience. The women's councils within the Soviet Union promoted anti-religious propaganda, political and economic mobilization, and social activism. In Tajikistan these agendas came into conflict with Muslim women's distinctive circumstances compared to women in western parts of the Soviet Union and urban women in general. Muslim women remained predominantly in rural areas of Tajikistan (over 80 per cent) and were less educated, more religious, and less culturally Sovietized compared to urban women. Rural women in Tajikistan came to see the women-only groups not only as an additional burden, but also as an imposition by urban women often of Slavic background and Russified Muslim women who largely constituted the *zhensoviety* leadership and active membership.[11] The *zhensoviety*'s centralized approach and their unpopular agenda in the Tajik periphery only widened the gap between urban and rural women. While the *zhensoviety* within the Soviet Union were taking more bottom-up approaches, especially compared to the Zhenotdel, in Tajikistan they retained their centralized approach in the countryside. Nonetheless, these women's committees illustrate the regime's change of approach to the woman question by appointing local regime and indigenous populations to oversee women's emancipation. The Central Committee, known as the republican *zhensoviet*, controlled the *zhensoviety* rather than the central regime in Moscow.[12]

The *Zhensoviety*'s Agenda in Soviet Tajikistan

As dictated by the central regime in Tajikistan, the *zhensoviety*'s objectives included a renewed attack on practices the regime associated with religion, and integration of Soviet culture in the countryside. These circumstances prevented women in Tajikistan from coming to together to challenge male hegemony in political and social spheres.[13] Thus, the regime's control over the *zhensoviety* averted these committees from potentially becoming a genuine venue for women's mobilization in Soviet Tajikistan. Expansion of the *zhensoviety* invigorated the woman question, which remained generally stagnant until the Khrushchev era. Khrushchev publicly declared the emancipation of Soviet women to be incomplete.[14] The regime identified general factors that prevented women's liberation and gender equality around the Soviet Union. First, women's double and triple burdens, namely women's full-time household chores combined with full-time jobs left them with less time than men for social and political activities. Secondly, traditional attitudes towards women persisted and led to sexual discrimination. Thirdly, women still lagged in terms of political consciousness.[15] As a result, the *zhensoviety* were responsible for addressing these and other factors the government came to view as major obstacles to women's complete liberation. The *zhensoviety* provided Soviet women with a seemingly workable institution for uniting and seeking their interests within the political and social spheres.

Historians have argued that the Khrushchev Thaw period, often seen as a time of liberalization of attitudes towards women, should be viewed in a different light. In fact, it was a period of increased state intrusion in domestic life. The Soviet government attempted to promote a vision of modernity that emphasized the importance of nuclear families and the role of women in the workforce. This involved a number of policies aimed at encouraging women's participation in the labour force, such as the provision of maternity leave and access to childcare facilities. However, these policies also reinforced traditional gender roles by placing the burden of domestic work and childcare on women, even as they pursued professional careers. Therefore, the Khrushchev Thaw should be understood as a period of intensified state regulation of gender roles and domestic life, rather than a period of liberalization.[16] As Victor Buchli notes, "If the Stalinist state was poised at the threshold of the 'hearth,' the Khrushchevist state walked straight in and began to do battle."[17] When a social welfare state intervenes to organize domestic life, it is usually women who face the consequences of these interventions first-hand.[18] Although the *zhensoviety* managed to bring millions of women into participating in various aspects of the state, economic, and cultural administration, their participation remained at the "low" or informal level of political activity.[19] Close examination of these committees across the Soviet Union shows that the agenda remained male-dominated because men continued to control access to political power and did not allow women to hold significant positions of power. As a result, the *zhensoviety* were constrained in their objectives and, more importantly, in their capacity to enact substantial changes in women's lives.[20]

During the Khrushchev era, the women's councils seemed more focused on the state's perception of what women needed to participate fully in the public life of the country, rather than what Soviet women actually wanted. This was part of the regime's ideological agenda, which aimed to highlight the Soviet Union's achievements in terms of gender equality by promoting certain women within the government.

It is worth noting that the Soviet Union had more women in positions of power than Western democracies. In terms of domestic policy, the regime relied on women's active participation in the economy.[21] The Khrushchev regime made promises to improve the working and living conditions of women workers through the *zhensoviety*. These promises included providing additional benefits for working mothers, such as longer periods of leave for pregnancy and childbirth. The government also recognized the need to increase childcare facilities, particularly in rural areas, and considered reducing the length of the working day for pregnant women and mothers with young children.[22] These promises remained largely unrealized.[23] Thus, a significant inconsistency between Soviet ideology and Soviet reality continued in the post-war period. Official ideology claimed that women were emancipated even though reality suggested otherwise. Nonetheless, Khrushchev's reopening of the woman question drew attention to women's everyday struggles to combine full-time work with childcare and household work.[24]

The existing works cite some data on *zhensoviety* activism in Muslim Central Asia, but there is no literature on the women's councils in Tajikistan. Browning has argued that in Central Asia the *zhensoviety*'s work was extremely important because they served to support women at the community level and the workplace, which did not exist previously.[25] While this was true in urban Tajikistan, it was not the case in rural parts of the country. This study of *zhensoviety* activism in Tajikistan illustrates that while the *zhensoviety* propagated universal messages to all Soviet women, their activities in Tajikistan resulted in series of contradictory outcomes.

The *zhensoviety* were vaguely based on the Zhenotdel. The major difference between these two women's organizations was based in the *zhensoviety*'s nominally grassroots nature. It was a volunteer organization that was theoretically independent from the regime.[26] The Khrushchev regime endorsed community-based organizations that worked in the spirit of volunteerism to promote social responsibility, notions of community, and public engagement. The *zhensoviety* provide an excellent example of this approach in action.[27] The *zhensoviety* existed before the Second World War, as part of the Soviet state feminism but the early women-only groups differed from the later ones in terms of location and membership.[28] Before the 1950s, the *zhensoviety* functioned only in urban areas and mostly represented the rights of working women in the industrial sector, provided support to widows and orphans.[29] The *zhensoviety* generally mobilized women across the Soviet Union around the same agenda, namely political, economic, and social activities.[30] Their mission was to introduce unemployed women into the workforce and to keep them employed, with an ultimate goal of their Sovietization. For instance, the *zhensoviety* report indicate that the women's councils in Tajikistan were actively leading educational activities among women to help engage them in production. It specified that it was doing so by creating all necessary conditions for women's education, labour, vacation, and motherhood.[31] This resembled the statement of the *zhensoviety*'s mission pronounced by an activist at the Women's Annual Congress in 1963:

> The *zhensoviety* unite thousands of women under a cohesive and powerful movement. They ensure that women have all the required conditions to enter and remain in the workforce. The *zhensoviety* engage women in political and social activities, they are responsible for helping party organizations in proper upbringing of Soviet women in the spirit of internationalism, high ideas, and low tolerance for laziness, bribery, localism, and dishonesty.[32]

The first women's committees were effective in representing women's interests in urban areas, particularly in garment and textile factories. They worked to safeguard women's labour rights, such as preventing pregnant women from getting fired during pregnancy and facilitated private rooms for female workers to breastfeed their children. They also controlled and maintained basic hygiene rules and regulations, and advocated for better working conditions, including heating systems and dust-absorbing technology.[33] The *zhensoviety* in urban Tajikistan also represented women at the community level. They often supported women in cases of physical abuse in the family, alcoholic husbands, and other private matters. They provided moral support and most importantly they negotiated possible solutions to women's family problems with *mahalla* elders. Often, they pressured the family or a certain member to address a domestic feud or a divisive issue using community elders' influence and support.[34] Yet the councils did not serve most of the indigenous female population, who lived in rural areas.[35]

These women's committees were expanded to the countryside only in the post-war period and under the Khrushchev regime. Urban activists were put in charge of guiding their rural counterparts since they were considered more experienced in women's social activism and culturally more Sovietized.[36] As a result, these grassroots organizations took up a top-down approach in rural Tajikistan.[37] Lower-level local councils were under the authority of the women's councils at higher levels and each local-level committee replicated activities of the higher-level council.[38] These local *zhensoviety* existed at various levels, including in regions (*oblasti*), districts (*raiony*), and residential areas (*mahallas*); on state and collective farms (*sovkhozy* and *kolkhozy*); and in other workplaces.[39] Based on this structure, which in many ways resembled that of the Communist Party, each higher-level *zhensoviet* in Tajikistan would receive information from the lower levels about their work and transmit orders from above to below.[40]

Most information about the *zhensoviety* comes from the "Reports of Work" (*otchety i doklady*) written by *zhensoviety* activists. Based on these reports, the *zhensoviety* did not have a national coordinating body based in Moscow. The Central Committee, known as the republican *zhensoviet*, was based in Dushanbe. The republican *zhensoviet* set the annual plan of action, including areas of focus and strategies to accomplish set agendas. It then assigned regional councils to accomplish this agenda.[41] The republican *zhensoviet* was in charge of ensuring that local committees accomplish set tasks by providing them with practical assistance.[42] A unique feature of the *zhensoviety*, as opposed to their predecessor, the Zhenotdel, was the predominance of non-party women within the organization. This resulted in more women, especially from rural areas, being included in women's committees therefore making the *zhensoviety* the largest women's organization in the history of Tajikistan. The lack of a national coordinating body hypothetically allowed the organization greater autonomy and diversity in organization and approach.[43]

All Soviet mass organizations were transmitters of party policies, and the *zhensoviety* were no exception to this rule.[44] While the initiative on part of the *zhensoviety* around the Soviet Union was encouraged, it was the successful implementation of the regime's agenda that received praise and attention.[45] So informally, the republican *zhensoviet* worked under the guidance of the central regime in Moscow and the lower-level council had to work in cooperation with local government administrations, trade unions, and party organizations such as the Komsomol. This arrangement was orchestrated partly through the *zhensoviety* leadership, which was drawn from the local and regional party membership.[46] The chair of the republican *zhensoviet* repeatedly echoed the regime's control of the organization; Nizoramo Zaripova, the head of the Presidium of the Supreme Soviet (in office 1982–4), and Guldzhakhon Bobosadykova, first secretary of the Komsomol in Tajikistan (in office 1979–87), presided over the republican *zhensoviet* during different periods in the 1970s and 1980s. This ensured the *zhensoviety*'s informal but expected identification with the regime's policies, both in general terms and specifically in respect to women.[47]

The women's councils' vague relations with the central regime remained unclear even to the *zhensoviety* leaders. Nizoramo Zaripova, the head of the republican *zhensoviet* on various occasions from the 1950s to the 1980s, even had to provide a response to a *zhensoviet* member's question regarding the nature of the women's councils' affiliation with the central regime at the Women's Annual Congress:

> The women's organizations always worked under the central regime's guidelines. In 1924–9, the Zhenotdel administered the Muslim women's emancipation campaign in Tajikistan.[48] When the regime abolished the Zhenotdel in 1930, the People's Commissariat of Labour and the Committees for the Improvement of the Life and Work of Women administered the woman question [*zhenskii vopros*]. During this period, the woman question was less centrally coordinated. In 1957, these departments were eliminated and united under *zhensoviety*, social, and volunteer-based organizations, without headquarters. So, an answer to your question as to who oversees the *zhensoviety* – the central regime in Moscow.[49]

Organizational discussions on how to strengthen the *zhensoviety* at all levels around the Soviet Union were frequently linked to making them more uniform and by establishing formal affiliation with the central regime.[50] Members claimed that the councils' voluntary basis and vague relationship with the regime in Moscow weakened their relationships with the local party organizations. Activists insisted that due to the *zhensoviety*'s informal nature, the Komsomol, trade unions, and other local government organizations did not take the committees' work and agenda seriously.[51]

At the 1986 Women's Annual Congress, Safieva, a member of the republican *zhensoviet* in Tajikistan, also spoke about the ineffectiveness of volunteer-based women-only groups. "We need to establish republican and regional women's committees with paid full-time members besides our volunteers. Life experiences have shown that some things cannot be done on a voluntary basis, this has been particularly the case with our work among women."[52] The *zhensoviety*'s vague relationship with the formal political structures and its voluntary basis reflects the low status assigned to women's issues in general.[53] This indicates that, similar to the 1920s and 1930s, in the post–Second World War period the regime and local officials allocated low priority to women's issues.[54] Nizoramo Zaripova recalled how her male colleagues in the Presidium of the Supreme Soviet of Tajikistan would jokingly refer to the *zhensoviety* as the appendix, implying its redundancy.[55] Women activists were aware of the sentiments held by local leadership and therefore sought a direct relationship with the regime in Moscow.[56]

Yet not all *zhensoviety* members and leaders desired formal affilia-tion with the central and local governments. For instance, Bikhodzhal Rakhimova, the assistant secretary of the Komsomol in the Soviet Tajik Republic and the head of the regional *zhensoviet* in the Leninabad region, explained the *zhensoviety*'s volunteer-based nature as a strate-gic approach: "The women-only groups elected female activists who were capable of combining their full-time professional duties, with household chores, and active input in volunteer activism," she insisted. "These activists were good multitaskers and could make organizational decisions while standing next to machine tools without any interrup-tions from production."[57]

Unlike their predecessor, the Zhenotdel, the *zhensoviety* included more Tajik and Uzbek cadres within leadership positions and general mem-bership.[58] Indigenous leaders like Bikhodzhal Rakhimova, Nizoramo Zaripova, Guldzhakhon Bobosadykova, Bakhti Shaidova, and others were educated and trained to fill governmental positions as part of the Soviet regime's *korenizatsiia* policy in the 1920s and 1930s. By the 1950s, for the first time in the history of Tajikistan indigenous women had arisen to prominent public positions in significant numbers.[59] Yet once educated and culturally Sovietized, these Muslim women professionals became outsiders culturally, political, and economically detached from the rest of the indigenous population, who remained predominantly in rural areas.[60]

The Dual Culture within the *Zhensoviety*

For most rural Muslim women, the transformation of urban native women was seen as a result of abandoning their cultural norms.[61] The socio-economic and cultural gap between urban and rural indigenous women remained considerable.[62] The "two-cultures" phenomenon – with one culture comprising the urban educated populace and the other consisting of the masses in the Tajik countryside – which was not as pronounced before the Soviet regime, was similar to the one that prevailed in Iran during the Pahlavi era. Similarly, it was reflected in such elementary spheres as dress, housing, styles of furnishing, means of transportation, among others.[63] The rural population of the Tajik countryside was also significantly behind urban areas in terms of education and career options. This was especially the case among women who unlike rural men could not easily seek these opportuni-ties in cities due to cultural norms.[64] These factors contributed to rural Muslim women remaining the least Sovietized segment of the popula-tion in Tajikistan.

Local actors played a crucial role in addressing issues that the central government in Moscow deemed low in priority, bringing specificity and substance to them. They were instrumental in determining which Central Asian–style goods would be considered "national," what would qualify as "culturedness," and shaping the new Central Asia model of gendered attire and family relations. This approach allowed the Soviet state to endorse specific familial relationships and gender roles in the Muslim periphery. Consequently, the Soviet borderlands of the 1970s exhibited vast diversity, with unique features distinctive to each region, village, and community, while still maintaining a recognizable Soviet character.[65]

The republican *zhensoviet* was responsible for setting the key organizational agenda. It was also assigned to ensure regional committees' attainment of set tasks and goals through practical and theoretical support.[66] Yet this liaison remained largely unregulated. The female activists, particularly from rural areas consistently appealed to the republican *zhensoviet* for guidance and practical support with administration of their work. The *zhensoviety*'s organizational reports indicate the futility of such requests.[67] M.K. Karimova, member of the republican *zhensoviet*, openly admitted at the 1972 Women's Annual Congress, "The republican *zhensoviet* does not collaborate and supervise the affiliate councils in rural areas. It does not study their reports or examine their work summaries." She maintained, "this leads to lack of direction in women's social and political activism in rural areas."[68]

This unregulated and ambiguous association between the committees in Tajikistan was based in the organization's voluntary nature and its members' double and triple burdens.[69] The voluntary foundation of the women's councils determined the organizational resources, or more accurately their lack thereof, to fund trips to rural areas to establish and strengthen relationships between urban and rural *zhensoviety*.[70] Most importantly, the lack of interaction between rural and urban women was due to female activists' double burden of responsibilities. Being forced to combine their volunteer work with their full-time jobs, childcare, and household chores made urban activists reluctant to commit to long trips and extensive interaction with their rural counterparts.[71] The *zhensoviety* members were women of various professions, including doctors, engineers, teachers, accountants, and many worked in administrative jobs within the various branches of the government. Their full-time professional responsibilities and chores at home often prevented republican members of the *zhensoviet* from visiting rural areas.[72]

These circumstances led the urban leaders of the republican *zhensoviet* to openly criticize and publicly shame rural members and leadership for unaccomplished tasks and lack of functioning work schedules.[73] As an urban activist, Maksimova, summarized her trip to the countryside, "The *zhensoviety* in rural areas do not take their work seriously. All of these shortcomings can be eliminated if the regional councils and the young girls' committee [*soviet devushek*] approach their responsibilities seriously and put together an annual work plan."[74] This approach enabled committee members to give the impression of thoroughly inspecting their rural colleagues' work in the short term, but did little to accomplish the goals of emancipation or Sovietization of rural Tajik women.[75]

Another illustration of the republican *zhensoviet*'s top-down approach in rural areas was criticism and public shaming of rural activists, particularly leaders for the failure to mobilize rural women and for not meeting set goals. This is how Usmanova, the head of the Propaganda Department, described her trip to the Leningrad, Kalinina, and Lenin collective farms: "The women's committees in rural areas are passive and not working based on protocol. They exist in name only. The head of the *zhensoviet* on *kolkhoz* Leningrad, Comrade Vahobova, organized only one meeting during the period 1962–3."[76] By criticizing specific leaders urban activists demonstrated familiarity with the regional affiliate councils and its activists but offered them little real assistance.[77]

Without practical help from the central committee and lack of experience in social activism, rural *zhensoviety* were indeed not active in mobilizing rural Tajik women. Like urban activists, rural women had to combine their full-time jobs, primarily on collective farms, with housework and childcare. They were also responsible for their private garden and livestock. Women's triple burden of responsibilities contributed to their perception of the *zhensoviety* activism as an additional burden.[78] This explains why rural activists and rural women in general were inactive and often physically unable to take part in social activism. As Zukhrokhon Negmatova, a member of the *zhensoviet* in an Arab village (*kishloq*) in the Kanibadam region, remembered, her family obligations and employment on the *kolkhoz* were one of many reasons she could not contribute to the women's committee activities. "After work I had to take care of my family, make dinner, clean our backyard, feed the cows, and take care of the chickens. I could not sneak out of the house, and away from the scrutiny of my in-laws, to attend women's evening gatherings." But to support her *zhensoviet* head, Savritdinnova, she agreed to attend the big gathering of women (the Annual Congress) in Dushanbe in 1979.[79]

Some urban activists argued that rural women's low input in social activism was due to their preoccupation with meeting seasonal production quotas (typically of cotton).[80] In response to this debate, Nizoramo Zaripova, the head of the Tajik Supreme Soviet who grew up in rural Kuliab (southern Tajikistan), advised women activists to be patient with their rural colleagues: "We need to keep in mind that these activists are barely educated, their level of political consciousness is low and it is reflected in the quality of their work."[81] For the same reason, M.K. Gafarova, member of the republic *zhensoviet* and the head of the pedagogical institute, proposed to find ways to bring the republican and rural *zhensoviety* closer together.[82]

The central committee relied on the regional councils to introduce and promote Soviet culture to rural areas. To bridge the urban-rural divide, including that between the councils, the central committee promoted Soviet culture and new practices to rural women in Tajikistan. Ibodat Rakhimova, a member of the republican *zhensoviet* and the assistant head of the Tajik Supreme Soviet, described this mission of the *zhensoviety* in her interview with the journal *Nauka i religiia* (Science and Religion). According to Rakhimova's account, "Rural *zhensoviety* have become the party's supporters in spreading the communist ideology." She explained that they did so by attracting women to production, engaging them in social activism, helping them with raising their children, and introducing new Soviet rituals and traditions to replace old norms and practices in the countryside.[83] According to Rakhimova, "So far they have succeeded in promoting Komsomol weddings (official government registration of the couples and a celebration afterward), celebratory send-offs of young men to the army, acceptance of Soviet passports, celebration of newborns, and honoring of veterans of revolution and labor."[84] She elaborated, "We demand great activism, flexibility, strength, and great understanding of ordinary women from rural women's councils. Today in Tajikistan there are over 900 *zhensoviety* in rural areas, in collective farms – *sovkhozes* and *kolkhozes*."[85] Rakhimova singled out Kanibadam city, where Habiba Karimova, head of the *zhensoviet* and secondary school principal, had been vigorously attracting women into the workforce from remote parts of her region (Kanibadam region, northern Tajikistan). "Some of these women are leaders in their place of employment. Today [referring to the mid-1970s], the Kanibadam *zhensoviet* is actively replacing old practices commonly based on feudal-boy traditions and religion with new Soviet practices and culture."[86]

The new Soviet practices also involved educating women about Western-style clothing, Soviet forms of household management, and ways to create a comfortable and cultured atmosphere for their families. These measures were based on the Khrushchev regime's goal of educating citizens on everyday behaviour, including hygiene habits, leisure pursuits, and consumption choices. Women were seen as the primary actors in helping the state promote these communist values to their families, particularly in the countryside. This type of intervention was a vital component of the Khrushchev regime's strategy for upholding its power and facilitating the shift to communism.[87]

The *zhensoviety* organizational reports commonly suggest that rural women had all the means to have a refined wardrobe and nicely furnished homes, but they were choosing not to do so. "Life in the countryside has improved substantially, but rural women have not learned to choose their clothes properly. They wear expensive dresses without underwear; many do not even own nightgowns or use proper bedding."[88] At the Women's Annual Congress, Safieva also pointed to rural women's clothing styles: "Our girlfriends wear the same dress to milk a cow, to go to sleep, and to visit relatives. We need to address this issue."[89] The *zhensoviety* activists also documented lack of basic hygiene in collective farm workers' homes.[90] Therefore, they called on their rural colleagues: "to support rural women in understanding and learning about benefits of hygiene." They asserted, "When a woman is dirty and is not used to cleaning herself, it is hard to fight for a culture of cleanliness. The women's committees need to pay serious attention to this issue."[91] To realize these objectives, Y.Y. Bazarbaeva and R.Z. Inoiatova suggested organizing lectures for rural women on themes such as: "What we need to know about clothing," "How to furnish your home," "Good taste in good quantities," and "What is family happiness?"[92] Kathryn Dooley's research shows that the Central Asian urban intelligentsia became identified as Europeanized and associated with Soviet ideals of "culturedness." Consumption habits, namely consumption of national goods – including traditional women's clothing, in the case of Tajikistan – came to signify the traits of rurality, traditionalism, tastelessness, and poverty.[93] The "Europeanization" of Central Asia, in a material cultural sense, was concentrated initially in urban areas and among the intelligentsia.[94]

The Khrushchev regime also aimed to shield women from the potentially corrupting influence of the growing availability of consumer goods through ideological campaigns. In essence, women's potential desire for household goods in their new homes had to align with the state-defined standards of rational consumption.[95] The assistant head of the Ministry of Commerce, H.G. Gufranova's, call to republican *zhensoviet* members attests to this: "Our women collective farm workers are earning thousands of rubles, but not spending their income on properly furnishing their homes." She particularly shamed rural party and Komsomol members for not supplying their families with basic home furniture. Gufranova justified her statement by asserting that these household items were not only for comfort, but were "essential for children's education so our future generation can easily do their homework."[96] Vera Dunham, in her analysis of "middle-class values" in the Soviet Union, has argued, "In postwar novels, objects, from real estate to perfume, took a voice of their own. They provide a material inventory of embourgeoisement."[97] The readers immersed themselves in descriptions of the interior, including the following: "Several brightly embroidered pillows were neatly arranged on her bed. Her small nightstand was covered with pink paper, scalloped at the edge."[98] Based on Reid's analysis of this passage, it identified the female occupant as cultured (*kulturnaia*) on account of her homemaking skills.[99] The *zhensoviety* reports seem to commonly point to lack of these skills among rural women in Tajikistan as an implication of absence of *kulturnost*.[100]

The new appetite for consumerism even triggered the central regime's appointment of authorized specialists to step in and reshape housekeeping practices related to domestic hygiene, thrift, efficiency, and taste.[101] Khrushchev asserted that it was necessary "not only to provide people with good homes, but also to teach them ... to live correctly, and to observe the rules of socialists communality." He maintained, "this will not come about of its own accord, but must be achieved through protracted, stubborn struggle for the triumph of the new communist way of life."[102] In Tajikistan, the republican *zhensoviet* approached this decree by organizing seminars in the countryside to educate women how to furnish their households. Nizoramo Zaripova who oversaw this initiative in Tajikistan, recalled, "We taught rural women proper ways to furnish their home, how to host guests, and informed them of the newly available household appliances. We lectured them about benefits of hygiene and maintenance of cleanliness around the house."[103] She recalled that the republican *zhensoviet* would send 3 or 4 women activists to specific villages ahead of time to arrange a sample room. "We wanted to show rural women how urban women were furnishing their homes,"[104] she explained. "Our primary goal was to introduce Soviet culture in rural Tajikistan."[105] The majority of the rural population in Tajikistan lived in one-storey houses that significantly differed from city apartment complexes. Rural women's dismal view of the urban *zhensoviety*'s trainings on proper furnishing of one's home was based partly on a widespread feeling of the irrelevance of these lectures for rural dwellings. It was also based on lack of resources, including scarcity of furniture in the countryside.[106]

The domestic skills trainings were intended only for women and girls, which reinforced the notion of housework as a female-only domain. This approach created obstacles for women in advancing their status outside the private domain. Consequently, the Bolshevik promises of women's emancipation rooted in Marxist ideology, specifically through women's introduction to the labour force and liberation from the confines of household chores, were no longer on the agenda.[107] Interviews with rural women revealed that they were rarely in charge of their household finances. Even fully employed women typically relied on male family members (fathers-in law and husbands) to make all the financial decisions.[108] It was commonly expected of a woman to bring her monthly salary to her husband, father, or mothers-in law. A Muslim woman would eventually gain independence with age, once her children grew up, her mother-in law was no longer alive and when she earned her husband's trust with financial matters.[109] The central *zhensoviety*'s focus on women, and not men, in their attempts to influence rural household's consumption choices confirms urban activists' misinterpretation of the situation on the ground.

Instead, the *zhensoviety* activists asserted that the government was helping rural women with social welfare and providing other all-encompassing support, yet women were not creating a cosy environment for their families. The report singled out the mother heroine, Gulbahor Odinaeva from *kolkhoz* Lenina. "She does not have any children's furniture, a desk, chairs, or books. Her children do their homework on the floor, but the family owns a brand-new car."[110] Essentially the activists were implying that the family purchased the car on social welfare allocated to Mother Heroines for having five or more children. Actually, the fact that a family owned a car typically signalled a man's decision since women traditionally did not drive in Tajikistan, especially in rural areas.[111] It was also a sign of prestige for men and not women. In fact, some activists were aware of this. They noted that heads of *kolkhozy* and *sovkhozy*, predominantly men, "are busy saving their salaries to keep up with neighbours in terms of cars and other unnecessary luxury goods. This comes at the expense of family members who have to sleep on the floors because they do not have beds." The author duly acknowledged, "Of course, everyone has a right to spend his/her money on what they desire. But it is our intelligentsia's mission to convince our rural sisters and brothers that expensive cars can wait and that they need to prioritize children's furniture."[112]

Urban activists insisted that intervention in the countryside was necessary because Tajik culture revolves around impressing others, especially neighbours and relatives, therefore rural households need guidance in their consumption habits. "Families save their money for lavish weddings, expensive funerals, and other occasions where they can display their wealth to their community." Authors of the report rationalized that rural women played an important role in promoting these social norms since they were customarily evaluated for their resourcefulness, and ability to save money and possessions for special occasions. Based on the report, "Women even save their nicer plates, kettle, and teacups for guests, as a result families do not have essential utensils for their daily use."[113] M.B. Shahobova's report also provided a detailed account of these cultural practices: "Lavish weddings are a serious problem in rural Tajikistan. Families have to produce an all-embracing dowry for celebrations that last 2–3 days."[114] Mothers started collecting dowry before their daughters reach adulthood. She explained that "They do so by cutting back on food and other everyday needs. Instead of giving children books and good education, they give them expensive plates, clothing, and carpets."[115] Yet these reports did not acknowledge the social pressure women faced to adhere to these established social norms, which also existed in urban areas. Browning has argued that the *zhensoviety*'s intervention raised questions about gender roles, but it focused primarily on expanding women's roles within existing societal structures rather than radically altering men's roles. The intention of the intervention also seemed to be limited to promoting cultural attitudes that aligned with European norms, rather than fully comprehending the circumstances in which rural women lived.[116]

Traditionally in Muslim households, in urban and rural areas, families saved their money for special occasions, including weddings and funerals, by economizing on food, home furniture, clothing, and other household goods. When a family failed to meet expenses for these celebrations, women would become the subject of community gossip.[117] To avoid this personal humiliation, women would start collecting their daughters' dowries and save resources for these special occasions early on.[118] The *zhensoviety* were thus exposing problems but not addressing their root causes or proposing culturally sensitive and effective solutions. These practices were also common in urban areas and the members of the *zhensoviety* knew it. Hence the interesting dilemma indigenous women activists faced. They were intimately familiar with the delicate aspects of the social norms and practices they were targeting as the cause of weak Sovietization in the countryside yet at home they typically adhered to these same practices.

Rural women were also criticized for not creating a cultured household for their family. I.R. Rakhimova, for instance pointed out, "Rural women do not buy classical literature and do not read books to their children. This impacts the culture of the household and its lack."[119] These reports rarely disclosed factors that kept rural women from reading classical literature and children's books. Instead, the women's councils called members to teach rural women how to spend their free time in a useful manner.[120] Nonetheless, more honest reports did recognize that there were still not enough dining halls, public showers, communal laundry rooms, and grocery stores where women could buy precooked food in rural areas. The fact that the country still faced a serious shortage of daycares and kindergartens and that the existing facilities were overcrowded and in dire conditions spoke to the lack of attention being paid to women's needs.[121] As a result, rural women faced these daily obligations with minimal family and government support. Surprisingly, urban activists' proposals for how to arrange women's free time implicitly recognized women's triple burden: "Firstly, to improve women's work and household situation with a goal of increasing their free time. Secondly, to organize their free time in such a manner that can help them increase their social life."[122]

About lack of culture in rural households, H. Halbaeva, the head of the Dzhirgatal *raion* women's council, asserted, "Few women in the countryside watch movies with their husbands. Girls do not play sports or engage in any kinds of athletic activities. Students rarely visit their local libraries. Rural women's culture is very low."[123] Reports by activists who had more exposure and knowledge of the rural realities informed, "We have many talented female athletes, yet due to the feudal mentality and strong influence of religion in the countryside, girls do not play sports. Many are reluctant to wear athletic clothes [Muslim women in Tajikistan did not wear pants or shorts]."[124] K.M. Mirzoalieva, the secretary of the Leninabad *obkom*, also recognized that rural girls did not attend local libraries or music schools, take dancing classes, or engage in extracurricular activities because these opportunities simply did not exist in the countryside.[125] "There are no movie or drama theatres, concert halls, and poetry clubs in the Tajik periphery," the author revealed.[126] To address these issues, the women's councils tried some of the Zhenotdel's approaches to mobilization through entertainment. The women's councils organized various events, including "na piialku chaia" (to a cup of tea) gatherings. This event aimed at political education of women though conversations about communism, discussion about women leaders' life experiences, poetry recitations, and staged plays. More commonly, these gatherings engaged women with homemaking lessons, childcare advice, and recipe sharing. The central *zhensoviety* claimed that this and other activities enabled them to expand in rural areas. "We are increasing women's cultural education, helping them with household questions, in upbringing of children, and organizing family vacations. Women's councils in rural areas are fighting for cultured and healthy living."[127]

Yet rural women conveyed a different reality. Firstly, rural councils' minimal experience with social activism and their lack of guidance from the republican committee made their work more challenging and less popular among their constituencies. Moreover, rural, and urban activists often did not personally adhere to the practices they promoted to their colleagues and neighbours in their attempts to promote Soviet culture and traditions in the countryside.[128] Several activists confessed that they ignored the republican zhensoviety's agenda. They explained it was due to numerous chores that consumed their daily hours. They also criticized the lack of practical assistance on the part of the zhensoviety in solving women's everyday problems, including their triple burden. The republican women's committee was aware of the women's committees' diminishing role starting in the mid- to late 1970s. As N. Mirzoeva, member of the republican zhensoviet and the head of the textile factory in Dushanbe, noted at the Women's Annual Congress, "The role of the zhensoviety in rural areas has weakened. We need to restore it through all possible means."[129]

Activists started frankly deliberating reasons why the women's councils' work was ineffective. According to the head of the Kayrakum carpet factory, S. Nurillaeva, it was because "the zhensoviety lack persistence." She asserted, "The women's councils follow the official protocol, but this approach is not achieving effective outcomes."[130] Abdullaeva, the secretary of the Komsomol in the Dzhirgatal region, shared same sentiments: "The zhensoviety's failure is due to its formal nature. They do not delve deep into rural women's every life, their workload, education, and vacation." She emphasized that "few women in the countryside increase their qualifications or engage in social activism because they do not have time. They have to care for children, fulfil their professional duties, and complete domestic chores on time."[131]

Some activists also pointed to the fact there were very few activists working in the countryside who were indigenous (Tajik or Uzbek). Based on this report, the majority of the zhensoviety activists working with rural activists were of Russian and Slavic backgrounds.[132] This contributed to the ineffectiveness of women's councils in the countryside since the majority of rural women in Tajikistan did not speak Russian.[133] In 1986, at the Women's Annual Congress, Guldzhakhon Bobosadykova, the head of the republican zhensoviet (in the 1970s and 1980s) excused these criticisms of the women's councils, namely their failure to effectively mobilize rural women. "The *zhensoviety* cannot take up responsibility for everything, we are not almighty. As you can see and know, we are not always aware of the situation on the ground."[134]

The republican *zhensoviet*'s reports from the 1980s openly discussed some of the achievements and failures of the *zhensoviety*. Successes included introducing more women into the workforce and ensuring that they were fulfilling their production quota.

The shortcomings included a lack of more practical actions in addressing women's burdens, ensuring that more indigenous girls pursued education, particularly at the university level, failure to eradicate the patriarchal approach to women, persisting shortages of daycares, introducing housewives into the workforce, and finally failing to introduce Soviet culture in the countryside.[135] Similar to state-directed women's organizations in Middle Eastern states, the *zhensoviety* in Soviet Tajikistan illustrate that when the state decrees social change for the population, indigenous women often viewed feminism as culturally "unauthentic," with little relevance to their lives.[136] The republican *zhensoviet* in Tajikistan retained a top-down approach to women in the countryside. Rural women were expected to take an active part in the *zhensoviety*'s activities while meeting their existing professional responsibilities, household duties, and child-rearing. As a result, women in the Tajik periphery came to view the *zhensoviety*'s work as a burden placed on them by urban women. The women's council's anti-religious propaganda, as dictated by the central regime in Moscow, came into conflict with rural Muslim women's distinctive circumstances compared to women in western parts of the Soviet Union and urban women in general.

6 "I Am Muslim and Soviet": The Soviet Anti-religious Campaign Aimed at Muslim Women, 1953–1982

After 1945, the Soviet regime largely succeeded in putting an end to the practices of veiling, polygamy, child marriage, and bride payments in urban areas. These, however, still existed in rural Tajikistan but were less commonly practised in comparison with the 1920s and 1930s. The Khrushchev government, like its predecessors, attributed patriarchal practices in Tajikistan to Islam and considered them the main reason for the low education levels and high unemployment rates among rural Muslim women. After a brief period of relaxation towards religion during and immediately after the Second World War, the Soviet regime renewed its efforts to eradicate Islam and feudal-boy practices. This led to the launch of an atheistic campaign in 1954.[1]

While this atheistic campaign was not as aggressive as the Bolshevik attack on religion in the 1920s and 1930s, the Khrushchev regime established a vast functioning apparatus for advancing atheism at all levels of society.[2] This chapter assesses the methods and rhetoric of the anti-religion campaign under Khrushchev, which specifically targeted women. It also examines some of its impact that became more evident under Brezhnev's regime (1964–82). The anti-religious campaign in rural Tajikistan was intimately connected with Khrushchev's wider plans to improve living conditions in the countryside and to boost agricultural productivity throughout the Soviet Union.[3] The regime considered the elimination of religion an essential prerequisite for rural population's participation in paid labour and commitment to rural productivity.[4] Hence the association between two major discourses of the post-war period: the emancipation of rural Muslim women and the attack on Islam. The Khrushchev administration believed that women's entry into the workforce would ensure their Sovietization and, most importantly, it would bring about the transformation of rural areas.[5] The regime's special focus on making atheists of rural women is most vividly reflected in its revival of the *zhensoviety*. The women's councils were expanded particularly in regions where religious influence was deemed strong: the Catholic regions of the Baltics, Muslim Central Asia, and areas in central Russia where the Russian Orthodox Church retained a strong foothold. In these places, women's social status was the most held back by social and economic realities, making it crucial to raise awareness of women's rights and opportunities.[6]

Before the 1950s, the *zhensoviety* functioned only in cities or towns and mostly represented the rights of working women in the industrial sector and provided support to widows and orphans of soldiers.[7] Under Khrushchev, the *zhensoviety* were actively expanded and established in rural areas, and urban activists were put in charge of guiding their rural counterparts since urban members were more experienced and culturally more Sovietized. As a result, these nominally grassroots organizations took up a centralized approach in rural Tajikistan.[8] The women's committees and other government institutions, including the Komsomol and trade unions, were directed to carry out the atheist campaign among women. Analysis of the *zhensoviety*'s anti-religious campaigns shows that the regime maintained its top-down approach to women's issues in the post-war period. It is also evident that the centre lacked a nuanced understanding of the many roles Islam served for the populace in Central Asia in general and Soviet Tajikistan in particular. Being a Muslim was not simply a religious identity but an essential element of one's perception of self and a critical component of Muslim men and women's sense of belonging to their community.[9] The infective tactics that primarily focused on descriptions of Islam as repressive and patriarchal eventually resulted in the Soviet regime's tacit acknowledgment of failure in the 1970s. This also followed up with a more relaxed approach to religion.

Soviet literature on Muslim women, both fiction and non-fiction, was based on two major premises. First, there was a broad assumption that gender equality and socialism were synonymous. The degree of women's integration into economic and political life was therefore an indicator of both social "progress" and women's "emancipation." This led to the promotion of the Bolshevik campaign of the 1920s and 1930s, namely women's education, paid employment, and participation in political institutions. Analyses of women's social status were based solely on these quantifiable indicators. Second, it was assumed that Muslim women's pre-revolutionary status was that of an exploited class, degraded by veiling, discriminated against in matrimonial laws and customs. Historical writings about Muslim women by Soviet authors clearly reflect these fundamental assumptions.[10]

Western scholarship has largely focused on men's role in preserving and practising Muslim traditions, namely attending secret mosques, Sufi-brotherhood congregations, male circumcision, and marriage ceremonies. Authors attribute the endurance of Muslim culture in the countryside to the relative lack of penetrative capacity by the Soviet state.[11] According to experts, the region's isolation from the wider Islamic world and the strict limitations on the accessibility of religious education have not only curtailed theological knowledge but also hindered engagement with Islam. Consequently, Islam in this context has become more of a symbolic aspect of secular national identity rather than a fully fledged religious practice.[12] Others have suggested that Islam as a system of belief became based on superstition. It became an expression of communal belonging expressed through celebrations of birth, marriage, death, and circumcision, among others. The practice of Islam also included visiting the shrines of Muslim saints in search of miraculous cures for illness and misfortunes, wearing amulets, visiting religious healers, and so on.[13] Anthropological study of rural Tajikistan and women's role in preserving Islamic practices and faith argues that unlike indigenous Muslim men, women were less affected by the Soviet regime's ban on public religious displays since they performed their religious duties at home. While few men rigorously observed Ramadan during the Soviet period, women almost universally observed it. As one elderly Muslim man in Obi-Safed village observed, "Before, if the men met together to pray, then there'd be trouble. The women, though – that was different. No one saw."[14] The author suggests that in Soviet Tajikistan, women were the main practitioners and guardians of traditional Tajik culture and Islamic practices. The distinction between public and private and male and female roles allowed most households in rural Tajikistan to reconcile their identities as both Muslim and communist, without perceiving them as contradictory.[15] There are similar findings in Soviet Russia, where Russian women promoted religious culture in the family through the maintenance of rituals, festivities, and diet. The celebration of Christmas and Easter, made special by traditional cuisine, remained central for Russian Orthodox families throughout the Soviet period.[16]

According to Johan Rasanayagam, the official and underground framework in Soviet Central Asia was based on the Soviet system's interpretation of Islam, which viewed it primarily as an individual belief and ignored its fundamental role as the foundation of social interactions. The author's study of Uzbekistan showed that there were no clear distinctions in the practice of Islam between public and private spaces. Both Uzbeks and Tajiks practised Islam in both officially designated spaces, such as mosques, and everyday ritual spaces within private households, all of which constitute Muslim practice.[17] In 1943, the regime approved the creation of the Muslim Spiritual Directorate for Central Asia and Kazakhstan (SADUM), which regulated and defined the religious activities in Muslim Central Asia.[18] Yet the population of Tajikistan understood and practised Islam within everyday life rituals as opposed to the textually defined Islam of the ulama or as directed by the SADUM.[19]

This bares certain resemblance to realities in other parts of the Muslim world. As James Grehan argues through his study of religious communities in the Ottoman Syria and Palestine demonstrations, prior to the focus on text and mass literacy, the religious culture disregarded formal theological distinctions. Through the spread of literacy, an obsession with and focus on the scriptures began. This eventually resulted in dismissal of the importance of saints and their veneration. Yet prior to this transition, agrarian religion (often referred to as "popular religion" or "folk religion") was both urban and rural.[20] "Druze visited the Virgin of the Mountain shrine, Christian women recited prayers on the Prophet Muhammad's birthday, and Muslims baptized their babies."[21] In the context of Tajikistan, where the majority of the populace during the Soviet period remained detached from religious texts, this describes the localized practice of Islam. Each region typically practised Islam based on unique geographic, environmental, and historic factors, among others. During the Soviet era, Islamic education was available only in a few urban areas of Central Asia and primarily abroad. Muslims in Tajikistan and the neighbouring countries received knowledge of Islam through the informal teaching of *mahalla* mullahs; female religious specialists, known as *otins* (in Tajik); and other religious workers.[22]

Otins, who lived in both rural and urban areas, were commonly known for leading prayers for women, teaching girls how to read and write Arabic script, and for transmitting important news from authoritative men in the community.[23] While the term for male and female religious and spiritual workers varies based by region, both rural and urban Muslims sought divine intervention with the help of religious and spiritual workers to overcome sickness, get pregnant, receive support following tragic life events, look into the future, connect with relatives who passed away, and otherwise manage life circumstances.[24] The widespread popularity of *otins*, mullahs, shamans, and other religious workers indicates that Islamic observance in Central Asia is tied not only to specific places but also to certain types of religious practitioners and their practices, which are performed in a range of settings, both private and public.[25] The Muslim populace consequently developed their sense of themselves based not on text or religious education but on their engagement in everyday life-cycle rituals, with religious and spiritual practitioners, and with spaces that created and confirmed them as members of their community. These practices typically changed and evolved over time, yet people continuously associated them with being Muslim.

Tajikistan stayed primarily agrarian during the Soviet period. For instance, the city of Khujand became an economic and trading centre during the Soviet era. However, like many other cities in Central Asia, Khujand did not completely shed its rural ties.[26] Even the capital city of Dushanbe had extensive rural parts to it. Rural and urban women shared experiences regarding religious obligations associated with celebrations, funerals, and more. Tajiks expressed their identity of being Muslim through the practice of circumcision of boys, the *janoza* (prayers said at funerals), and marriage ceremonies, which commonly included the *nikoh* (Muslim marriage ritual), and other ceremonies. For many in Tajikistan and neighbouring Uzbekistan, practices associated with Islam were central in their daily routines and contributed to their evolving sense of social morality. This was particularly true in rural areas, where the majority of the population lived and remained.[27] Consequently, during the Soviet period, Islam remained a collective enterprise, which essentially made one Muslim by birth rather than by belief.[28]

Compared to the 1920s and 1930s, the late Stalinist regime created a more favourable environment for religious revival. During the Second World War, the regime relaxed its approach to Islam and religious traditions, largely to mobilize the Muslim men of Central Asia for the war effort. Registered mosques were permitted to operate in a limited fashion, and private religious practices were tolerated. Rather than seeking to eliminate all religious practices, Stalin opposed only those that directly challenged the regime.[29] Even after 1945, Stalin retained this less confrontational approach to religion. After 1954, Khrushchev publicly denounced Stalin and, along with his ideological advisers, sought to restore the early Bolshevik approach to religion. The Khrushchev regime launched a renewed attack against religion to eradicate the remaining archaic traditions particularly in the countryside and mostly among rural women. No scholarship on the tactics, extent, and impact of the renewed anti-religious campaign in Muslim Tajikistan or Central Asia, however, has yet appeared.

The party removed the old staff who had established friendly relations between religious institutions and the state. The state criticized local and central authorities for leniency towards religious activism and proposed a program for a crackdown on religion.[30] The renewed campaign was followed by closure of unauthorized places of worship and persecution of unregistered clergy. The government ordered the Department of Propaganda and Agitation to conduct a series of lectures at universities and to train cadres of anti-religion propagandists. The Ministries of Culture of all the Soviet republics and the Znanie (Knowledge) society were tasked with producing detailed plans for the improvement of atheist work. At the government's initiative, Znanie established a monthly popular journal, *Nauka i religiia* (Science and Religion), with a print run of seventy-five thousand.[31] The state instructed the republic-level ministries of education and the trade unions to strengthen their promotion of atheism among youths and workers, with special attention to women.[32]

Khrushchev's Anti-religious Campaign in the Countryside

Khrushchev's anti-religious campaign was intimately connected with his wider policies of rural modernization and cultural change. While travelling through the countryside in 1953 and 1954, Khrushchev observed economic and social degradation and viewed rural problems as rooted in the religiosity of the local people.[33] The Soviet state considered religion as a significant barrier to mobilizing the rural population, especially women, for the workforce. Khrushchev believed that a modern socialist countryside needed citizens who were genuinely Soviet and atheist.[34] He promised to create a model of socialist modernity in rural areas.[35] Yet these promises of rural reforms were not accompanied by infrastructural changes, such as the creation of daycare facilities, secondary schools, career training centres, and employment beyond manual jobs on collective farms. "The regime reinvigorated the 'woman question' in the Soviet Union, but it by no means solved it."[36]

Khrushchev presented Muslim women as victims of patriarchal society and objects of male manipulation. Islam was continually depicted in official reports as the main source of oppressive patriarchal traditions.[37] Propagandists called for an intensified anti-religious campaign and the dissemination of more information on subjects such as science and culture through the mass media.[38] With few exceptions, the Soviet government's approach to Islam claimed that fathers, brothers, and husbands were the perpetrators and enforcers of patriarchal practices. Collective farm workers and farmers committed 85 per cent of all patriarchal crimes, including polygamy, underage marriages, and bride payments. In the early 1960s, a secret report by the head of the Tajik SSR Supreme Court underpinned these assumptions with statistical data on rural criminality, which showed that most of the feudal-boy crimes in Tajikistan occurred in rural areas.[39] Working-class men and those in administrative positions committed the remainder.[40] The report identified the southern regions of Regar, Kuibeshevskii, Moskovskii, Shaartuzskii, and Sovietskii and the northern regions of Ura-Tiube, Kanibadam, Isfara, and Pendzhakent as the epicentres of these crimes.[41]

Subsequent atheistic messages portrayed indigenous men as the main obstacles to women's full involvement in social and economic life:

> Men with old mentalities are to blame for the persistence of patriarchal practices. They force their wives, daughters, and sisters to wear the *paranji*. We know of many cases in which a young woman who grew up in Soviet society with new values is forced into early marriage and required to take up veiling. Why? Because her husband, father, or brother prohibits her from walking in public without the *paranji*.... We assert that most women still wearing a veil do so because of men. After all, most of our leaders are indigenous men. These men have forgotten that they live in the Soviet Union.[42]

The propagandists implied that patriarchal practices persisted in rural society because indigenous government officials were not genuinely interested in eradicating them. The secretary of Pendzhakent publicly acknowledged this:

> We still see a feudal-boy approach to women, including *chapanchi* and violence against women. While the Soviet regime introduced major reforms in the lives of our female comrades, Tajik women are not completely liberated. This is chiefly because indigenous men are the administrators of our laws and policies, including those pertaining to women's organizations and activities.[43]

Reports claimed that party members and government officials were not interested in challenging feudal practices because they personally took part in bride payments, polygamy, and women's seclusion, and often forced their wives and daughters to veil when in public.[44]

Government reports also described cases of women's seclusion as a reality in most households, even in the homes of political leaders and members of the intelligentsia: "A woman is not allowed to welcome guests who come to her house. Sometimes she may enter the room to bring food but must leave immediately. We vigorously fight against these traditions that are disrespectful to women."[45] Stories identifying specific indigenous men in leadership positions who enforced patriarchal practices were featured in the mass media, including the journal *Molodoi kommunist* (Young Communist):

> Pulatova Gulchekhra was an active member of the Komsomol in the Tadzhikabad *raion* [southern region of Tajikistan]. Now she is the wife of the head of *kolkhoz* Pobeda in Piandzh *raion*, Khasanov. He married her when she was fifteen years old, while she was in the seventh grade. After marriage, she stopped her social activism and quit school. She is no longer paying her Komsomol membership fees. Her husband interrupted her from her studies and forced her to forget about Komsomol duties. As a Soviet leader instead of serving as a respectable example, Khasanov committed a severe crime. When the head of the Komsomol attempted to enter Khasanov's home to investigate the case, Khasanov's family denied him permission. They explained it as due to cultural traditions, which strictly prohibit male strangers to talk to female members of the household. It is sad that some of our leaders, including teachers are often the carriers of the feudal mentality.[46]

If local Communist Party members and prominent leaders upheld these practices, there can be little doubt why so few rural women entered the workforce and continued their education. Propaganda claimed that because these Communist Party members, Komsomol activists, members of local party organizations, teachers, and secretaries were forcing their wives, sisters, and daughters to wear the *paranji* and imposing their seclusion, these women were not able to attend school and enter the workforce.[47] As in earlier campaigns, women were seen as helpless victims who acted based on men's instructions.[48] No female agency was acknowledged.

When urban women activists visited rural areas and observed a significant percentage of rural women wearing the *paranji*, they described it as a forced practice. These rural women were rarely interviewed or asked to explain why they wore the *paranji* and practised Islamic traditions. Urban activists described veiling as "imposed by men" and "loathed by women."[49] One report noted:

> Our socialist culture and the *paranji* cannot be combined. Veiling makes it difficult for women to adjust to the new Soviet life and hides them from the light of our constitution. The *paranji* is not women's fault. We know that our girlfriends take off their *paranjis* when they arrive in urban areas and observe the new Soviet life with open faces and happy eyes. Our women are tired of the black veil. This veil is a gloomy remnant of the past, loathed by our women, including those who have not been brave enough to take it off.[50]

These sources indicate that unlike in Uzbekistan, where, as Northrop describes, veiling was an urban practice, in post-war Soviet Tajikistan veiling was equally common in rural areas.[51] Urban women activists who had direct conversations with rural women in Zafarabad, the northern region of Tajikistan, were told that the situation had calmed down during the war (referring to the Second World War) and nobody was making remarks about women wearing the *paranji* anymore. So, women were able to freely walk around the town wearing the *paranji* again.[52]

Veiling was not simply a remnant of the feudal past but also a major obstacle to women's entry into and active participation in the paid labour force. By the 1950s, it was clear that collectivization had largely failed to establish modern agriculture. Women's labour was regarded as an essential element for the revitalization of the countryside. As a result, calls to Muslim women to take off their veils were consistently accompanied by appeals for them to join the workforce and help increase production:

> Women in rural areas are a major workforce. To keep this labour force away from production is a crime.... Let's deliver cotton for the freedom we have received from the Koran and sharia. Women's oppression is now a forgotten tale. The Soviet regime gave women a new life, a bright future, and a happy life. The state drew a new path for us. We shouldn't delay the construction of this great work. I call on our rural girlfriends to join our fight against feudal-boy practices, throw off your *paranji*, and promise to deliver twelve thousand kilograms of cotton per season.[53]

In the state-sponsored attack against Islam, it was veiling that received the most attention. Writers wrote novels, filmmakers produced movies, and theatres staged plays about women's struggles, most notably against the *paranji*.[54] The prominent Tajik poet Mirzo Tursunzoda dedicated a poem to the subject called "The Three Beauties":

> In *paranji* like in the tomb, Tajik women buried their youth
> Mother and daughter, daughter-in-law, and sister were hidden by the veil from the world
> Black like cloud hid spring from young girls' faces
> The land was a desert where you were a slave
> For us this is a faraway history now.[55]

The Khrushchev regime's focus on women in its drive against religion also had pedagogical and disciplinarian dimensions. The Soviet state proudly pronounced its campaign as a struggle against social injustice and oppression, promising to bring women to a fulfilling and meaningful life outside the prison of religion. As a result, the atheistic crusade consistently compared Muslim women's new lives with the pre-revolutionary past:

Before the Russian Revolution, Muslim women of the East had no rights. Their exploiters convinced them that they were men's slaves. Islam not only allowed men to sell women but also permitted their murder. The archaic mentality considered the birth of girls a curse. It was better to give birth to a rock. With these words parents celebrated a baby girl's birthday. There were various religious laws that humiliated the human dignity of women. One such custom was women's isolation from the outside world through the *paranji* – a black prison of slavery. She was completely separated from public life. It was not easy for our women to take off the *paranji....* The most oppressed of all oppressed – Eastern women – outlasted obstacles and overcame their subjugation. Take off your veils, sisters, and get in line with the builders of happiness and freedom.[56]

These messages were aimed at mobilizing rural women's support in the fight against Islam and feudal-boy practices by reminding them about their destitute lives before the October Revolution. They were likewise intended to make Muslim women appreciate and value their new, happy lives under the Soviet regime. According to Paert, by emphasizing women's liberation from religion, Khrushchev's regime also claimed a revolutionary role.[57]

Members of the intelligentsia and public figures reinforced the regime's positions that Islam was the foundation of patriarchal practices and the main source of female oppression. They portrayed Islam as a dark past from which Soviet women no longer had to suffer. As the Soviet Uzbek poet Zulfiia's message in *Literaturnaia gazeta* asserted, with the assistance of Central Asian intellectuals and party members, that young women's future would be brighter.[58] The new Soviet Tajik woman had a happy life and a bright future.[59] The Tajik poet Boki-Rakhimzada, speaking at the Women's Annual Congress, proclaimed, "Under the exploitation of Islam, women were deprived of basic human rights. Their words did not have any value. They were entitled to receive only one-eighth of an inheritance. Islam and religious officials preached that women should remain blind and deaf, so they could not exit the home, talk to strangers, or listen to their inner voice."[60] Interestingly, at the end of his speech Rakhimzada concluded that "the definition of gender equality does not mean that the women do not have to do their household chores any more, but it means that they have equal rights to education and work."[61] Descriptions of Muslim women's lives before and after the Bolshevik Revolution were the most commonly used rhetoric in the post-war assault on Islam.

Unlike the earlier Bolshevik campaign, government institutions promoted a new image of the Soviet Tajik woman. One new Soviet woman personally declared war against patriarchal practices and publicly condemned her patriarchal husband. Female leaders used this story as one of their speaking points at the Women's Annual Congress in 1956:

> My husband's a communist and a promoter of feudal practices. He often uses physical force against our children and me. He banned our daughters from attending school. When I express objection to his demands, he forces me out of the house and threatens to marry a younger woman. I've been living like this for eighteen years now. I'm here to seek the party organization's assistance.[62]

This message was most vividly conveyed in the famous Tajik film *Zumrad*, produced in 1961 by the state-controlled film industry. After graduating from secondary school, the eponymous Zumrad travels to Dushanbe to continue her education. Soon she meets and falls in love with her professor, Kadyrov, who charms her with his progressive communist views and his familiarity with Persian poetry. However, after the pair marry, he shows his true face as a *fiodal* ("patriarch" in Tajik). He isolates Zumrad from the outside world and forces her to quit her studies. After she gives birth to a daughter (not a son), Kadyrov becomes aggressive and begins beating her. Zumrad breaks with traditional mores and runs away to her native village. There she becomes a respected collective farm brigadier and cultivates cotton. She eventually reunites with her secondary school sweetheart, Jalil. *Zumrad* was screened around the country for free.[63]

Zumrad was part of a post-war campaign that called on women to fight against religious traditions and patriarchal social norms at a personal level.[64] Zumrad depicted a proactive communist woman who determined her and her daughter's future by leaving an oppressive husband. Eventually she found happiness by dedicating herself to full-time work and social activism. As part of this campaign, women were entreated to "Take off your *paranji* without fear!" and were assured that "Laws will protect you!"[65] These slogans followed appeals to women to learn the constitutional rights granted to them by the Soviet regime. Authors of propaganda literature maintained that it was women's fault for allowing men to abuse them. The reports insisted, "We severely punish men and government officials who undermine women's rights and create obstacles to women's active participation in social and political life of the republic, yet often women personally choose not to practise their legal rights."[66]

The women's committees retained this position after the tragic death of one of their members. Dzhanat Rakhimova, a Communist Party member and deputy to the Leninabad city council (*gorsoviet* in Russian), was murdered by her husband, Iskandar Ataev. According to the Supreme Court records, Ataev had a feudal mentality and regularly prevented his wife from fulfilling her professional duties. He killed her when she came late from work on 17 February 1961.[67] The women's committees maintained:

> We have increased women's participation in social work. Yet we still have cases in which exemplary female workers are respected more at work than at home. Often such circumstances lead to tragic outcomes. Such outcomes need to be viewed as women's expression of weakness. It is essential to increase our women's awareness of their rights. It is important for every woman to know that Soviet laws are on her side.[68]

Dzhanat Rakhimova was one of many indigenous female activists who learned to "speak Bolshevik" and closely identified with the regime's policies. Dzhanat was staying late at work to serve her nation and by doing so breaking traditional notions of a good wife. As Bakhti Shaidova, assistant secretary of Komsomol in the Leninabad region, explained, public shaming of one's husband or of an immediate family member remained a cultural taboo in Soviet Tajikistan. Indigenous women who publicly criticized their husbands, brothers, or fathers for patriarchal acts were socially ostracized, often by other women.[69] This was against the traditional concepts of female modesty (in Tajik, *sharm/nomus*, "modesty"). Official reports also suggest that the regime failed to convince the local population that the husband's use of violence against his wife was a criminal act. These reports indicate that local administrators rarely followed up on reports of domestic abuse.[70] Even indigenous female activists like Dzhanat who strongly identified with the Soviet ideology did not or simply could not turn against social norms, which the regime continually identified as patriarchal.

The post-war Soviet state's clampdown on religious custom ensured that the most visible practices had disappeared by the late 1950s, thus dramatically changing the visual image of Muslim women. Veiling and polygamy were probably harder to hide from the state than underage marriage, bride payments, and other traditions. As a result, there were fewer reports about veiling from the late 1960s through to the 1980s. Muslim women eventually replaced *paranjis* with small headscarves that covered only the hair.[71] As for polygamy, the official problems associated with having two wives increased over time, especially if both produced children who had to be registered with the state. Marrying an underage girl, however, could be kept secret until she reached the authorized marriage age of eighteen. This practice was also featured in *Molodoi kommunist*:

> Mekhriniso Narzulaeva is the only girl among fourteen boys to graduate from the Gorky secondary school in Iava region. For this reason, she is facing social disapproval. All her female classmates dropped out of the school after the sixth grade in order to get married. Parents obtain fake birth certificates to marry their daughters before the legal age. Mekhriniso's parents were not an exception to this social norm. While her father was happy that she was able to continue her education, her mother was in a hurry to marry her off. Only with her father's support and Komsomol assistance was Mekhriniso able to pursue a degree from the Shevchenko Pedagogical Institute. She was the first woman in her region to continue her education beyond secondary school.[72]

Women Guardians of Tradition

As the article accurately suggests, Muslim women were the primary actors in charge of maintaining and endorsing traditional customs. Practices such as early marriage, bride payments, and lavish weddings and traditional funeral ceremonies remained a significant part of rural and urban lifestyle. Mothers oversaw their children's arranged marriages. It was usually women from the groom's household who made the first move. The groom's mother would approach the bride's mother. Negotiations took place primarily between the mothers of the two families. Some official reports noted that it was women who insisted that practices such as male circumcision, religious wedding ceremonies, and other traditions be carried out.[73] Dzhamilia Ismailova recalled a funeral she attended in Isfara in the 1960s where the deceased man, a prominent doctor in the village, left a will strictly instructing his family, "When I die, make sure that nobody wears mourning clothes. My wife and three daughters should wear mourning clothes but only for three days." The deceased man explained in his note that he wanted to be buried according to Islamic tradition, but this mourning tradition was not based on the Koran.[74] After the will was read, the *mahalla* men nodded in agreement and promised to acknowledge this last wish, yet the women present at the funeral objected to it. One loudly declared, "Why wouldn't this family wear mourning cloth? We all had to do it in the past. Our grandmothers practised this tradition, why does this family have to be an exception?"[75] Along with women's agency in practising and maintaining rituals commonly associated with Islam such as funeral processions and obligations, this story conveys the importance community members, and women in particular, attached to these ceremonies. They regarded these practices as both their personal obligation and their family and ancestorial duty, part of being a good Muslim.

An example of the discontinuity between the centre and the periphery in the regime's anti-religion campaign is reflected in the atheistic literature's explanations of women's religiosity. According to this propaganda, in addition to age, lack of education and employment opportunities, unfulfilled emotional needs were also significant drivers that attracted rural women to religion.[76] Although the authors denied biological causes of female religiosity, they nevertheless emphasized women's aesthetic desire for beauty. Official reports claimed that for this reason religious officials were able to mobilize women's support.[77] As a result, women were actively encouraged to participate in music, dancing, and other creative activities.[78] The regime believed that women's engagement in such activities could provide an outlet for their need for artistic fulfilment.[79] During the post-war era, the Soviet regime recruited women to art and music clubs, and to theatre and dance performances. Official reports proudly claimed, "Hundreds of indigenous women were recruited to work in the sphere of culture and literature. One could not even imagine this in the feudal darkness of the Bukhara."[80] These announcements were accompanied by stories of rural girls who had never attended the theatre or opera.[81] There was a lack of cultural activities for women and girls in the countryside; there were no theatres or dance, music, or poetry clubs in rural areas.[82] Urban women could take advantage of Soviet cultural activities and facilities, but these remained unavailable outside the cities.

Diverse Understanding of Being a Muslim

Soviet sociologists' characterization of rural women's religiosity as more common in older, uneducated, and unemployed women was not necessarily incorrect.[83] Yet the various factors the central regime used to explain women's religiosity remained generally inaccurate. One such instance was the regime's interpretation of female healers' role in society. These women were popular among the female populace, even though it is difficult to know the extent of their influence on average Muslim women's religiosity. The propaganda reports described a rural religious woman who called herself a *hur giz* ("girl from paradise" in Uzbek). "She greets her female visitors covered in a white blanket," the report described. "This woman performs religious rituals such as *mushkil kusho*, *bibi sishanbe*, and other traditional religious customs. She claims that she can forecast the future. Even urban women seek her services. She clouds women's heads with religious lies," the report emphasized.[84] Another woman spiritual leader was registered in Stalinabad region. Tuycheeva Huriniso claimed that she could heal sick women, especially those who could not get pregnant. She made belts with prayers written on them, which guaranteed a deceased person a spot in heaven. She called the belt "kiyomat kiik" ("attire for judgment day" in Uzbek), which cost up to six hundred rubles, but she also accepted cattle as payment.[85] The report noted that while medical services were free and easily available, rural women, especially those who are not able to get pregnant preferred these healers.[86]

Men and women in Tajikistan developed their sense of themselves as Muslims based on their engagement in everyday rituals. Some, like the *hur giz*, also expressed themselves through engagement in working with spirits.[87] Others claimed they could have direct encounters with divine power while sick, healing, or in dreams and visions.[88]

The case of Sanubar Qasimova (b. 1969), a healer who resides outside Khujand, a city in northern Tajikistan, provides a glimpse into how these individuals take up these roles and achieve prominence within their community.[89] At the age of thirteen, Qasimova had an encounter with a snake while cleaning the entryway to her father's store. Even though she remained unharmed, the experienced caused Sanubar mental distressed compelling her parents to take her to a séance session of the famous hypnotist Anatoly Kashpirovsky (b. 1939) in Tashkent. When that did not work, her parents consulted with a local spiritual worker, who informed them that Qasimova was destined to eventually take up his profession. Now she communicates with the dead and local people speak highly of her abilities.[90] The popularity of religious healers is reflected in a study of Oshoba, a rural village in Tajikistan. When the Soviet hospitals arrived, local practices of treating illness by connecting to spirits, with herb-based remedies, targeting evil eye, and others did not disappear. In fact, doctors with Soviet training did not discourage local medical practices and tended to include them in their thinking about the treatment.[91]

Mixing local rituals and beliefs with Soviet ideas and practices was not uncommon among Muslim professionals. Even though publicly these officially frequently called on the public to extend a helping hand to women who had fallen victim to these so-called religious healers and officials:

> We need to help women who have mistakenly fallen into the trap of religious officials. We need to put them on a right path. To end the shameful feudal traditions, we need to organize a massive educational campaign. We need to publicly shame these individuals who still promote and practice patriarchal practices. We must declare a ruthless war not just through legal means but also through community action. We need to educate these women's morals and values, direct them towards a communist path, honest labour for the benefit of society, collectivism, simplicity, and modesty in public and in private life.[92]

The new Soviet Tajik woman was portrayed as completely different from the previous religious woman who was seen as being under the influence of the feudal regime. Propaganda declared that there was no place for such women in the new, modern, Soviet communist village.[93] However, these descriptions of religious women as rural, backward, and uneducated did not accurately reflect the diversity of women's experiences during this period. In fact, urban women also participated in rituals associated with Islam, including those that involved spiritual healers.

Consequently, the image of an emancipated Tajik woman determined to be successful professionally and personally, produced by the secular culture of the Khrushchev era, competed with images maintained by popular memory.[94] Consider, for example memories retained by Bikhodzhal Rakhimova's, a prominent government official. Based on her memory of post-war Soviet Tajikistan, women, including urban and rural government officials, identified themselves as both Muslim and Soviet. "Combining these two identities did not preclude one from utilizing official Soviet discourse and leading a normal Soviet life,"[95] she noted.

> I was a government official, which often involved hosting senior officials at my house. Based on our Tajik tradition before sending guests off, my mother would have to say a blessing; instead of mentioning Allah, she'd mention Lenin, Marx, and Engels. Instead of concluding with "Amin," she'd say, "Proletarians of all countries unite," and would run her hands over their faces. These were tough times; one couldn't express any religious sentiments, especially me since I worked for the Communist Party, which preached universal atheism. But I'd constantly say, "Bismillohu

Rahmoni Rahim" [In the name of Allah, the most gracious, the most mer-
ciful]. I'd observe these traditions but get on the podium and criticize people who practised religion, I'd punish those who attended mosques and
read prayers.[96]

Uttering Islamic phrases such as *bismillah* (in the name of God) before
or after a meal, greetings such as *salaam alaikum* (peace upon you), and
other everyday rituals remained part of the regular routine all Muslims
participated in.[97] While Soviet ideology emphasized the dramatic differences in the images of new and old Tajik women, they overlooked the
fact that Muslim women, including government officials and members
of the intelligentsia, continued to take part in both religious and Soviet
cultural events, without necessarily adhering to the supposedly contradictory meaning of either.[98]

All men and women regardless on their geographic location observed
and celebrated Soviet holidays including International Women's Day
(8 March), Labour Day (1 May), Victory Day (9 May), October Revolution Day (7 November), which symbolized their belonging to the Soviet
Union.[99] Urban and rural women also seamlessly combined these secular holidays with celebrations associated with Islam such as marriage
and circumcision of boys festivities, hosting of guests, funeral processions, honouring ancestors who passed away, celebration of Ramadan,
and more. These practices and celebrations remained at the core of
Muslim men and women's being part of their community and practising sociality.[100] The highest Soviet officials of Muslim background rou-
tinely participated in these customs.

Analysis of these celebrations in rural Tajikistan during the Soviet
period illustrates the evolving nature of these ceremonies. For instance,
wedding festivities are commonly associated with being a Muslim
and, during the Soviet regime, it came to include a secular element of
ZAGS, a required registration of the marriage with the government.
After ZAGS, the newlyweds typically paid tribute to the local statue
of Lenin.[101] The traditional wedding lasted for three days (the length
of the ritual varies by location in Tajikistan) and served to strengthen
social networks, established a system of social support and debt obligations, and served as a critical practice of sociality.[102] Tajiks adjusted
their traditions and made new meanings of everyday routines and
celebratory occasions to take part in both "Islamic" and Soviet traditions.[103] In most Muslim societies, men and women regularly debate
what constitutes 'real' or 'genuine' Islam but in Soviet Central Asia
such discussions are rare. As Rasanayagam posits, the Soviet regime
in Muslim Central Asia, including Tajikistan, demonstrates that the

relationship between Islam and Soviet ideology was not inherently contradictory, and the same can be said for the interplay between culture and religion.[104]

Muslim officials executed state policy and orders based on their own shifting priorities. During aggressive state clampdowns on religion, Muslim male and female leaders felt a need to act assertively yet during periods of calmness, many adjusted accordingly.[105] For instance, at the Tenth Women's Annual Congress in 1972, when a doctor, Sofia Hafizovna Khakimova, suggested embracing some Islamic norms to facilitate good habits among rural women. After all, she insisted, "the Koran prohibits women from fasting when they're breastfeeding.... Maybe we should utilize these useful aspects of religion to teach our women good practices, especially in terms of hygiene."[106] This public figure freely proposing the incorporation of useful aspects of religion in ideological work, among other things, speaks of the non-threatening nature of the post-war attack on religion.

Nonetheless, Khakimova's suggestion provoked uproar in the auditorium. Most women activists disagreed with her. M. Gafarova, professor of philosophy and head of the pedagogical institute in Dushanbe, responded first, "We have to be cautious about using old traditions since they can turn against us, especially positive aspects of Islam. We need to address these questions with a highly scientific approach, not with religion and the Koran."[107] Comrade Fadeeva followed:

All nations have well-established traditions but as Comrade Gafarova rightly pointed out some of these traditions have dangerous powers. Orthodox Christianity also has useful aspects to it. It preaches not to harm, not to steal, not to kill, but we shouldn't use that either. We must only use our communist positions to address our problems since communism has the moral codes that form the basis of our lives, not religion.[108]

H.F. Gafarova, assistant head of the *zhensoviet* presidium and deputy minister of commerce, ended the discussion by thanking Khakimova for her presentation and told her to avoid using the Koran and Islam in the future and to base everything on scientific facts.[109] Khrushchev's anti-religious campaign was ultimately a failure, not because it did not manage to eliminate religious expression in public, but because it failed to convince believers in Russia and Muslims in the periphery that religion and the Soviet system were incompatible.[110] Most importantly, the state failed to understand the role Islam played in daily lives of the practitioners.

While the regime forced women to enter the workforce and women eventually threw off their veils, fasting, and traditional practices continued in the countryside. In the mid-1970s and 1980s, the failure of central and local governments to eradicate Islam and religious practices among women in Tajikistan was evident. In 1973, Z. Muradova and M.K. Karimova, members of the Gissar *zhensoviet*, reported that anti-religious work among rural women had been ineffective: "Rural women still practise religion, women take pilgrimage trips, practise circumcision celebrations, take part in religious wedding ceremonies."[111] V. Ahmedova, head of the culture department, similarly declared, "Our women are still religious; this is especially evident during religious holidays, when the production level declines drastically and women skip work."[112]

As a result, in the 1980s, Karimova called for increasing rural women's access to education and cultural facilities in order to fight effectively against Islam in the countryside:

> The majority of women in rural areas practice Islam and force their children, especially their daughters, to observe religious rituals and practices, including Ramadan, when women and children fast. Over 75.6 per cent of women celebrate Ramadan in the countryside. The atheistic education of women should be our priority.[113]

The ineffectiveness of the anti-religious campaigns in rural areas triggered a new approach in the 1970s. Journals and newspapers, including *Zanoni Tojikiston* ("Women of Tajikistan" in Tajik), *Nauka i religiia*, and *Kommunist Tadzhkistan* ("Communist of Tajikistan" in Russian), as well as other forms of mass media, published articles about these new approaches to their anti-religious work. In 1974, *Nauka i religiia* published an interview with Ibodat Rakhimova, member of the Presidium of the Tajik Supreme Soviet (in office 1978–82) regarding the government's new tactic:

> The household is a very delicate sphere. Before we enter it with our ideological information, we must have a thorough understanding of its taboos. A single insensitive word can trigger rejection and make a woman indifferent and immune to atheistic campaigns. The party calls on us to increase our attack on religion, to apply diverse approaches, to stop using the same ideological propaganda, to apply approaches that are individually tailored, influence person's feelings and consciousness, to speak from the heart and use emotions, persistently introduce Soviet rituals and traditions. We are currently trying to mobilize new women campaign workers but there are still not enough of them. Before we assign a woman to carry out an atheistic campaign, we must ensure that she is articulate and knows

how to carry out atheistic work properly, to ensure that she does not do more damage than good.[114]

Rakhimova pointed out that any future anti-religious campaign would

specifically clarify that feudal traditions have nothing to do with Tajik heritage, that these are local and regional customs. What can expensive religion-based funerals have in common with Tajik heritage and national ethics? Or what can wedding rituals, when a mullah preaches to a young bride about family, have in common with our modern principles and progressive traditions of the Tajik nation?[115]

During the Brezhnev period and under his successors, the Soviet regime shifted its approach to Islam and traditional practices in the Muslim periphery. Customs and traditions frequently associated with being a Muslim, such as wedding celebrations, funerals, circumcision of boys, eating with one's hands instead of utensils, and other practices, became increasingly acceptable during this time. This change in policy was tacit, but it marked a significant departure from previous Soviet attitudes towards religion and cultural practices.[116]

The post-war Soviet campaign against Islam in Tajikistan centres around the state's belief that introducing women to Soviet lifestyle and rituals would not only ensure their entry into the labour force, but also result in their complete transformation to emancipated secular Soviet women. The Khrushchev and Brezhnev regimes eventually managed to pressure rural Muslim women to enter the workforce and replace their veils with small headscarves. However, this dramatic visual transformation was not accompanied by the eradication of practices linked to being a Muslim in Tajikistan. For most indigenous people in Tajikistan, urban and rural, Islam and religious practices remained a core part of their daily lives, despite, or possibly because of, the Khrushchev regime's overt attempt to eliminate these practices. Julie McBrien's work on Kyrgyzstan shows that Soviet secularism further encouraged Central Asian people to think of religion as a belonging. Essentially, the regime's secularism created a purpose for Islam. This harmoniously coincided with notions of collectivity over individualism and independent economic agency. Promotion of ethnic groups centred around religious traditions such as Islam and Orthodox Christianity providing particular scripts about religion, the community and person, and generative action. This contributed to the idea of religion as the basis of the Muslim population's notion of collective belonging and sociality.[117] As a result, the *zhensoviety*'s activism around the anti-religious campaign only added to the challenges the organization faced in becoming a genuine voice for women it was created to represent. Slogans targeting entrenched practices associated with being a Muslim and practising sociality contributed to rural women's perception of the women's organizations as superficial and not serious in their attempt to introduce meaningful and lasting chance in women's lives.

Epilogue

In the 1920s, the Bolshevik regime introduced the most progressive gender reforms in the world. The regime intended to bring women out of the household realm and encourage participation in the public sphere and the workforce, a prerequisite for industrialization and state modernization. In Central Asia, the campaign focused on eradicating "Islamic" traditions, which the regime viewed as the primary obstacles to women's entry into the public domain. Chapter 1 of this study focused on the initial stages of the Bolshevik campaign in the 1920s. It illustrated that, while they were intended to mobilize Muslim women, the gender reforms were accompanied by contradictory outcomes and violent resistance from the local population. During this period, the campaign illustrates the regime's trial-and-error-style administration of the region, including the women's liberation campaign.

Despite the retreat from the liberal Bolshevik gender reforms, Stalin's regime created a new understanding of gender among its female populace. During the 1930s and 1940s, women throughout the Soviet Union zealously contributed to the regime's efforts in the industrial and agrarian sectors. Chapter 2 focused on Tajik women's experiences of developing a new identity as collective farm workers. Sources illustrate that these women nurtured genuine feelings of affection for their leader, Stalin, and worked hard for the future prosperity of their nation. Chapter 3 drew connections between rural women's lack of educational and career opportunities and the strengthening of patriarchal social structures in the region. In Tajikistan, socio-economic circumstances, cultural norms, and the passport and residency systems restricted rural women's ability to migrate to urban areas.

Indigenous women who managed to urbanize more easily benefitted from the opportunities created by the Soviet regime. Chapter 4 centred on these women. Despite being in the best position to advance the cause of women, urban and educated elite women often failed to do so. This was consistent with the Iranian experience.[1] In Soviet Tajikistan, these outcomes were beyond the power of Muslim women leaders. Female professionals were expected to combine their demanding careers with strict gender norms and domestic duties. Urban women's educational and professional achievements placed them in a separate social category and isolated them from their female peers in the countryside. The growing divide between urban women and rural women is vivid in the analysis of the *zhensoviety*'s work in the post–Second World War period. Chapter 5 explored how rural women in Tajikistan came to view the *zhensoviety*'s activism as an imposition by urban activists.[2] The women's councils' approaches and activism only widened the gap between urban Slavic and Sovietized indigenous women and rural Muslim women. One of the *zhensoviety*'s missions included the anti-religious campaign aimed primarily at rural women of Soviet Tajikistan. The final chapter of the book focused on Khrushchev's renewed attack on Islam in the countryside. Analysis of the anti-religious campaign illustrates that, despite the *zhensoviety*'s grassroots nature, the regime maintained its centralized approach to women's issues from the 1950s to the 1980s. The propaganda messages convey the regime's inadequate understanding of the Muslim periphery.

While this study has analysed the many challenges rural Muslim women faced in pursuing education in the cities, women born and raised in urban areas also had to abide by similar social expectations and confronted similar limitations. The biggest advantage urban women enjoyed was proximity to university education and industrial sector jobs. I grew up in the second-largest city in Tajikistan, Khujand, and it was only because of my father's unexpected death that I was allowed to pursue education outside my community, in the neighbouring country of Kyrgyzstan. His unfortunate passing led my mother to break away from his family's control and allowed me to ignore my aunts' insistence that I follow all the norms expected of my gender. When my mom took me to seek the blessing of my eldest aunt to pursue education at AUCA, she refused. She loudly proclaimed that I would bring shame to my family and harm my sisters' marriage prospects. I was a middle child and my oldest sister's marriage was already secured, so my breaking away from the established norms affected only my youngest sibling's marriage choices. My mother assured me that, because my youngest sister was attractive, I should not worry about her. Even the most progressive urbanite women in Tajikistan are expected to adhere to the societal norms established for women. The rigidity and enforcement of these norms is continuously changing due to fluid social, political, and economic dynamics. Based on conversations with my interviewees and family members, women are taking up veiling to negotiate more opportunities outside the private domain for themselves and their daughters.

Today urban women in Tajikistan often attend university only until their marriage is arranged, which commonly happens during the second year of college. After the wedding, there is a renegotiation of terms, and the bride is pressured to abandon her studies to prioritize her new family obligations. For most rural girls, attending a university in a city is harder than it was during the Soviet period. Those who do attend university face challenges, including food insecurity, poor quality of education, sexual harassment, and lack of transportation and housing. Most importantly, their families will not allow them to live away from home before marriage. Some women use the veil to safely pursue education or work in public spaces. The veil allows women to avoid male attention and sexual harassment and signals modesty and unapproachability for dating outside marriage.

In the aftermath of the civil war (1992–7), which took the lives of many men, Tajikistan experienced a distorted gender ratio. This disparity has only widened with Tajik men's migration to Russia in search of work due to high unemployment at home. There is an established perception of veiled women as modest, traditional, and obedient: characteristics associated with improved marriage prospects. These same factors explain the increasing numbers of polygamous marriages and child brides. The lack of men further contributes to the wide acceptance of polygamous relationships and compels parents to rush their daughters into early marriages to secure a life partner.[3]

Following the collapse of the Soviet Union, Tajikistan experienced an economic and political crisis. It was accompanied by electricity shortages and lack of basic utilities around the country. In rural areas, these shortages lasted for extended periods and led to considerable rural-to-urban migration. This migration continues to this day since there is no longer a passport or residency system that restricts citizen's internal mobility. Most residents of the countryside are leaving their native hinterlands in search of better prospects for themselves and their families. Similar to findings in Egypt, today the majority of Tajik women who veil are from rural areas, with lower levels of education and stronger religious beliefs.[4] As Leila Ahmed explains, mothers who were born in rural areas and have retained "a strong dose of religion and tradition" are the main influences on young Egyptian women's decision to veil.[5] Rural women in Tajikistan are moving to the cities, taking up veiling, and convincing their daughters to do the same in order to seek affiliation with a broader Islamic community during the transition to a new urban setting. This also provides women with a sense of safety in a new environment while in public and around male strangers.[6] In short, reasons for the re-emergence of veiling vary and are individually based.

Ghodsee's findings in post-socialist Bulgaria show that the resurgence of Islam and practices associated with being a Muslim (such as veiling) are not solely based on religiosity but are often grounded in socio-economic considerations, political causes, and historical background. The author illustrates that mosques have replaced former employment in local mines as a vehicle for men to express masculinity. Muslim women encouraged this development to combat alcoholism and violence at home.[7] Comparably, in Tajikistan, women are taking up veiling and practising piety based on present and future calculations more than past circumstances. Nonetheless, the Soviet past still serves as a critical foundation of daily life in Tajikistan. As Kandiyoti poignantly notes, "There was a great deal more to the 'traditionalism' attributed to Central Asian societies than could not be explained with references to either anti-colonial resistance or the supposed failure of modernization."[8]

Today Islam is celebrated as part of a national heritage and the rapid building of mosques has served as a sign of national rebirth.[9] The government of Tajikistan, similar to that in neighbouring Uzbekistan, is attempting to police women's fashion choices, approving a national style of dress (*kurta uzor* in Tajik) and disapproving of foreign-style clothing by linking it to extremism or "Wahhabism."[10] The current regime is actively reinventing the national image and using women as central actors in this nation-building project. Traditional feminine roles are utilized to construct a national identity of "law-abiding citizenry thriving under the guidance of the father of the nation."[11] As part of this new narrative, the most famous female politician in Tajikistan, Zaripova, is only ever quoted in the Tajik press about a woman's role in the family, not her extensive and unprecedented political career (see figure E.1).[12]

Figure E.1. The author with Nizoramo Zaripova, June 2014

Notes: Zaripova was a prominent political figure in Soviet Tajikistan, serving as chair of the Presidium of the Tajik Supreme Soviet from 1982 to 1984. This photograph captures an important moment of connection between the author and a historical figure whose legacy is explored in the pages of this book.

Source: Photograph taken by the author.

Notes

Introduction

1 Reference to Muslim, Tajik, or indigenous women includes a diverse range of ethnicities, religions, and other significant identifications, including Tajik, Uzbek, Pamiri, Garmi, Kuliubi, and Khujandi (previously Leninabadi), the majority of whom are Sunni Muslim, except for Pamiri women, who are predominantly Ismaili. Tajik women also include Jewish minority women who converted to Islam, especially following the collapse of the Soviet Union.

2 I refer to the Bolshevik regime to distinguish the earlier Soviet regime (1917–24) under Lenin from the subsequent regimes under Stalin, Khrushchev, and other Soviet leaders.

3 Edgar, "Bolshevism, Patriarchy, and the Nation," 264.

4 Moghadam, *Modernizing Women*, 22.

5 Edgar, "Bolshevism, Patriarchy, and the Nation," 252.

6 Bride payments usually consist of animals, money, and goods from the groom's family to the bride's family. This tradition persisted during the Soviet regime. Prior to the Soviet regime, Muslim girls who reached puberty were considered of marriageable age; the Soviet regime changed it to eighteen and above for both genders.

7 Tekeli, *Women in Modern Turkish Society*, 185, cited in Fleischmann, "Other Awakening," 120.

8 *Itogi vsesoiuznoi perepisi naseleniia*, 79–83.

9 Heyat, *Azeri Women in Transition*, 4–5.

10 Heyat, 4–5. Marfua Tokhtakhodjaeva, in *Slogans of Communism*, identifies similar conditions in Soviet Uzbekistan.

11 Interviews with Muslim women who held government positions, conducted by the author: Bihodzhal Rakhimova (October 2012), Zaragul Mirasanova (August 2012), Nizoramoh Zaripova (June 2013), and others.

12 Gerstenzang and Getter, "Laura Bush Addresses State of Afghan Women"; also see Abu-Lughod, "Do Muslim Women Really Need Saving?"

13 Massell, *Surrogate Proletariat*. According to Massell, the Soviet government used Muslim women as a means to dismantle established social structures in Central Asia and expected newly emancipated women to become the indigenous working class that the region lacked. Douglas Northrop's book *Veiled Empire* largely supports Massell's argument. However, Northrop also suggests that local resistance against the colonial power mobilized Uzbeks and united them under a national identity. More recent studies by Edgar, Kamp, Khalid, and others challenge the view that indigenous Central Asian actors were unimportant and uninvolved. In particular, Marianne Kamp's *New Woman in Uzbekistan* provides a women-centred perspective on the Bolshevik unveiling campaign. Kamp argues that some Uzbek women, influenced by local Muslim reformers (Jadids) who had a particular view on modernity and women's roles, joined the Soviets to promote the women's liberation campaign.

14 See Massell, *Surrogate Proletariat*; and Northrop, *Veiled Empire*.

15 Massell, *Surrogate Proletariat*; and Northrop, *Veiled Empire*.

16 Ersanli-Behar, *Iktidar ve Tarih*, cited in Adeeb, "Backwardness," 249.

17 Khalid, "Backwardness and the Quest for Civilization," 250; also see Edgar, "Bolshevism, Patriarchy, and the Nation," 271.

18 Edgar, 257.

19 Cronin, "Coercion or Empowerment?," 25–6; also see Kamp, "Women-Initiated Unveiling," 223.

20 Keller, "Trapped between State and Society," 20.

21 Kamp, *New Woman in Uzbekistan*, 157–8; Kamp, "Women-Initiated Unveiling"; and Cronin, "Coercion or Empowerment?," 26; also see Keller, "Trapped between State and Society."

22 Edgar, "Bolshevism, Patriarchy, and the Nation," 264.

23 Kandiyoti, *Women, Islam, and the State*, 9.

24 Edgar, "Bolshevism, Patriarchy, and the Nation," 255; and Kamp, *New Woman in Uzbekistan*.

25 Cronin, "Coercion or Empowerment?," 3. Modernization programs included mass mobilization, nation building, political centralization, and radical interventions and reforms within society and culture, including emancipation of women, literacy campaigns, and secularization; also see Khalid, "Backwardness," 234.

26 Cronin, "Coercion or Empowerment?," 3.

27 Edgar, "Bolshevism, Patriarchy, and the Nation," 255.

28 Khalid, "Backwardness," 234.

29 Khalid, 250.

30 Edgar, "Bolshevism, Patriarchy, and the Nation," 252; also see Cronin, "Coercion or Empowerment?," 27.

31 Edgar, 252.

32 Moghadam, *Modernizing Women*, 77.
33 Edgar, "Bolshevism, Patriarchy, and the Nation," 256.
34 Edgar, "Nationality Policy," cited in Edgar, "Bolshevism, Patriarchy, and the Nation," 271.
35 Cronin, "Coercion or empowerment?," 25–7.
36 Cronin, 27.
37 Edgar, "Bolshevism, Patriarchy, and the Nation," 271. The Zhenotdel was put in charge of the women's emancipation campaign in Muslim Central Asia.
38 Ghodsee, *Second World, Second Sex*, 53–75.
39 Charrad, "Tunisia at the Forefront," 113; also see Charrad, *States and Women's Rights*; and Kallander, *Tunisia's Modern Woman*.
40 Charrad, "Tunisia at the Forefront," 113.
41 Kamp, *New Woman in Uzbekistan*, 7.
42 Muslim women in Tajikistan were ethnically either Tajik or Uzbek women. Therefore, I refer to them as either Muslim or indigenous urban or rural women.
43 See Martin, *Affirmative Action Empire*, 10.
44 Massell, *Surrogate Proletariat*.
45 See Martin, *Affirmative Action Empire*, 10, 19–20.
46 Krylova, "Stalinist Identity," 640; also see Krylova, *Soviet Women in Combat*.
47 Ilič, "Introduction," 2.
48 Geiger, *Family in Soviet Russia*; Buckley, *Women and Ideology*; and Juviler, "Women and Sex in Soviet Law."
49 Heyat, *Azeri Women in Transition*, 121; also see Goldman, *Women, the State and Revolution*.
50 Sedghi, *Women and Politics in Iran*, 5.
51 Sedghi, 130.
52 Kandiyoti, "Sex Roles and Social Change"; "Urban Change and Women's Roles"; and "Bargaining with Patriarchy."
53 Moghadam, *Modernizing Women*, 64.
54 White, "State Feminism," 156.
55 Ecevit, "Shop Floor Control." In this study, the author illustrates how participation in the labour force positively affected young women. They were able to retain family support to postpone marriage and childbearing; as a result, they were able to enjoy more experiences in terms of professional and personal growth.
56 Goskomstat SSSR, *Narodnoe khoziaistvo SSSR za 10 let* (1988).
57 Kalinovsky, *Laboratory*, 63.
58 "Urbanization," in Curtis, *Tajikistan*.
59 "Urbanization," in Curtis, 3.
60 Jones and Grupp, *Modernization*, 77.

61 Moghadam, *Modernizing Women*, 109.
62 Moghadam, 109.
63 Guboglo, *Sovremennee ethnoiazykovye protsessy*, 114; also see Kaiser, "Social Mobilization," 271–2, 274.
64 Youseff, *Women and Work*, 37; also see Sacks, "Work Force Composition," 190.
65 Youseff, *Women and Work*, 37.
66 Patnaik, "Women in Uzbekistan."
67 See *Itogi vsesoiuznoi perepisi naseleniia*, 79–83.
68 Fleischmann, "Other 'Awakening,'" 119–20.
69 Moghadam, *Modernizing Women*, 64.
70 Sedghi, *Women and Politics in Iran*, 163.
71 Corcoran-Nantes, *Lost Voices*, 59.
72 Interview with Dzhamilia Ismailova, conducted by the author, October 2012; also see Rakowska-Harmstone, *Russia and Nationalism*, 99.
73 Interviews with Nizoramo Zaripova (June 2012), Bikhodzhal Rakhimova (October 2012), and Bakhti Shaidova (September 2012), conducted by the author.
74 The *zhenskie soviety* – commonly known as the *zhensoviety* – were women's councils. These councils were the successor organizations to their predecessor, the Zhenotdel. The *zhensoviety* were the only women's organizations in charge of Muslim women's transformation in Central Asia in the post–Second World War period.
75 Interviews with rural women in Kanibadam, Varzob, Isfara, and Sugd regions, conducted by the author, June 2010–August 2014.
76 Browning, *Women and Politics*, 92–3.
77 Kandiyoti, "Emancipated but Unliberated?," 323.
78 Kandiyoti, 323.
79 Kandiyoti, "Politics of Gender," 613.
80 Kandiyoti, 616.
81 Epkenhans, *Origins of the Civil War*, 12.
82 McAndrew, "Soviet Women's Magazines," 80.
83 In Tajikistan, the term *kelnoya* is applied to all married women.
84 Krylova, "Stalinist Identity," 640.

1. The Attack

1 Moghadam, *Modernizing Women*, 69.
2 Cronin, "Coercion or Empowerment?," 18.
3 Edgar, *Tribal Nation*, 242–4.
4 Tett, "Ambiguous Alliances," 111.
5 Moghadam, *Modernizing Women*, 78–9.

6 Lenin, quoted in Moghadam, 88.
7 Kollontai, *Trud zhenshchiny*, 146, 161–2, quoted in Hoffmann, "Mothers in the Motherland," 35.
8 Tett, "Ambiguous Alliances," 38–9.
9 Goldman, *Women, the State and Revolution*, v, 3–5, 10–12, 340–2.
10 Goldman, 3, 337.
11 Goldman, 3–12.
12 Wood, *Baba and the Comrade*, cited in Ghodsee, *Second World, Second Sex*, 40.
13 Clements, "Utopianism of the Zhenotdel," 485.
14 Ghodsee, *Second World, Second Sex*, 41.
15 Tett, "Ambiguous Alliances," 39.
16 Kamp, *New Woman of Uzbekistan*, 11.
17 Khalid, "Backwardness," 241.
18 Edgar, "Bolshevism, Patriarchy, and the Nation," 252.
19 Kamp, *New Woman of Uzbekistan*, 29. Also see Khalid, *Making Uzbekistan*, 203.
20 Kandiyoti, "Women and the Turkish State," cited in Khalid, *Making Uzbekistan*, 198.
21 Khalid, *Making Uzbekistan*, 357.
22 Khalid, 197.
23 Khalid, "Backwardness," 241.
24 Khalid, 243; also see Kamp, *New Woman in Uzbekistan*, 43.
25 Kamp, *New Woman in Uzbekistan*, 229.
26 Kamp, 86, 93.
27 Kamp, 93.
28 Kamp, 229.
29 Khalid, *Making Uzbekistan*, 208.
30 Khalid, 361–2.
31 Corcoran-Nantes, *Lost Voices*, 49.
32 [Sredazburo, Zhenotdel], *Besh yil*, 5, cited in Khalid, *Making Uzbekistan*, 204.
33 Massell, *Surrogate Proletariat*, xxxii–xxxiii.
34 Shulman, *Stalinism on the Frontier*, 18.
35 Khalid, *Making Uzbekistan*, 205.
36 G'ilozquova, "Ochilgan o'zbek xotin-qizlariga ko'makga," 5, cited in Khalid, *Making Uzbekistan*, 358.
37 Madzhidov, *Osobennosti formirovaniia*, 32.
38 Corcoran-Nantes, *Lost Voices*, 51.
39 PAIPI TsK KP RT, f. 1, op. 1, d. 5, l. 32; f. 1, op. 1, d. 724, l. 36.
40 PAIPI TsK KP RT, f. 1, op. 1, d. 724, l. 79. All translations of quotations from non-English sources throughout the book are the author's own.
41 Buckley, *Women and Ideology*, 71, cited in Corcoran-Nantes, *Lost Voices*, 50.

42   Massell, *Surrogate Proletariat*, 244–5.
43   Tett, "Ambiguous Alliances," 41.
44   PAIPI TsK KP RT, f. 1, op. 1, d. 4, l. 63.
45   PAIPI TsK KP RT, f. 1966, op. 1, d. 46, l. 7.
46   Tokhtakhodjaeva, *Slogans of Communism*, 51–3; also see Corcoran-Nantes, *Lost Voices*, 53.
47   Buckley, *Women and Ideology*, 71; also see Khalid, *Making Uzbekistan*, 204.
48   Edgar, *Tribal Nation*, 221.
49   PAIPI TsK KP RT, f. 1, op. 1, d. 4, l. 102.
50   PAIPI TsK KP RT, f. 1, op. 1, d. 4, l. 102; also see Kamp, "Unveiling Uzbek Women," 253–8; and Edgar, *Tribal Nation*, 221.
51   PAIPI TsK KP RT, f. 1, op. 1, d. 4, l. 102.
52   PAIPI TsK KP RT, f. 1, op. 1, d. 4, l. 63.
53   PAIPI TsK KP RT, f. 1, op. 1, d. 4, l. 63.
54   PAIPI TsK KP RT, f. 1, op. 1, d. 724, l. 36.
55   PAIPI TsK KP RT, f. 3, op. 1, d. 862, ll. 2–5.
56   PAIPI TsK KP RT, f 1, op. 1, d. 30, l. 71.
57   PAIPI TsK KP RT, f. 1, op 1, d. 464, l. 31.
58   Stavrakis, "Women and the Communist Party," 172–87; Ilbert, *Klara Tsetkin*, 182–6; *Pravda stavshaia legendoi*, 125–31; and Chamberlin, *Soviet Russia*, 378–80; all cited in Stites, *Women's Liberation Movement*, 340.
59   PAIPI TsK KP RT, f. 3, op. 5, d. 139, l. 79.
60   PAIPI TsK KP RT, f. 3, op. 5, d. 139, l. 79.
61   PAIPI TsK KP RT, f. 1, op. 1, d. 832, l. 5.
62   PAIPI TsK KP RT, f. 1, op. 1, d. 30, ll. 28–33.
63   PAIPI TsK KP RT, f. 1, op. 1, d. 862, l. 2.
64   PAIPI TsK KP RT, f. 1, op. 1, d. 30, ll. 28–33.
65   PAIPI TsK KP RT, f. 1, op. 1, d. 464, l. 22.
66   Kamp, *New Woman of Uzbekistan*, 71.
67   PAIPI TsK KP RT, f. 1, op. 1, d. 464, l. 29.
68   Stites, *Women's Liberation Movement*, 340; Massell, *Surrogate Proletariat*, 213; and Ergasheva, "Challenges for Women," 4, cited in Corcoran-Nantes, *Lost Voices*, 50.
69   Corcoran-Nantes, *Lost Voices*, 53.
70   Corcoran-Nantes, 56.
71   Corcoran-Nantes, 56–7.
72   Bergne, *Birth of Tajikistan*, 149; also see Wheeler, *Modern History*, 134.
73   Aminova, *October Revolution*, 121.
74   Aminova, 131–3.
75   Aminova, 151. For more on Koshchi/Qoshchi in Uzbekistan, see Khalid, *Making Uzbekistan*, 205.

76 Edgar, *Tribal Nation*, 222.
77 Aminova, *October Revolution*, 161.
78 Patnaik, *Perestroika and Women Labour Force*, 29–30.
79 PAIPI TsK KP RT, f. 1, op. 1, d. 457, l. 1.
80 PAIPI TsK KP RT, f. 1, op. 1, d. 39, l. 88.
81 Tett, "'Guardians of the Faith?,'" 137.
82 Tett, 138.
83 Zaripova, interview, June 2012.
84 Zaripova, interview, June 2012.
85 PAIPI TsK KP RT, f. 1, op. 1, d. 4, l. 64. The Komsomol (a syllabic abbreviation of the Russian *Vsesoiuznyi Leninskii Kommunisticheskii Soiuz Molodozhi*) was the youth division of the Communist Party.
86 PAIPI TsK KP RT, f. 1, op. 1, d. 862, l. 20.
87 See Massell, *Surrogate Proletariat*; and Keller, *To Moscow, Not Mecca*.
88 Tett, "Ambiguous Alliances," 41.
89 PAIPI TsK KP RT, f. 1, op. 1, d. 862, l. 21.
90 PAIPI TsK KP RT, f. 1, op. 1, d. 862, l. 98.
91 PAIPI TsK KP RT, f. 1, op. 1, d. 1206, l. 5.
92 PAIPI TsK KP RT, f. 3, op. 61, d. 295, l. 1.
93 Kamp, *New Woman of Uzbekistan*, 201.
94 Stites, *Women's Liberation Movement*, 340.
95 Aminova, *October Revolution*, 99.
96 Massell, *Surrogate Proletariat*, 259–64.
97 RGASPI, f. 62, op. 2, d. 1691, l. 113, cited in Kamp, *New Woman of Uzbekistan*, 212.
98 Quoted in Kisch and Reil, *Changing Asia*, 140–6, cited in Rakowska-Harmstone, *Russia and Nationalism*, 296.
99 Quoted in Kisch and Reil, 140–6, cited in Rakowska-Harmstone, 298.
100 Tett, "Ambiguous Alliances," 41; also see Kamp, *New Woman of Uzbekistan*, 201.
101 PAIPI TsK KP RT, f. 1, op. 1, d. 724, l. 41.
102 Keller, "Trapped between State and Society," 25–6.
103 Stites, *Women's Liberation Movement*, 340.
104 Keller, "Trapped between State and Society," 25.
105 Keller, 25.
106 Kamp, *New Woman of Uzbekistan*, 201.
107 Tett, "Ambiguous Alliances," 42.
108 PAIPI TsK KP RT, f. 1, op. 1, d. 464, l. 22.
109 PAIPI TsK KP RT, f. 1, op. 1, d. 464, l. 22.
110 PAIPI TsK KP RT, f. 1, op. 1, d. 862, l. 10.
111 Cronin, "Coercion or Empowerment?," 25.
112 PAIPI TsK KP RT, f. 1, op. 1, d. 1206, l. 53.

113 PAIPI TsK KP RT, f. 1, op. 1, d. 1206, l. 53.

114 Kamp, *New Woman of Uzbekistan*, 69.

115 PAIPI TsK KP RT, f. 1966, op. 1, d. 46, l. 4.

116 PAIPI TsK KP RT, f. 1966, op. 1, d. 46, l. 4.

117 RGASPI, f. 62, op. 2, d. 1234, l. 49, cited in Edgar, *Tribal Nation*, 240.

118 RGASPI, f. 62, op. 2, d. 440, ll. 93–4, 109–10, cited in Edgar, 240.

119 RGASPI, f. 62, op. 2, d. 440, ll. 3, 93–4; d. 1237, ll. 68–9, cited in Edgar, 240.

120 Edgar, 240–1; f. 1966, op. 1, d. 46, l. 5.

121 PAIPI TsK KP RT, f. 1966, op. 1, d. 46, l. 5.

122 PAIPI TsK KP RT, f. 1966, op. 1, d. 46, l. 5.

123 Edgar, *Tribal Nation*, 244.

124 Edgar, 244.

125 PAIPI TsK KP RT, f. 1966, op. 1, d. 46, l. 6.

126 Edgar, *Tribal Nation*, 244.

127 Corcoran-Nantes, *Lost Voices*, 40.

128 Northrop, *Veiled Empire*, 127.

129 Northrop, 127.

130 Makhmudov, *Semeino-pravovye sredstva obespecheniia stabilnosti brak*, 58, cited in Tett, "Ambiguous Alliances," 111.

131 Corcoran-Nantes, *Lost Voices*, 41.

132 Northrop, "Subaltern Dialogues," 126–9, cited in Kamp, *New Woman of Uzbekistan*, 72.

133 As noted above (see chapter 1), the Soviet regime also increased the marriage age for men and women from nine for girls and twelve for boys to eighteen for both.

134 Interviews with rural women in Kanibadam, Varzob, Isfara, and Sugd regions, conducted by the author, June 2010–August 2014.

135 Tett, "Ambiguous Alliances," 111.

136 Tett, 196.

137 Roberts, "Old Elites under Communism," 8.

138 Roberts, 5.

139 Wheeler, *Modern History*, 206.

140 Akiner, "Between Tradition and Modernity," 272.

141 See Massell, *Surrogate Proletariat*.

142 Kassymbekova, *Despite Cultures*, 203.

2. The Retreat

1 Goldman, *Women, the State and Revolution*, 338.

2 Hoffmann, "Mothers in the Motherland," 35.

3 Krylova, "Stalinist Identity"; also see Dunham, *In Stalin's Time*, 41. The term "Great Retreat" is associated with Nicholas Timasheff's *Great Retreat*.

4 Stites, *Women's Liberation Movement*, cited in Ghodsee, *Second World, Second Sex*, 41.
5 Eden, *God Save the USSR*, 126–32.
6 Khalid, *Islam after Communism*, 133.
7 Existing literature includes Dudoignon and Noack, *Allah's Kolkhozes*. This is a collection of case studies that analyse the forced migrations that occurred in Soviet Tajikistan during the post–Second World War period. The assessments cover various topics, such as the state's efforts to homogenize communities, the resistance of some communities, and the re-emergence of religious practices in the late 1980s. Also see Roche, *Family in Central Asia*.
8 See Martin, *Affirmative Action Empire*.
9 Interviews with Muslim women who held government positions during the Soviet period, all conducted by the author: Bikhodzhal Rakhimova (October 2012), Zaragul Mirasanova (August 2012), Nizoramo Zaripova (June 2012), Guldzhakhon Bobosadykova (July 2012), Bakhti Shaidova (September 2012), Makhfirat Dadabaeva (September 2012), Masuda Usmonova (September 2012), and others.
10 Patnaik, *Perestroika and Women Labour Force*, 87–8.
11 Krylova, "Stalinist Identity," 640.
12 Ilič, "Introduction," 2.
13 Holland, *Soviet Sisterhood*, 39.
14 See Timasheff, *Great Retreat*.
15 According to Richard Stites and Heather DeHaan, the Bolsheviks did not have the intention of liberating women from their domestic responsibilities. Stites specifically points out that some of the earlier Bolshevik leaders, including Lenin and his wife, Nadezhda Krupskaia, held conservative views about gender roles and family dynamics. See Stites, *Women's Liberation Movement*; and DeHaan, "Engendering a People," 440.
16 Gail Lapidus, Sheila Fitzpatrick, Roberta Manning, Wendy Goldman, Barbara Holland, and others view the Stalinist state as a radical break from the Bolshevik reforms of the 1920s. See Lapidus, *Women in Soviet Society*; Fitzpatrick, "Middle-Class Values"; Manning, "Women in the Soviet Countryside"; Goldman, *Women, the State and Revolution*; and Holland, *Soviet Sisterhood*. On the other hand, David Hoffmann suggests that the Soviet regime's evolving approach to family and marriage from the 1930s to the 1950s was similar to the changes that were happening in other European countries during that period. Hoffmann's article "Mothers in the Motherland" delves into this topic in more detail.
17 Krylova, "Stalinist Identity," 640; also see Dunham, *In Stalin's Time*, 41; Reid, "All Stalin's Women," 154; Shulman, *Stalinism on the Frontier*, 14; Neary, "Mothering Socialist Society"; and Buckley, "Untold Story."

18 Shulman, *Stalinism on the Frontier*, 16. Neary, Shulman, and Buckley have demonstrated a more complex picture of the Movement of Wife-Activists and shown that it was more than merely a movement of socially active middle-class women.

19 Krylova, "Stalinist Identity," 639.

20 Hellbeck, *Revolution on My Mind*, 361.

21 Hellbeck, 361.

22 Ilič, "Introduction," 2.

23 The state allocated families in rural areas small plots of land for individual gardening; see Siegelbaum, "Double Burden."

24 McAuley, *Women's Work and Wages*, 166.

25 Nikolaeva and Karaseva, *Zhenshchina v boiakh za kommunizm*, 7, cited in Clements, "Utopianism of the Zhenotdel," 496.

26 Clements, 496.

27 Tokhtakhodjaeva, *Slogans of Communism*, 92.

28 Kandiyoti, "Politics of Gender," 607.

29 Taagepeva, "National Differences"; and Heer and Bryden, "Family Allowances"; both cited in Kandiyoti, "Politics of Gender," 607. Also see Goldman, *Women at the Gates*, 279.

30 Falkingham, "Women and Gender Relations," 9. For more on Heroine Mother and Motherhood Glory awards, see Kandiyoti, "Politics of Gender," 607.

31 Kandiyoti, 608.

32 PAIPI TsK KP RT, f. 36, op. 4, d. 10, l. 10.

33 PAIPI TsK KP RT, f. 3, op. 93, d. 14, l. 41.

34 Ilič, "Introduction," 5.

35 Reikhel, "Voprosy semeinogo prava," 85, 84; Volfson, "Semia v sotsialisticheskom gosudarstve," 39, 43; and G.A., "Semia i brak v SSSR"; all cited in Goldman, *Women, the State and Revolution*, 343.

36 Ilič, "Introduction," 4.

37 PAIPI TsK KP RT, f. 3, op. 71, d. 24, l. 6.

38 PAIPI TsK KP RT, f. 3, op. 246, d. 6, l. 17.

39 PAIPI TsK KP RT, f. 3, op. 246, d. 6, l. 17.

40 PAIPI TsK KP RT, f. 3, op. 4, d. 10, l. 8.

41 PAIPI TsK KP RT, f. 3, op. 71, d. 24, l. 6. For more on Tajik women during the Second World War, see Direnberger, "Representations of Armed Women." Direnberger's analysis of the Tajik-language magazine *Zanoni Tojikiston*, and Soviet research on women published in Tajikistan after the Second World War, suggests that narratives about women's agency through their participation in the Soviet army can be found in local press and studies written in the Tajik language. However, these narratives are not reflected in the central Soviet ideology.

42 PAIPI TsK KP RT, f. 66, op. 1, d. 4643, l. 18.

43 PAIPI TsK KP RT, f. 3, op. 93, d. 14, l. 10.

44 PAIPI TsK KP RT, f. 3, op. 246, d. 6.

45 Ilič, "Introduction," 4. This was also a common sentiment among the women I interviewed.

46 PAIPI TsK KP RT, f. 3, op. 93, d. 9, l. 60.

47 PAIPI TsK KP RT, f. 3, op. 93, d. 9, ll. 59–61.

48 Cohn, "Sex and the Married Communist," 431.

49 Ilič, "Introduction," 4.

50 PAIPI TsK KP RT, f. 3, op. 93, d. 9, ll. 59–61.

51 For more on female modesty in Soviet Central Asia, see Edgar, *Intermarriage and the Friendship of Peoples*, 96–8.

52 Zaripova, interview, June 2012.

53 Zaripova, interview, June 2012.

54 Zaripova, interview, June 2012.

55 Zaripova, interview, June 2012.

56 PAIPI TsK KP RT, f. 3, op. 71, d. 213, l. 1.

57 A kulak was officially a "rich peasant," as distinct from a "middle peasant" (*serednika*) and a "poor peasant" (*bedniak*). The kulaks were generally divided into three groupings: "counter-revolutionaries," who had all their property confiscated and were prosecuted; "exploiters," who were charged with supposedly exploiting their neighbours and deported, but were permitted to keep some of their possessions; and kulaks, who could remain on their land but did not join collective farms, and were therefore subject to partial dekulakization. See Buckley, *Mobilizing Soviet Peasants*, 18; Lewin, *Russian Peasants and Soviet Power*, 496–7; and Davies, *Socialist Offensive*, 234–6.

58 PAIPI TsK KP RT, f. 3, op. 71, d. 213, l. 1.

59 Collectivization of agriculture brought about a radical transformation of the countryside, including the confiscation of land, animals, and equipment. Dekulakization was one aspect of this process. The state forced "rich peasants" to turn in their property, including clothing and footwear. Many of these peasants were deported. The seized property of the kulaks was meant to go towards creating collective farms, with poor peasants benefitting immediately through their membership of these collectives. See Buckley, *Mobilizing Soviet Peasants*, 8, 18; Lewin, *Russian Peasants and Soviet Power*, 496–7, 505–6; and Davies, *Socialist Offensive*, 234–6.

60 PAIPI TsK KP RT, f. 3, op. 71, d. 213, l. 21.

61 Interviews with Muslim women who held government positions, conducted by the author: Bikhodzhal Rakhimova (October 2012), Zaragul Mirasanova (August 2012), Nizoramo Zaripova (June 2012), and others.

62 Zaripova, interview, June 2012.
63 Zaripova, interview, June 2012.
64 PAIPI TsK KP RT, f. 3, op. 71, d. 24, l. 9.
65 *Gorkom* (short for *gorodskoi komitet*) was the name given to a city government committee in the Soviet Union, while *raikom* (short for *regionalnyi komitet*) was the term for a district government committee.
66 PAIPI TsK KP RT, f. 3, op. 71, d. 24, l. 9. In the *obkom*, in 1948, there were 235 women, including 79 Tajik women, compared to 1,302 women in 1945, of whom 262 were Tajik. In the *raikom* there were 1,475 women in 1948, including 395 Tajik women, compared to 2,907 women in 1945, including 884 Tajik and Uzbek women.
67 PAIPI TsK KP RT, f. 3, op. 71, d. 24, l. 9.
68 PAIPI TsK KP RT, f. 3, op. 93, d. 34, l. 26. Another example is the textile factory in Dushanbe, which in 1950 had 2,400 workers, including 1,676 women, only 62 of whom were Tajik and 18 Uzbek. See PAIPI TsK KP RT, f. 66, op. 1, d. 4643, l. 27.
69 PAIPI TsK KP RT, f. 3, op. 71, d. 24, l. 7.
70 Patnaik, *Perestroika and Women Labour Force*, 40.
71 PAIPI TsK KP RT, f. 3, op. 93, d. 34, l. 26.
72 PAIPI TsK KP RT, f. 66, op. 1, d. 4643, l. 10.
73 PAIPI TsK KP RT, f. 36, op. 4, d. 10, l. 11.
74 PAIPI TsK KP RT, f. 3, p. 93, d. 14, l. 44.
75 Chatterjee, "Soviet Heroines," 53.
76 Chatterjee, 53.
77 PAIPI TsK KP RT, f. 3, op. 93, d. 14, l. 91.
78 *Pravda*, no. 11 (March 1936); no. 10 (March 1938); *Rabotnitsa i krestianka*, no. 14 (1936): 14, cited in Chatterjee, "Soviet Heroines," 63.
79 Tokhtakhodjaeva, *Slogans of Communism*, 107.
80 PAIPI TsK KP RT, f. 3, op. 93, d. 14, ll. 12–13.
81 PAIPI TsK KP RT, f. 3, op. 93, d. 5, l. 40.
82 Interview with Gulsun Tursunova, conducted by the author, October 2012.
83 Chatterjee, "Soviet Heroines," 64.
84 PAIPI TsK KP RT, f. 66, op. 1, d. 4658, l. 4.
85 PAIPI TsK KP RT, f. 66, op. 1, d. 4658, l. 5.
86 PAIPI TsK KP RT, f. 66, op. 1, d. 4658, l. 5.
87 Ilič, "Introduction," 2.
88 Ilič, 2.
89 PAIPI TsK KP RT, f. 3, op. 105, d. 330, l. 14.
90 PAIPI TsK KP RT, f. 3, op. 93, d. 14, l. 90.
91 PAIPI TsK KP RT, f. 66, op. 1, d. 4658, l. 5.
92 Ilič, "Introduction," 2.

93 Chatterjee, "Soviet Heroines," 64.
94 PAIPI TsK KP RT, f. 66, op. 1, d. 4658, l. 41.
95 PAIPI TsK KP RT, f. 66, op. 1, d. 4658, l. 45.
96 PAIPI TsK KP RT, f. 3, op. 93, d. 14, l. 41; f. 3, op. 93, d. 27, ll. 7, 12; f. 66, op. 1, d. 4585, ll. 29, 60.
97 PAIPI TsK KP RT, f. 3, op. 4, d. 1055, l. 5.
98 PAIPI TsK KP RT, f. 66, op. 1, d. 4643, l. 23.
99 PAIPI TsK KP RT, f. 3, op. 4, d. 1055, l. 5.
100 PAIPI TsK KP RT, f. 3, op. 93, d. 27, l. 5.
101 PAIPI TsK KP RT, f. 3, op. 93, d. 27, l. 4.
102 PAIPI TsK KP RT, f. 3, op. 93, d. 5, l. 13.
103 PAIPI TsK KP RT, f. 3, op. 93, d. 5, l. 14.
104 PAIPI TsK KP RT, f. 3, op. 93, d. 5, l. 77.
105 PAIPI TsK KP RT, f. 66, op. 1, d. 4676, l. 37.
106 PAIPI TsK KP RT, f. 3, op. 30, d. 46, l. 118.
107 PAIPI TsK KP RT, f. 3, op. 4, d. 1055, l. 4.
108 PAIPI TsK KP RT, f. 3, op. 71, d. 167, l. 20.
109 PAIPI TsK KP RT, f. 3, op. 4, d. 1055, l. 4.
110 PAIPI TsK KP RT, f. 3, op. 30, d. 46, l. 117.
111 PAIPI TsK KP RT, f. 3, op. 93, d. 14, ll. 9–10.
112 PAIPI TsK KP RT, f. 3, op. 4, d. 1055, l. 5.
113 PAIPI TsK KP RT, f. 3, op. 4, d. 1055, l. 6.
114 PAIPI TsK KP RT, f. 3, op. 93, d. 14, l. 46.
115 PAIPI TsK KP RT, f. 3, op. 93, d. 14, l. 12.
116 PAIPI TsK KP RT, f. 66, op. 1, d. 4643, l. 21.
117 PAIPI TsK KP RT, f. 3, op. 71, d. 24, l. 11.
118 PAIPI TsK KP RT, f. 66, op. 1, d. 4643, l. 37. Another report suggested similar findings in the Kuybesheva region (present-day Khatlon province, southern Tajikistan): "In 1946, there were 789 girls in the first grade, 378 continued into the second grade, 231 in the third grade, and today [1950] there are only 78 female students in the fourth grade."
119 PAIPI TsK KP RT, f. 66, op. 1, d. 4643, ll. 32–3.
120 At the Stalinabad Nursing School, there were 185 female students in 1951, of whom only 5 were Tajik. Of these female students, 55 graduated, only two of whom were Tajik. In the same year, at the Stalinabad Pedagogical Institute, there were a total of 305 female students, of whom 171 were Tajik; of these, 99 graduated, only 8 of whom were Tajik. See PAIPI TsK KP RT, f. 8, op. 12, d. 341, l. 26.
121 PAIPI TsK KP RT, f. 3, op. 93, d. 8, ll. 23–4.
122 PAIPI TsK KP RT, f. 3, op. 93, d. 8, l. 26.
123 The state promoted two main types of farm: collective farms (*kolkhozy*) and state farms (*sovkhozy*). The main difference between

them was that the former were normally cooperatives, and the latter were under the command of the administrative system, organized on the factory principle. This meant that the state paid *sovkhoz* workers, or *sovkhozniki* wages. By contrast, *kolkhozniki* received their wages based on the output of their *kolkhoz*. See Buckley, *Mobilizing Soviet Peasants*, 20.
124 PAIPI TsK KP RT, f. 3, op. 93, d. 8, l. 29.
125 Chatterjee, "Soviet Heroines," 64.

3. The Triple Burden

1 Kandiyoti, "Sex Roles and Social Change"; Deniz Kandiyoti "Urban Change and Women's Roles"; and Kandiyoti, "Bargaining with Patriarchy."
2 Jones and Grupp, *Modernization*, 77.
3 Jones and Grupp.
4 Stone, "'Overcoming Peasant Backwardness,'" 298.
5 Patnaik, *Perestroika and Women Labour Force*, 43.
6 Interviews with rural women around Tajikistan, conducted by the author: Aziza Erkaeva (June 2013), Gulsun Tursunova (September 2012), Hamro Kiikova (August 2013), Khikoiat Toshmatova (September 2012), Muyitabar Pochoeva (September 2012), Tukhfa Ergasheva (September 2012), Tutikhon Aminova (August 2012), Ulfatniso Abdukakharova (August 2012), and Zukhrokhon Negmatova (June 2012).
7 Interview with Tukhfa Ergasheva, conducted by the author, September 2012.
8 *Itogi vsesoiuznoi perepisi naseleniia*, 79–83. For more on the use of child labour for cotton picking in Soviet Tajikistan, see Kalinovsky, *Laboratory*, 193–4.
9 Interviews with rural women in Kanibadam, Varzob, Isfara, and Sugd regions, conducted by the author, June 2010–August 2014.
10 Patnaik, *Perestroika and Women Labour Force*, 43.
11 *Itogi vsesoiuznoi perepisi naseleniia*, 79–83.
12 See Poliakov, *Everyday Islam*, 15.
13 Zaripova, interview, June 2012.
14 Zaripova, interview, June 2012.
15 Tokhtakhodjaeva, *Slogans of Communism*, 138.
16 See Dienes, *Soviet Asia*; Rumer, *Soviet Central Asia*; and Hodnett, "Technology and Social Change."
17 Dienes, *Soviet Asia*, 133, 12. Leslie Dienes characterizes Soviet Tajikistan as a "plantation province" due to its reliance on importing food and light industry products from the USSR while exporting cotton. Dienes

emphasizes the contrast between the significant amount of cotton exported and the low proportion of cotton textiles manufactured in Tajikistan, which amounted to only 6.5 per cent of total Soviet production.

18 Hodnett, "Technology and Social Change," 95–6. Hodnett's analysis is similar to Dienes's and emphasizes that industrial development in Tajikistan was closely tied to cotton production, specifically ginning, textile manufacturing, and related industries.

19 Rumer, Soviet Central Asia, 184, 40. The author insists the Soviet regime's interests in Tajikistan centred on the production of cotton.

20 Interviews conducted by Zamira Abman.

21 Tokhtakhodjaeva, Slogans of Communism, 104; also see Kalinovsky, Laboratory, 123.

22 Kalinovsky, 123.

23 Tokhtakhodjaeva, Slogans of Communism, 104.

24 Tett, "Ambiguous Alliances," 56.

25 Kalinovsky, Laboratory, 124–5.

26 Kalinovsky, 121.

27 Sacks, "Work Force Composition," 190–204; also see Sacks, Work and Equality.

28 Seniavskii, Rost rabochego klassa SSSR, 223, cited in Filtzer, "Women Workers," 32.

29 Heyat, Azeri Women in Transition, 144; also see Lubin, Labor and Nationality.

30 Haggag Youseff, Women and Work, 37.

31 Sacks, "Work Force Composition," 189–90.

32 Roy, New Central Asia, cited in Kandiyoti, "Politics of Gender," 608.

33 For more on this subject, see Keller, "Puzzle of Manual Harvest."

34 Kalinovsky, Laboratory, 177.

35 Kalinovsky, 177.

36 Ergasheva, "Rural Central Asia," 5, cited in Corcoran-Nantes, Lost Voices, 88.

37 Goskomstat SSSR, Narodnoe khoziaistvo SSSR za 10 let (1987); Goskomstat SSSR, Narodnoe khoziaistvo SSSR za 10 let (1988); and Goskomstat SSSR, Naselenie SSSR, cited in Ata-Mirzayev and Kayumov, "Demography of Soviet Central Asia," 221.

38 Interviews with rural women in Kanibadam, Varzob, Isfara, and Sugd regions, conducted by the author, June 2010–August 2014.

39 Faizulloev, "Mahalla," 76.

40 Kandiyoti, "Politics of Gender," 608.

41 Filtzer, "Women Workers," 31; also see Filtzer, Soviet Workers and De-Stalinization.

42 Sacks, "Work Force Composition," 204.

43 Kazakh SSR and Goskomstat SSSR, *Narodnoe khoziaistvo Kazakhstana*; and Goskomstat SSSR, *Selskoe khoziaistvo SSSR* (1988), 60–1; both cited in Craumer, "Agricultural Change," 149.

44 Goskomstat SSSR, *Naselenie SSR 1987*, cited in Craumer, 153.

45 Bridger, *Women in the Soviet Countryside*, 89–90.

46 *Zhenshchiny v SSSR*, 92–5.

47 Anderson, "Life Course."

48 Ata-Mirzayev and Kayumov, "Demography of Soviet Central Asia," 213.

49 Ziuzin, "Prichiny nizkoi mobilnosti," cited in Ata-Mirzayev and Kayumov, "Demography of Soviet Central Asia," 244.

50 Patnaik, *Perestroika and Women Labour Force*, 43–5.

51 *Itogi vsesoiuznoi perepisi naseleniia*, 2:24, table 3.

52 *Chislennost i sostav naseleniia SSSR*.

53 Interview with Muyitabar Pochoeva, conducted by the author, September 2012.

54 Wheeler, *Modern History*, 206.

55 Bridger, *Women in the Soviet Countryside*, 156–7.

56 PAIPI TsK KP RT, f. 3, op. 338, d. 79, l. 93.

57 Interview with Hamro Kiikova, conducted by the author, August 2012.

58 Bridger, *Women in the Soviet Countryside*, 68–9.

59 PAIPI TsK KP RT, f. 3, op. 246, d. 10, l. 24.

60 Rakowska-Harmstone, *Russia and Nationalism*, 249.

61 Tokhtakhodjaeva, *Slogans of Communism*, 78; Guboglo, *Sovremennyee ethnoiazykovyye protsessy*, 114; and Kaiser, "Social Mobilization," 261.

62 Guboglo, 114; also see Kaiser, 265.

63 Guboglo, 114; also see Kaiser, 265.

64 Kalinovsky, *Laboratory*, 231.

65 *Vestnik statistiki*, no. 5 (1991): 74, cited in Nourzhanov and Bleur, *Tajikistan*, 174; also see Kalinovsky, 231.

66 Tokhtakhodjaeva, *Slogans of Communism*, 78; and Guboglo, *Sovremennyee ethnoiazykovyye protsessy*, 114; also see Kaiser, "Social Mobilization," 261.

67 Interview with Tutikhon Aminova, conducted by the author, August 2012.

68 Aminova, interview, August 2012.

69 Interview with Hamro Kiikova, conducted by the author, August 2013.

70 Joseph, "Brother/Sister Relationships."

71 Interview with Aziza Erkaeva, conducted by the author, June 2013.

72 On 4 December 1935, the Kremlin hosted a gathering in honour of forty-three Tajik and thirty-three Turkmen "progressive" *kolkhozniki* who had distinguished themselves during the last cotton harvest. The most important members of the Politburo were all present, including Stalin,

Molotov, Kaganovich, and Voroshilov. The Soviet leadership listened
to speeches from the participants about their accomplishments. Stalin
made traditional promises of aid. A ten-year-old pioneer girl, Mamlakat
Nakhangova, gave Stalin a copy of the Tajik translation of his own book,
Questions of Leninism. According to *Pravda*'s correspondent, "Stalin is
touched.... With rapid steps he approaches the pioneer girl, Mamlakat,
and gives the happy girl a gold watch and then, in a fatherly fashion, he
embraces and kisses her." See "Velikaia druzhba," *Pravda*,
5 December 1935, 1, cited in Martin, *Affirmative Action*, 437.

73 Konchalovsky and Lipkov, *Inner Circle*, 74.
74 "Meet Mamlakat," 28. For more on Mamlakat, see Kassymbekova, *Despite Cultures*, 182–3.
75 PAIPI TsK KP RT, f. 3, op. 338, d. 78, l. 51.
76 Sacks, "Work Force Composition," 190; also see *Tsentralnoe statisticheskoe upravlenie SSSR*.
77 Tett, "'Guardians of the Faith?,'" 137; also see Tett, "Ambiguous Alliances," 101.
78 Tett, "'Guardians of the Faith?,'" 137–8; also see Tett, "Ambiguous Alliances," 101.
79 Pochoeva, interview, September 2012.
80 See Mernissi, *Women's Rebellion*; El-Feki, *Sex and the Citadel*; and Eltahawy, *Headscarves and Hymens*.
81 Pochoeva, interview, September 2012.
82 Tolmacheva, "Muslim Woman in Soviet Central Asia," 542.
83 Tett, "Ambiguous Alliances," 95; also see Tett, "'Guardians of the Faith?,'" 137–9.
84 Tett, "Ambiguous Alliances," 43.
85 Tolmacheva, "Muslim Woman in Soviet Central Asia," 538.
86 PAIPI TsK KP RT, f. 3, op. 246, d. 14, l. 8.
87 PAIPI TsK KP RT, f. 3, op. 338, d. 3, ll. 132–3.
88 Zaripova, interview, June 2012.
89 Erkaeva, interview, June 2013.
90 Tokhtakhodjaeva, *Slogans of Communism*, 138.
91 PAIPI TsK KP RT, f. 3, op. 105, d. 330, l. 71.
92 Tolmacheva, "Muslim Woman in Soviet Central Asia," 542.
93 PAIPI TsK KP RT, f. 3, op. 359, d. 161, ll. 57–8.
94 Tolmacheva, "Muslim Woman and Atheism," 194.
95 Pochoeva, interview, September 2012.
96 Interviews with rural women in Kanibadam and Isfara regions, conducted by the author, June 2010–August 2014.

97 Tolmacheva, "Muslim Woman in Soviet Central Asia," 544.

98 Tolmacheva, 537.

99 Goskomstat SSSR, *Naselenie SSSR*, 174–89, cited in Ata-Mirzayev and Kayumov, "Demography of Soviet Central Asia," 216.

100 Interviews with rural woman conducted by the author, June 2010–August 2014.

101 Poliakov, *Everyday Islam*, 55.

102 "Society," in Curtis, *Tajikistan*.

103 Goskomstat SSSR, *Narodnoe khoziaistvo SSSR za 70 let*, cited in Ata-Mirzayev and Kayumov, "Demography of Soviet Central Asia," 213.

104 "Tajikistan – Society," *The Library of Congress*, 2009.

105 Anderson, "Life Course."

106 Hoffman, *Stalinist Values*, 88.

107 PAIPI TsK KP RT, f. 3, op. 246, d. 3, l. 5.

108 PAIPI TsK KP RT, f. 3, op. 246, d. 1, l. 34.

109 Jones and Grupp, *Modernization*, 245–9.

110 Interview with Zukhrokhon Negmatova, conducted by the author, June 2013.

111 PAIPI TsK KP RT, f. 3, op. 246, d. 5, l. 42.

112 PAIPI TsK KP RT, f. 3, op. 246, d. 3, l. 49.

113 Islamov, *Semia i byt*, 66, 135, cited in Tett, "Ambiguous Alliances," 65. Also see interview with Karamat H. from Kokand in Tokhtakhodjaeva, *Slogans of Communism*, 114.

114 Interview with Kurbonbibi Ibragimova, conducted by the author, June 2013.

115 Dienes, *Soviet Asia*, 151.

116 "Kogda rabota ne zhdet," 2.

117 PAIPI TsK KP RT, f. 3, op. 246, d. 10, l. 5.

118 "Zhenshchiny i deti v SSSR," 60; cited in Kaiser, "Social Mobilization," 271.

119 *Tsentralnoe statischeskoe upravlenie SSSR*, 157–72.

120 PAIPI TsK KP RT, f. 3, op. 116, d. 381, l. 62; f. 3, op. 246, d. 5, l. 39.

121 PAIPI TsK KP RT, f. 3, op. 116, d. 381, l. 62; f. 3, op. 246, d. 5, l. 39.

122 Bridger, *Women in the Soviet Countryside*, 155–9.

123 Zaripova, interview, June 2012.

124 "Advocates of Old Traditions," cited in Ilič, "Women in the Khrushchev Era: An Overview," 14.

125 "Advocates of Old Traditions," cited in Ilič, 68–9.

126 Corcoran-Nantes, *Lost Voices*, 88.

127 Pomfret, "State-Directed Diffusion of Technology"; and Abashin "'Idealnyi kolkhoz,'" cited in Keller, "Puzzle of Manual Harvest," 302.

128 Keller, 302.

129 PAIPI TsK KP RT, f. 3, op. 359, d. 161, l. 70.

130 PAIPI TsK KP RT, f. 3, op. 338, d. 44, l. 94.
131 PAIPI TsK KP RT, f. 3, op. 359, d. 161, ll. 72–3.
132 PAIPI TsK KP RT, f. 3, op. 338, d. 44, l. 31.

4. The Beneficiaries

1 Interviews with Nizoramo Zaripova (June 2012), Guldzhakhon Bobosadykova (July 2012), and Bikhodzhal Rakhimova (October 2012), conducted by the author; also see Tokhtakhodjaeva, *Slogans of Communism*, 91.
2 Tekeli, *Women in Modern Turkish Society*, 185, cited in Fleischmann, "Other Awakening," 120.
3 See Martin, *Affirmative Action Empire*, 19–20.
4 Lapidus makes this argument in *Women in Soviet Society*.
5 Fleischmann, "Other Awakening," 119–20.
6 Corcoran-Nantes, *Lost Voices*, 59; also see interviews with Nizoramo Zaripova (June 2012), Bikhodzhal Rakhimova (October 2012), Bakhti Shaidova (September 2012), Zaragul Mirasanova (August 2012), and others, all conducted by the author.
7 Heyat, *Azeri Women in Transition*, 4. See interviews with Nizoramo Zaripova (June 2012), Bikhodzhal Rakhimova (October 2012), and Bakhti Shaidova (September 2012), all conducted by the author.
8 Tokhtakhodjaeva and Turgumbekova, *Daughters of Amazons*, 27. See interviews with Nizoramo Zaripova (June 2012), Bikhodzhal Rakhimova (October 2012), and Bakhti Shaidova (September 2012), all conducted by the author.
9 See Jancar, *Women under Communism*; Lapidus, *Women in Soviet Society*; Ilič, "What Did Women Want?"; and Browning, *Women and Politics*.
10 Lapidus, *Women in Soviet Society*. Gail Lapidus's analysis of gender in the Soviet Union is well regarded in scholarship on the subject. Her argument that Soviet women were unable to develop an independent space or political consciousness within patriarchal political and social structures is supported by recent findings. These findings suggest that despite Soviet policies promoting gender equality, women were often excluded from decision-making processes and were unable to form independent organizations to advocate for their interests. As a result, women were often limited to roles assigned to them by men and were unable to develop their own autonomous identity.
11 Lapidus, *Women in Soviet Society*; Heitlinger, *Women and State Socialism*; and Einhorn, *Cinderella Goes to Market*.
12 Dodge, *Women in the Soviet Economy*; Dunn and Dunn, *Study of the Soviet Family*; and Lapidus, *Women in Soviet Society*.

13 Heyat, *Azeri Women in Transition*, 5.
14 Heyat, 5; also see Lubin, *Labor and Nationality*.
15 Heyat, *Azeri Women in Transition*, 135–7, 139–41.
16 Heyat, 135–7, 139–41.
17 Keller, "Trapped Between State and Society," 20.
18 Rakowska-Harmstone, *Russia and Nationalism*, 133.
19 Fuqua, *Politics of the Domestic Sphere*, 18.
20 Stalin, *Marksizm i natsionalno-kolonialnyi vopros*, 62; *Tainy natsionalnoi politiki TsK RKP*, 102; and *Dvenadtsatyi sezd RKP/b/*, 481–2; all cited in Martin, *Affirmative Action Empire*, 12.
21 Martin, *Affirmative Action Empire*, 12, 19–20.
22 Tokhtakhodjaeva, *Slogans of Communism*, 91.
23 Tokhtakhodjaeva, 91.
24 Corcoran-Nantes, *Lost Voices*, 166–8.
25 Rakowska-Harmstone, *Russia and Nationalism*, 96.
26 PAIPI TsK KP RT, f. 3, op. 276, d. 1, l. 13.
27 Tokhtakhodjaeva, *Slogans of Communism*, 92.
28 PAIPI TsK KP RT, f. 3, op. 202, d. 1, ll. 23–4.
29 It is common in Tajikistan for children to take either their father's or their grandfather's first name as their last name. In Soviet Tajikistan, a person's last name usually consisted of the suffix *-ov* or *-ova* (for males and females, respectively), followed by their father's or grandfather's first name. For example, if a man's father was named Muhammad, his last name would be *Muhammadov*, and if a woman's grandfather was named Ali, her last name would be *Alieva*.
30 Zaripova, interview, June 2012.
31 Tokhtakhodjaeva, *Slogans of Communism*, 138.
32 Edgar, *Tribal Nation*, 231.
33 The All-Union Pioneer Organization, named after Vladimir Lenin, was a Soviet youth organization that catered to children aged ten to fifteen. Established in 1922, the organization operated until 1991. Upon reaching the age of fifteen, members of the Pioneer Organization could join the Komsomol, which was the youth wing of the Communist Party.
34 Interview with Guldzhakhon Bobosadykova, conducted by the author, July 2012.
35 The term "speaking Bolshevik" was coined by Stephen Kotkin in *Magnetic Mountain*.
36 Neary, "Mothering Socialist Society." Neary's work on the Movement of Wives in Industry and Wives of Red Army Commanders in Soviet Russia demonstrates how women activists came to believe in their mission and became loyal representatives of the regime. Similarly, Buckley's *Mobilizing Soviet Peasants* showcases the transformation of young peasant women who

proved themselves in competitions to raise productivity in agriculture and viewed themselves as equals to men. Hellbeck's *Revolution on My Mind* further traces these adaptations in ordinary Soviet citizens, including women, through an analysis of their diaries. Krylova's study on Soviet women in combat during the Second World War also highlights this phenomenon.

37 Rakowska-Harmstone, *Russia and Nationalism*, 242; also see Martin, *Affirmative Action Empire*, 26–7.

38 Martin, 26–7.

39 For more on Russian as the primary professional language, see Kalinovsky, *Laboratory*, 231.

40 Ismailova, interview, October 2012.

41 GARF, f. 9606, op. 1, d. 3568, cited in Kalinovsky, *Laboratory*, 56.

42 GARF, f. 9606, op. 1, d. 8234, cited in Kalinovsky, 56.

43 Bogumanova, "Pomoshch bratskikh respublik Tadzhikistanu," 16, cited in Kalinovsky, 56.

44 Kalinovsky, 56.

45 Rakowska-Harmstone, *Russia and Nationalism*, 284.

46 Ismailova, interview, October 2012.

47 Interview with Bikhodzhal Rakhimova, conducted by the author, October 2012.

48 Rakowska-Harmstone, *Russia and Nationalism*, 288–9.

49 Tokhtakhodjaeva, *Slogans of Communism*, 78.

50 Rakowska-Harmstone, *Russia and Nationalism*, 284.

51 Tett, "'Guardians of the Faith?,'" 138; also see Tett, "Ambiguous Alliances," 79, 85–6.

52 Tett, "'Guardians of the Faith?,'" 138.

53 Interview with Bakhti Shaidova, conducted by the author, September 2012. The term *Russified* was also used to describe other ethnic groups who came to accept the Soviet lifestyle and spoke fluent Russian, including Tatars, Kyrgyz, Kazakhs, Armenians, and other nationalities. Also see Rakowska-Harmstone, *Russia and Nationalism*, 283–5. For more on the tension felt by Russified women in Tajikistan, see Kalinovsky, *Laboratory*, 229.

54 Shaidova, interview, September 2012.

55 Asozoda, *Dostoni zindagi*, 324–5, cited in Kalinovsky and Scarborough, "Oil Lamp and the Electric Light," 131.

56 Asozoda, 324–5, cited in Kalinovsky and Scarborough, 131.

57 Corcoran-Nantes, *Lost Voices*, 59.

58 PAIPI TsK KP RT, f. 3, op. 71, d. 213.

59 PAIPI TsK KP RT, f. 3, op. 71, d. 213.

60 Corcoran-Nantes, *Lost Voices*, 79.

61 Rakowska-Harmstone, *Russia and Nationalism*, 99.

62 Corcoran-Nantes, *Lost Voices*, 168.

63 Zaripova, interview, June 2012; also see Rakowska-Harmstone, *Russia and Nationalism*, 288–9.
64 Rakowska-Harmstone, *Russia and Nationalism*, 111.
65 Rakowska-Harmstone, 133.
66 Rakowska-Harmstone, 140.
67 Ismailova, interview, October 2012.
68 Heyat, *Azeri Women in Transition*, 141.
69 Zaripova, interview, June 2012.
70 Browning, *Women and Politics*.
71 Heyat, *Azeri Women in Transition*, 116.
72 Heyat, 140.
73 Rakhimova, interview, October 2012.
74 Rakhimova, interview, October 2012.
75 Patnaik, *Perestroika and Women Labour Force*, 111.
76 Interview with Zaragul Mirasanova, conducted by the author, August 2012.
77 PAIPI TsK KP RT, f. 3, op. 73, d. 324, l. 1.
78 PAIPI TsK KP RT, f. 3, op. 73, d. 324, l. 1.
79 Cohn, "Sex and the Married Communist," 431.
80 Mirzo Tursunzoda was a prominent Soviet Tajik poet and an academic (1911–77).
81 Interview with Guldzhakhon Bobosadykova, conducted by the author, August 2012.
82 Zaripova, interview, June 2012.
83 PAIPI TsK KP RT, f. 3, op. 269, d. 18, ll. 34–5.
84 Tokhtakhodjaeva, *Slogans of Communism*, 138.
85 Tokhtakhodjaeva, 60–1.
86 Heyat, *Azeri Women in Transition*, 141.
87 Corcoran-Nantes, *Lost Voices*, 165.
88 PAIPI TsK KP RT, f. 3, op. 202, d. 1, l. 32.
89 Rakhimova, interview, October 2012.

5. The Thaw Era

1 Reid "Women in the Home," 154.
2 PAIPI TsK KP RT, f. 3, op. 338, d. 79, l. 18.
3 Buckley, *Women and Ideology*, 155–6; and Racioppi and O'Sullivan See, "Organizing Women," cited in Corcoran-Nantes, *Lost Voices*, 14.
4 Corcoran-Nantes, *Lost Voices*, 14.
5 In 1979 census shows that Tajiks constituted 39.1 per cent, Russians 32.4 per cent, Uzbeks 10 per cent, Tatars 4.1 per cent, and Ukrainians 3.5 per cent of Dushanbe's population, which totalled around 602,000. See

Goskomstat SSSR, *Naselenie SSR*, cited in Rowland, "Demographic Trends," 236.

6 Over 80 per cent of the *zhensoviety* reports I have uncovered at the Communist Party Archive of the Tajik Republic are in Russian.

7 Ismailova, interview, October 2012.

8 Based on oral history interviews with *zhensoviety* members in Tajikistan (June 2012–August 2013). Also, as noted above, over 80 per cent of the *zhensoviety* reports I have uncovered at the Communist Party Archive of the Tajik Republic are in Russian.

9 Guboglo, *Sovremennyee ethnoiazykovye protsessy*, 114; also see Kaiser, "Social Mobilization," 265.

10 Browning, *Women and Politics*, 11.

11 Based on interviews with rural women conducted by the author (June 2010–July 2014).

12 I discussed the structure of the *zhensoviety* most extensively with women who administered this organization in Tajikistan: Bikhodzhal Rakhimova (October 2012), Nizoramo Zaripova (June 2012), and Guldzhakhon Bobosadykova (August 2012). For more on the structure of the *zhensoviety* in the USSR, see Browning, *Women and Politics*.

13 Jancar, *Women under Communism*.

14 Ilič, "What Did Women Want?," 118.

15 Ilič, 118.

16 Buchli, *Archaeology of Socialism*, 138; also see Reid, "Women in the Home," 154.

17 Buchli, 138; also see Reid, 154.

18 Wilson, *Women and the Welfare State*, 9, cited in Reid, 156.

19 Browning, "Where Are the Women?," 208.

20 Browning, 233.

21 Ilič, "What Did Women Want?," 118.

22 See "Speeches at the Party Congress – Concluded," cited in Ilič, "Women in the Khrushchev Era: An Overview," 9.

23 Ilič, 22.

24 Ilič, 22.

25 Browning, "Zhensovety Revisited," 100; also see Corcoran-Nantes, *Lost Voices*, 163.

26 Browning, *Women and Politics*, 70.

27 Browning, 49.

28 Browning, 58.

29 Zaripova, interview, June 2012.

30 Browning, *Women and Politics*, 65–6.

31 PAIPI TsK KP RT, f. 3, op. 359, d. 161, l. 18.

32 PAIPI TsK KP RT, f. 3, op. 202, d. 1, l. 28.

33 Ryndina and Kopeiko, *Reshaet zhensoviet.*
34 PAIPI TsK KP RT, f. 3, op. 338, d. 69, l. 63; and Rakhimova, interview, October 2012.
35 Browning, *Women and Politics*, 58.
36 Zaripova, interview, June 2012; also see Ilič, "What Did Women Want?," 118.
37 Zaripova, interview, June 2012.
38 Browning, *Women and Politics*, 67.
39 The largest unit was the entire union, followed by the republic (in this case, the republic of Soviet Tajikistan), region (*oblast*), district (*raion*), and then village, town, or workplace. Thus, within the Communist Party, the village party "cell" acted as a subdivision of the *raikom*, which was a subdivision of the *obkom*, which in turn was a part of the republican party – itself a division of the union party.
40 Interviews with Nizoramo Zaripova, Guldzhakhon Bobosadykova, and Bikhodzhal Rakhimova, conducted by the author. Tajikistan was a part of the Soviet Union's administrative system, with Moscow as its centre. Within this system, Tajikistan was effectively one level of governance. Political decisions were made by the central regime in Moscow and communicated to the Tajik leadership through various ministries. The Tajik leadership would then implement these decisions through the *raion* or *oblast* committees. Despite this centralized system, the Tajik leadership had some flexibility to manoeuvre politically at all levels within the hierarchy. See Humphrey, *Karl Marx Collective*, 2.
41 Based on *zhensoviety* regional reports and interviews with members in urban and rural areas.
42 PAIPI TsK KP RT, f. 3, op. 338, d. 77, l. 25.
43 Browning, *Women and Politics*, 92.
44 Barbara Jancer, "Book review of Genia Browning's *Women and Politics in the USSR*," *Soviet Studies* 4, vol. 40 (October 1998): 667–8.
45 Browning, *Women and Politics*, 73.
46 Ilič, "What Did Women Want?," 111.
47 Browning, *Women and Politics*, 123.
48 During this period, Tajikistan was an autonomous republic within the Soviet Republic of Uzbekistan (1924–9). The majority of the Zhenotdel staff were based in the capital of Soviet Uzbekistan, Tashkent, as well as other major cities.
49 PAIPI TsK KP RT, f. 3, op. 359, d. 176, l. 3.
50 Browning, *Women and Politics*, 61.
51 Browning, 73.
52 PAIPI TsK KP RT, f. 3, op. 359, d. 161, ll. 78–80.
53 Browning, *Women and Politics*, 123.
54 For the 1920s–30s, see Edgar, *Tribal Nation*, 222.

55 Zaripova, interview, June 2012.
56 Browning, *Women and Politics*, 61; also see Browning, "Zhensovety Revisited"; and Racioppi and O'Sullivan See, "Organizing Women," cited in Corcoran-Nantes, *Lost Voices*, 14.
57 Interview with Bikhodzhal Rakhimova, conducted by the author, October 2012.
58 PAIPI TsK KP RT, f. 3, op. 338, d. 61, l. 92.
59 These included Mariam Bazarbaeva (minister of education, 1966–73), Habiba Gufranova (assistant minister of commerce, 1960–73), Ibodat Rakhimova (assistant chair of the Presidium of the Tajik Supreme Soviet, 1978–82), Nizoramo Zaripova (chair of the Presidium of the Tajik Supreme Soviet, 1982–4), Guldzhakhon Bobosadykova (first secretary of the Tajik VKLSM, 1961–84), and Mahfirat Karimova (chair of the Council of Ministers, 1961–74).
60 Corcoran-Nantes, *Lost Voices*, 59.
61 Tett, "'Guardians of the Faith?,'" 138.
62 Corcoran-Nantes, *Lost Voices*, 59.
63 Keddie, *Modern Iran*, 170.
64 The prevalence of patriarchal social and cultural norms in rural areas has resulted in a disproportionate number of women as compared to men. These norms promote obedience and modesty among Muslim girls and women, encourage early marriage practices, and create cultural expectations for women to have large families. These factors have contributed to a higher number of women living in rural areas.
65 Dooley, "Selling Socialism," 414.
66 PAIPI TsK KP RT, f. 3, op. 338, d. 77, l. 25.
67 PAIPI TsK KP RT, f. 3, op. 246, d. 15, l. 163.
68 PAIPI TsK KP RT, f. 3, op. 246, d. 15, ll. 160–8.
69 Bobosadykova, interview, August 2012.
70 Interview with Bakhti Shaidova, conducted by the author, October 2012.
71 Interviews with Bakhti Shaidova (September 2012) and Nizoramo Zaripova (June 2012), conducted by the author.
72 Zaripova, interview, June 2012.
73 Shaidova, interview, September 2012.
74 PAIPI TsK KP RT, f. 3, op. 246, d. 15, l. 172.
75 Shaidova, interview, September 2012.
76 PAIPI TsK KP RT, f. 3, op. 149, d. 320, l. 152.
77 Interviews with *zhensoviety* members and rural women, conducted by the author, June 2010–July 2014.
78 Browning, *Women and Politics*, 125.
79 Negmatova, interview, June 2013.
80 PAIPI TsK KP RT, f. 3, op. 246, d. 10, l. 22.
81 PAIPI TsK KP RT, f. 3, op. 246, d. 15, l. 143.

82 PAIPI TsK KP RT, f. 3, op. 338, d. 76, ll. 4–6.
83 Rakhimova "Spiritual Emancipation of Women," 6.
84 Rakhimova, 7.
85 Rakhimova, 6.
86 Rakhimova, 7.
87 Reid, "Women in the Home," 155–6.
88 PAIPI TsK KP RT, f. 3, op. 338, d. 45, ll. 87–8.
89 PAIPI TsK KP RT, f. 3, op. 359, d. 161, l. 78.
90 PAIPI TsK KP RT, f. 3, op. 338, d. 46, l. 7.
91 PAIPI TsK KP RT, f. 3, op. 246, d. 15, l. 161.
92 PAIPI TsK KP RT, f. 3, op. 338, d. 55, l. 83.
93 Dooley, "Selling Socialism," 411.
94 Bourdieu, *Distinction*, cited in Dooley, "Selling Socialism," 412.
95 "Summary of XXI (Extraordinary) Party Congress," 90; and Hanson, *Advertising and Socialism*, 7–8, 72; both cited in Reid "Women in the Home," 165.
96 PAIPI TsK KP RT, f. 3, op. 105, d. 330, l. 24.
97 Dunham, *In Stalin's Time*, 41.
98 Dunham, 42.
99 On *kulturnost* (lit. "culturedness"), see Kelly and Volkov, "Directed Desires"; also see Reid, "Women in the Home," 151.
100 Dooley, "Selling Socialism," 411.
101 Reid, "Women in the Home," 164.
102 Reid, "Cold War in the Kitchen," 244.
103 Zaripova, interview, June 2012.
104 Zaripova, interview, June 2012.
105 Zaripova, interview, June 2012.
106 Kiikova, interview, August 2013.
107 Cowan, *More Work for Mother*, 70–101; also see Reid, "Women in the Home," 170.
108 Interview with rural women in Tajikistan, conducted by the author, June 2010–July 2014.
109 Ergasheva, interview, September 2012.
110 PAIPI TsK KP RT, f. 3, op. 338, d. 47, l. 10.
111 Interview with rural women in Tajikistan, conducted by the author, June 2010–July 2014.
112 PAIPI TsK KP RT, f. 3, op. 246, d. 17, l. 26.
113 PAIPI TsK KP RT, f. 3, op. 338, d. 56, l. 217.
114 PAIPI TsK KP RT, f. 3, op. 338, d. 54, l. 13.
115 PAIPI TsK KP RT, f. 3, op. 319, d. 150, l. 26.
116 Browning, *Women and Politics*, 108.

117 Interview with Zukhrokhon Negmatova, conducted by the author, June 2012.
118 Negmatova, interview, June 2012.
119 PAIPI TsK KP RT, f. 3, op. 338, d. 59, ll. 5, 7; f. 3, op. 338, d. 45, l. 88.
120 PAIPI TsK KP RT, f. 3, op. 338, d. 47, l. 21.
121 PAIPI TsK KP RT, f. 3, op. 246, d. 1, l. 75.
122 PAIPI TsK KP RT, f. 3, op. 338, d. 63, l. 133.
123 PAIPI TsK KP RT, f. 3, op. 338, d. 59, l. 21.
124 PAIPI TsK KP RT, f. 3, op. 105, d. 330, ll. 22–3.
125 PAIPI TsK KP RT, f. 3, op. 269, d. 18, l. 30.
126 PAIPI TsK KP RT, f. 3, op. 338, d. 47, l. 25.
127 PAIPI TsK KP RT, f. 3, op. 338, d. 53, l. 54.
128 Interviews with Zukhrokhon Negmatova (June 2012), Bakhti Shaidova (September 2012), and Hamro Kiirova (August 2012), conducted by the author.
129 PAIPI TsK KP RT, f. 3, op. 246, d. 8, l. 57.
130 PAIPI TsK KP RT, f. 3, op. 338, d. 39, l. 29.
131 PAIPI TsK KP RT, f. 3, op. 338, d. 69, l. 103.
132 PAIPI TsK KP RT, f. 3, op. 338, d. 61, l. 92.
133 Guboglo, *Sovremennyee ethnoiazykovye protsessy*, 114.
134 PAIPI TsK KP RT, f. 3, op. 338, d. 62, l. 59.
135 PAIPI TsK KP RT, f. 3, op. 338, d. 40, l. 80.
136 Fleischmann, "Other Awakening," 120.

6. "I Am Muslim and Soviet"

1 Grossman, "Khrushchev's Anti-religious Policy," 383.
2 Grossman, 386.
3 Stone, "'Overcoming Peasant Backwardness,'" 301.
4 Stone, 298–9.
5 Stone, 301; also see Taubman, *Khrushchev*, 228–9.
6 Browning, *Women and Politics*, 55; also see Ilič, "What Did Women Want?," 118.
7 Zaripova, interview, June 2012.
8 Ilič, "What Did Women Want?," 118.
9 Abashin, *Sovietskii kishlak*.
10 For Uzbekistan, see Aminova, *October Revolution*. Soviet scholars S.A. Khalikova and R.M. Madzhidov attributed the persistence of Islam, particularly among women, to the rural female population's attachment to tradition, lack of education, and high unemployment. See Khalikova, *Zhenshchiny sovietskogo Tadzhikistana*.

11 D'Encausse, *Great Challenge*; Bennigsen, *Islam in the Soviet Union*; Bennigsen and Broxup, *Islamic Threat*; Bennigsen and Wimbush, *Mystics and Commissars*; and Bennigsen and Wimbush, *Muslim National Communism*.

12 Khalid, "Secular Islam"; Ro'i, "Secularism of Islam"; and Shahrani, "'Scientific Atheism.'" cited in Rasanayagam, *Islam in Post-Soviet Uzbekistan*, 79.

13 Akiner, "Islam, the State and Ethnicity." cited in Rasanayagam, *Islam in Post-Soviet Uzbekistan*.

14 Tett, "Ambiguous Alliances," 94.

15 Tett, 196.

16 Paert, "Demystifying the Heavens," 207.

17 Rasanayagam, *Islam in Post-Soviet Uzbekistan*, 91.

18 Ro'i, *Islam in the Soviet Union*, 20–1.

19 Louw, *Everyday Islam*, cited in Rasanayagam, *Islam in Post-Soviet Uzbekistan*, 166.

20 Grehan, *Twilight of the Saints*, 16.

21 Grehan, 179.

22 For more on *otin/otincha*, see Peshkova, "Otinchalar in the Ferghana Valley."

23 Fathi, *Femme d'autorité*, cited in Tasar, *Soviet and Muslim*, 21.

24 Rasanayagam, *Islam in Post-Soviet Uzbekistan*, 88. Also see Abashin, *Sovietskii kishlak*, 439–40. In Tajikistan, individuals who engage in traditional healing and spiritual practices are commonly referred to as *folben*, regardless of their gender. However, in some regions, women practitioners may be called *biotun*. The use of the term *shaman* is rare, while *bakhsi* is specific to certain regions of the country.

25 Tasar, *Soviet and Muslim*, 21.

26 Faizulloev, "Mahalla in Northern Tajikistan," 76.

27 Rasanayagam, *Islam in Post-Soviet Uzbekistan*, 85.

28 Rasanayagam, 163. Abashin's book *Sovietskii kishlak* is a study of the village of Oshoba in the northern region of Tajikistan that highlights the influence of Islam on the daily life of rural communities in the Sugd region.

29 Ro'i, *Islam in the Soviet Union*, 12.

30 Grossman, "Khrushchev's Anti-religious Policy," 378.

31 Znanie was established in 1947 to replace the League of the Militant Godless. During the Khrushchev era, it focused primarily on the anti-religious campaign. In September 1959, the society began publishing its monthly atheist journal, *Nauka i religiia*.

32 Grossman, "Khrushchev's Anti-religious Policy," 378.

33 Grossman, 375.

34 Grossman, 375.

35 Whitney, *Khrushchev Speaks*, 38–53.

36 Ilič, "Women in the Khrushchev Era: An Overview," 22.

37 See, e.g., PAIPI TsK KP RT, f. 3, op. 155, d. 3/81.

38 PAIPI TsK KP RT, f. 3, op. 155, d. 3/81.

39 PAIPI TsK KP RT, f. 3, op. 155, d. 30, ll. 122–3.

40 PAIPI TsK KP RT, f. 3, op. 155, d. 30, l. 129.

41 PAIPI TsK KP RT, f. 3, op. 155, d. 30, l. 130.

42 PAIPI TsK KP RT, f. 3, op. 93, d. 14, l. 48.

43 PAIPI TsK KP RT, f. 3, op. 178, d. 14, l. 40. A *chapanchi* is a horsehair veil that covers the entire face.

44 PAIPI TsK KP RT, f. 3, op. 130, d. 103, l. 102.

45 PAIPI TsK KP RT, f. 36, op. 6, d. 447, l. 28.

46 Kronov, "Tadzhikskie devushki," 71.

47 PAIPI TsK KP RT, f. 36, op. 6, d. 447, l. 28.

48 Stronski, *Tashkent*, 192.

49 PAIPI TsK KP RT, f. 3, op. 129, d. 385, l. 169.

50 PAIPI TsK KP RT, f. 3, op. 93, d. 14, l. 47.

51 Northrop, *Veiled Empire*.

52 PAIPI TsK KP RT, f. 3, op. 149, d. 320, l. 105.

53 PAIPI TsK KP RT, f. 3, op. 93, d. 14, l. 92.

54 PAIPI TsK KP RT, f. 3, op. 246, d. 1, ll. 41–3.

55 PAIPI TsK KP RT, f. 3, op. 246, d. 6, l. 7.

56 PAIPI TsK KP RT, f. 3, op. 130, d. 103, l. 11.

57 Paert, "Demystifying the Heavens," 217.

58 Stronski, *Tashkent*, 193.

59 PAIPI TsK KP RT, f. 3, op. 246, d. 1, l. 41.

60 PAIPI TsK KP RT, f. 3, op. 319, d. 150, l. 79.

61 PAIPI TsK KP RT, f. 3, op. 233, d. 54, l. 1.

62 PAIPI TsK KP RT, f. 3, op. 93, d. 14, l. 91.

63 PAIPI TsK KP RT, f. 3, op. 155, d. 30, l. 9.

64 PAIPI TsK KP RT, f. 3, op. 93, d. 14, l. 91.

65 PAIPI TsK KP RT, f. 3, op. 93, d. 14, l. 49.

66 PAIPI TsK KP RT, f. 3, op. 202, d. 1, l. 98.

67 PAIPI TsK KP RT, f. 3, op. 155, d. 30, ll. 122–3.

68 PAIPI TsK KP RT, f. 3, op. 276, d. 1, l. 29.

69 Shaidova, interview, September 2012.

70 PAIPI TsK KP RT, f. 3, op. 178, d. 29, l. 34.

71 Interviews with women from Tajikistan, conducted by the author, June 2010–July 2014.

72 Kronov, "Tadzhikskie devushki," 69–71.
73 PAIPI TsK KP RT, f. 3, op. 130, d. 103, l. 36.
74 Ismailova, interview, October 2012. Per Tajik cultural practices, it is customary for female immediate family members to wear black or dark-coloured clothes for a year as part of the mourning process.
75 Ismailova, interview, October 2012.
76 Paert, "Demystifying the Heavens," 216.
77 PAIPI TsK KP RT, f. 3, op. 246, d. 15, l. 38.
78 PAIPI TsK KP RT, f. 3, op. 269, d. 18, l. 30.
79 Pismannik, *Otnoshenie religii k zhenshchine*, 31–2, cited in Paert, "Demystifying the Heavens," 216. See also Igmen, *Speaking Soviet with an Accent*.
80 PAIPI TsK KP RT, f. 3, op. 246, d. 1, l. 41.
81 PAIPI TsK KP RT, f. 3, op. 269, d. 18, l. 28.
82 PAIPI TsK KP RT, f. 3, op. 338, d. 47, l. 25.
83 Anderson, "Out of the Kitchen," 209–11, cited in Paert, "Demystifying the Heavens," 206.
84 PAIPI TsK KP RT, f. 3, op. 129, d. 385, l. 90.
85 PAIPI TsK KP RT, f. 3, op. 129, d. 385, l. 91.
86 PAIPI TsK KP RT, f. 3, op. 129, d. 385, l. 169.
87 Bowen, *Muslims through Discourse*, 229–50, cited in Rasanayagam, *Islam in Post-Soviet Uzbekistan*, 89.
88 Rasanayagam, 89.
89 In Tajik, the proper pronunciation is *Sanavbar*.
90 During and Khudoberdiev, *La voix du chamane*, 22, cited in Tasar, *Soviet and Muslim*, 21.
91 Abashin, *Sovietskii kishlak*, 437, 453, 448–9.
92 PAIPI TsK KP RT, f. 3, op. 246, d. 1, l. 69.
93 Paert, "Demystifying the Heavens," 217–18.
94 Paert, 218.
95 Rakhimova, interview, October 2012.
96 Rakhimova, interview, October 2012.
97 Rasanayagam, *Islam in Post-Soviet Uzbekistan*, 44.
98 Stone, "'Overcoming Peasant Backwardness,'" 320.
99 Florin, "Many Ways of Being Soviet."
100 Rasanayagam, *Islam in Post-Soviet Uzbekistan*, 85.
101 This practice is well documented and is also based on the personal experience of the author, who grew up in the late 1980s in the Soviet Union.
102 Abashin, *Sovietskii kishlak*, 590.
103 Abashin, 568, 576–611.

104 Rasanayagam, *Islam in Post-Soviet Uzbekistan*, 90.
105 Rorlich, "Islam and Atheism."
106 PAIPI TsK KP RT, f. 3, op. 246, d. 8, ll. 55–6.
107 PAIPI TsK KP RT, f. 3, op. 246, d. 8, l. 56.
108 PAIPI TsK KP RT, f. 3, op. 246, d. 8, l. 56.
109 PAIPI TsK KP RT, f. 3, op. 246, d. 8, l. 56.
110 Stone, "'Overcoming Peasant Backwardness,'" 319.
111 PAIPI TsK KP RT, f. 3, op. 338, d. 11, l. 69.
112 PAIPI TsK KP RT, f. 3, op. 338, d. 62, l. 30.
113 PAIPI TsK KP RT, f. 3, op. 338, d. 79, l. 128.
114 Rakhimova, "Spiritual Emancipation of Women," 6.
115 Rakhimova, 6–7.
116 Khalid, *Islam after Communism*, 99.
117 McBrien, *From Belonging to Belief*, 176.

Epilogue

1 Sedghi, *Women and Politics in Iran*, 163.
2 These women's councils attempted to mobilize Soviet women under
   the guidance of the patriarchal regime and around notions of gender
   equality constructed by men. As a result, instead of alleviating women's
   responsibilities at work and at home, the *zhensoviety* only reinforced
   these roles. In fact, the activism of these women's committees became an
   additional burden for Soviet women, since they were expected to actively
   take part in *zhensoviety* activities while juggling their existing responsibilities
   of full-time work, household chores, and child-rearing, known as women's
   double burden. In rural areas, women faced a triple burden, since they were
   also responsible for work on their individual plots of land.
3 Interviews with rural women, conducted by the author, June 2010–August
   2014.
4 Ahmed, *Women and Gender in Islam*, 222. Also see interviews with rural
   women, conducted by the author: Aziza Erkaeva (June 2013), Gulsun
   Tursunova (September 2012), Hamro Kiikova (August 2013), Khikoiat
   Toshmatova (September 2012), Muyitabara Pochoeva (September 2012),
   Tukhfa Ergasheva (September 2012), Tutikhon Aminova (August 2012),
   Ulfatniso Abdukakharova (August 2012), Zukhrokhon Negmatova (June
   2012), and others.
5 Ahmed, *Women and Gender in Islam*, 222.
6 Interviews with rural women, conducted by the author, June 2010–August
   2014. Also see Ahmed, *Women and Gender in Islam*, 222.
7 Ghodsee, *Muslim Lives in Eastern Europe*.

8 Kandiyoti, "Politics of Gender," 616.
9 Kandiyoti, 609.
10 Abramson, "Engendering Citizenship," n. 57, cited in Kandiyoti, "Politics of Gender," 609.
11 Kandiyoti, 671.
12 See, e.g., Kasimov, "Nizoramo Zaripova."

Bibliography

Primary Sources

Archival Sources

STATE ARCHIVE OF THE RUSSIAN FEDERATION (GOSUDARSTVENNYI ARKHIV ROSSIISKOI FEDERATSII, GARF)

f. 9606, op. 1, d. 3568. Cited in Kalinovsky, *Laboratory*, 56.
f. 9606, op. 1, d. 8234. Cited in Kalinovsky, *Laboratory*, 56.

PARTY ARCHIVE OF THE INSTITUTE FOR POLITICAL RESEARCH OF THE REPUBLIC OF TAJIKISTAN COMMUNIST PARTY CENTRAL COMMITTEE (PARTIINYI ARKHIV INSTITUTA POLITICHESKIKH ISSLEDOVANII TSK KOMPARTII RESPUBLIKI TADZHIKISTANA, PAIPI TSK KP RT)

f. 1, op. 1, d. 4 (1924–5).
f. 1, op. 1, d. 5 (1924–5).
f. 1, op. 1, d. 30 (1925–6).
f. 1, op. 1, d. 39 (1924–5).
f. 1, op. 1, d. 464 (1927–9).
f. 1, op. 1, d. 724 (1927).
f. 1, op. 1, d. 832 (1928).
f. 1, op. 1, d. 1206 (1929).
f. 3, op. 4, d. 10 (1948).
f. 3, op. 4, d. 1055 (1946).
f. 3, op. 5, d. 139 (1929–30).
f. 3, op. 30, d. 46 (1940).
f. 3, op. 61, d. 295 (1934).
f. 3, op. 71, d. 167 (1948).
f. 3, op. 71, d. 213 (Bazarbaeva's case: letters addressed to Gafurov, secretary of TsIK of Tajikistan, 1948–50).
f. 3, op. 71, d. 24 (1948).
f. 3, op. 73, d. 324 (1951).

f. 3, op. 93, d. 5 (1948).

f. 3, op. 93, d. 8 (Teacher's meetings, 1948).

f. 3, op. 93, d. 9 (1948).

f. 3, op. 93, d. 14 (1950).

f. 3, op. 93, d. 27 (1948–51).

f. 3, op. 93, d. 34 (1955–6).

f. 3, op. 105, d. 330 (Materials from Women's Sixth Congress, 1955).

f. 3, op. 116, d. 381 (1958).

f. 3, op. 129, d. 385 (1960).

f. 3, op. 130, d. 103 (Reports from Women's Seventh Congress, 1960).

f. 3, op. 149, d. 320 (1958).

f. 3, op. 155, d. 3/81 (1961).

f. 3, op. 155, d. 30 (Reports from Supreme Court of Tajik SSR, 1962).

f. 3, op. 178, d. 14 (Reports from party organizations on accomplishments of Tajik SSR TsIK regarding inspections of Iava region, 1962).

f. 3, op. 178, d. 29 (Material on work among women for Women's Eighth Congress, 1963).

f. 3, op. 202, d. 1 (Reports from Women's Eighth Annual Congress, 1963).

f. 3, op. 233, d. 54 (Reports from Young Women's Congress, 1968).

f. 3, op. 246, d. 1 (Reports on women's progress towards accomplishing decrees of the KPSS Twenty-Second Congress in Tajik SSR, 1963).

f. 3, op. 246, d. 3 (Information in preparation for Women's Ninth Congress, 1967).

f. 3, op. 246, d. 5 (Republican *zhensoviet* inspection of work among women in Moscovskie *raion*, Tajik SSR, December 1967).

f. 3, op. 246, d. 6 (1967–9).

f. 3, op. 246, d. 8 (Protocols and reports from meeting of republican *zhensoviet*, 1968–72).

f. 3, op. 246, d. 10 (Republican *zhensoviet* inspection of work among women in Tajik SSR, 1969).

f. 3, op. 246, d. 14 (Protocols from meetings of republican *zhensoviet*, 1972).

f. 3, op. 246, d. 15 (Protocols and reports from republican *zhensoviet*, 1972–3).

f. 3, op. 246, d. 17 (Republican *zhensoviet* inspection of work among women, 1971).

f. 3, op. 269, d. 18 (Materials from Women's Annual Congress, 1971).

f. 3, op. 276, d. 1 (Materials from Women's Tenth Congress, 1973).

f. 3, op. 319, d. 150 (Reports from Women's Eleventh Congress, 1978).

f. 3, op. 338, d. 3 (1971).

f. 3, op. 338, d. 11 (Materials from Women's Ninth Congress, 1973: preparation work, Comrade I.P. Rakhimova's presentation text, reports of the committee, etc.).

f. 3, op. 338, d. 39 (1982).

f. 3, op. 338, d. 40 (1982).

f. 3, op. 338, d. 44 (1979–83).

f. 3, op. 338, d. 45 (1973).

f. 3, op. 338, d. 46 (1975–8).

f. 3, op. 338, d. 47 (1979–81).

f. 3, op. 338, d. 53 (1985).

f. 3, op. 338, d. 54 (1972–85).

f. 3, op. 338, d. 55 (1973–5).

f. 3, op. 338, d. 56 (1976–8).

f. 3, op. 338, d. 59 (1976–7).

f. 3, op. 338, d. 61 (Reports from Bobosadykova, head of republican *zhensoviet*, 1980).

f. 3, op. 338, d. 62 (Protocols and reports from meeting of republican *zhensoviet*, with material from Women's Tenth and Eleventh Congresses, 1982–5).

f. 3, op. 338, d. 63 (1978–9).

f. 3, op. 338, d. 69 (1985–6).

f. 3, op. 338, d. 76 (1986).

f. 3, op. 338, d. 77 (1986).

f. 3, op. 338, d. 78 (1986).

f. 3, op. 338, d. 79 (Materials from Women's Twelfth Congress, 1986).

f. 3, op. 359, d. 161 (Materials from Women's Twelfth Congress, 1986).

f. 3, op. 359, d. 176 (Nizoramo Zaripova's speech at Women's Twelfth Congress, 1986).

f. 8, op. 12, d. 341 (1951).

f. 36, op. 4, d. 10 (1948).

f. 36, op. 6, d. 447 (Reports and information from head of the regional governments and Komsomol about work with young women in the Tajik SSR, 1958).

f. 66, op. 1, d. 4585 (1948).

f. 66, op. 1, d. 4643 (1950).

f. 66, op. 1, d. 4658 (1950).

f. 66, op. 1, d. 4676 (1950)

f. 1966, op. 1, d. 46 (1929).

RUSSIAN STATE ARCHIVE OF SOCIAL AND POLITICAL HISTORY (ROSSIISKII GOSUDARSTVEN-NYI ARKHIV SOTSIALNO-POLITICHESKOI ISTORII, RGASPI)

f. 62, op. 2, d. 440, ll. 3, 93–4, 109–10; d. 1237, ll. 68–9. Cited in Edgar, *Tribal Nation*, 240.

f. 62, op. 2, d. 1234, l. 49. Cited in Edgar, *Tribal Nation*, 240.

f. 62, op. 2, d. 1691, l. 113. Cited in Kamp, *New Woman of Uzbekistan*, 212.

Oral Histories: 2009–14 Interviews

All interviews were conducted by the author. All interviewees are identified by first and last name, birth date, and city of birth.

Abdukakharova, Ulfatniso. Born 1953; grew up in Khujand. Interviewed 2012, Khujand. Tajik.

Aminova, Tutikhon. Grew up in Kanibadam region. Interviewed 2012, Kanibadam. Uzbek.

Azizova, Samiia. Born 1926; grew up in Khujand. Interviewed 2012, Khujand. Tajik.

Bobosadykova, Guldzhakhon. Born 1937; grew up in Isfara, Sugd region. Interviewed 2012, Dushanbe. Tajik.

Dadabaeva, Makhfirat. Born 1945; grew up in Khujand. Interviewed 2012, Khujand. Tajik.

Ergasheva, Tukhfa. Born 1948; grew up in Isfara. Interviewed 2012, Isfara. Tajik.

Erkaeva, Aziza. Born 1946; grew up in Arab *kishlak*, Kanibadam region. Interviewed 2013, Kanibadam. Uzbek.

Ibragimova, Kurbonbibi. Born 1947; grew up in Arab *kishlak*, Kanibadam region. Interviewed 2013, Kanibadam. Tajik.

Ismailova, Dzhamilia. Born 1952; grew up in Khujand. Interviewed 2012, Khujand. Tajik.

Khadzhimuratova, Rakhimakhon. Born 1947; grew up in Isfara. Interviewed 2012, Isfara. Tajik.

Kiikova, Hamro. Born 1939; grew up on *sovkhoz* Khamzaalieva (previously *kolkhoz* Kalinina), Sugd region. Interviewed 2012, Pralitarsk. Tajik.

Mirasanova, Zaragul. Born 1954; grew up in Pamir, Gorno-Badakhshan region. Interviewed 2012, Dushanbe. Tajik.

Negmatova, Zukhrokhon. Born 1953; grew up in Arab *kishlak*, Kanibadam region. Interviewed 2012–13, Kanibadam. Uzbek.

Pochoeva, Muyitabar. Born 1954; grew up in Bobojon Garufov district. Interviewed 2012, Khujand. Tajik.

Rakhimova, Bikhodzhal. Born 1941; grew up in Khujand. Interviewed 2012, Khujand. Tajik.

Shaidova, Bakhti. Born 1946; grew up in Pul'chukur village, Bobodzon Gafurova district. Interviewed 2012, Khujand. Tajik.

Toshmatova, Khikoiat. Born 1931; grew up in Sartukai, Sugd region. Interviewed 2012, Khujand. Tajik.

Tursunova, Gulsun. Born 1940; grew up in Iava, Sugd region. Interviewed 2012, Iava. Uzbek.

Usmonova, Masuda. Born 1949; grew up in Khujand. Interviewed 2012, Khujand. Tajik.

Zaripova, Nizoramo. Born 1925; grew up on *kolkhoz* Ishtimoet, Pakhtakor village, Kuliab region. Interviewed 2012, Dushanbe. Tajik.

Statistical Sources

Chislennost i sostav naseleniia SSSR po dannym vsesoiuznoi perepisi naseleniia 1979 goda [The Size and Composition of the Population of the USSR, Based on Data from the 1979 All-Union Census]. Moscow, 1984.

Goskomstat SSSR. *Natsionalnyi sostav naseleniia* [The National Composition of the Population]. Moscow, 1989.

– *Narodnoe khoziaistvo SSSR za 70 let* [The National Economy of the USSR over Seventy Years]. 1987. Cited in Ata-Mirzayev and Kayumov, "Demography of Soviet Central Asia," 213.

– *Narodnoe khoziaistvo SSSR za 10 let* [The National Economy of the USSR over Ten Years]. Moscow, 1987.

– *Narodnoe khoziaistvo SSSR za 10 let* [The National Economy of the USSR over Ten Years]. Moscow, 1988. Cited in Ata-Mirzayev and Kayumov, "Demography of Soviet Central Asia," 221.

– *Naselenie SSR* [The Population of the SSR]. Moscow: Finansy i Statistika, 1987. Cited in Rowland, "Demographic Trends," 236.

– *Naselenie SSR 1987* [The Population of the SSR, 1987]. Moscow, 1988.

– *Naselenie SSR 1987. Statisticheskii sbornik* [The Population of the SSR, 1987: Statistical Digest]. Moscow, 1988. Cited in Craumer, "Agricultural Change," 153.

– *Naselenie SSSR* [The Population of the USSR]. Moscow, 1988.

– *Selskoe khoziaistvo SSSR. Statisticheskii sbornik.* Moscow: Finansy i Statiska, 1988. Cited in Craumer, "Agricultural Change," 149.

– *Vsesoiuznoi perepisi naseleniia SSSR, 1987* [The All-Union Census of the USSR, 1987]. Moscow, 1988.

Itogi vsesoiuznoi perepisi naseleniia [Results of the All-Union Census]. Moscow, 1970.

Itogi vsesoiuznoi perepisi naseleniia 1959 goda [Results of the All-Union Census, 1959]. Moscow, 1962.

Itogi vsesoiuznoi perepisi naseleniia 1970 goda [Results of the All-Union Census, 1970]. Moscow, 1972–4.

Kazakh SSR, Tsentralnoe Statisticheskoe Upravlenie and Goskomstat SSSR. *Narodnoe khoziaistvo Kazakhstana. Statisticheskii ezhegodnik.* Alma-Ata, Kazakhstan, 1960–88. Cited in Craumer, "Agricultural Change," 149.

Narodnoe khoziaistvo SSSR (statisticheskii ezhegodnik) [The National Economy of the USSR (Statistical Yearbook)]. Moscow, various years.

Narodnoe obrazovaniia, nauka i kultura v SSSR [National Education, Science, and Culture in the USSR]. Moscow, 1977.

Selskoe khoziaistvo SSSR [Agriculture in the USSR]. Moscow, 1971.
Tsentralnoe statisticheskoe upravlenie SSSR [The Central Statistical
  Administration of the USSR]. 1984. Cited in Kaiser, "Social Mobilization,"
  273–4.
Vestnik statistiki (vsesoiuznoi perepisi naseleniia) [Statistical Bulletin (All-Union
  Census)]. Various issues, 1980–2.
Zhenshchina i deti v SSSR [Woman and Children in the USSR]. Moscow, 1963.
Zhenshchina v SSSR [Woman in the USSR]. Moscow, 1937, 1980.
"Zhenshchiny i deti v SSSR" [Women and Children in the USSR]. *Vestnik
  statistiki*, no. 1 (1988): 57–76. Cited in Kaiser, "Social Mobilization," 271.
Zhenshchiny v SSSR. Statisticheskii sbornik [Women in the USSR: Statistical
  Digest]. Moscow, 1975.

Periodicals and Newspapers

"Advocates of Old Traditions." *Current Digest of the Soviet Press*, no. 36 (1962):
  23–4 (complete text from *Pravda*, 4 September 1962). Cited in Ilič, "Women
  in the Khrushchev Era: An Overview," 14.
Izvestiia. Moscow.
"Kogda rabota ne zhdet" [When Work Cannot Wait]. *Pravda*, 1 June 1975.
Kommunistka. Moscow.
Koster. Saint Petersburg.
Krestianka. Moscow.
Kronov, A. "Tadzhikskie devushki i zamaskirovannyie feodali" [Tajik Girls
  and Masked Patriarchs]. *Molodoi kommunist*, no. 6 (1962): 67–74.
"Poznakomit' s Mamlakat" [Meet Mamlakat]. *Koster*, 1967, 27–9.
Pravda, 11 March 1936. Cited in Chatterjee, "Soviet Heroines," 63.
Pravda, 10 March 1938. Cited in Chatterjee, "Soviet Heroines," 63.
Rabotnitsa i krestianka, no. 14 (1936). Cited in Chatterjee, "Soviet
  Heroines," 63.
Rabotnitsa. Moscow.
Rakhimova, Ibodat. "Dukhovniaa emansipatsiia zhenshchin" [The Spiritual
  Emancipation of Women]. *Nauka i religiia*, no. 3 (1974): 6–7.
"The Speeches at the Party Congress – Concluded." *Current Digest of the Soviet
  Press*, no. 20 (1956): 23 (complete text from *Pravda*, 26 February 1956). Cited
  in Ilič, "Women in the Khrushchev Era: An Overview," 9.
Zanoni Tojikiston, 6–7. Dushanbe, Tajikistan.

Secondary Sources

Abashin, Sergei. "'Idealnyi kolkhoz v Sovietskoi Srednei Azii: Istoriia
  neudachi ili uspekha?" [The Ideal *kolkhoz* in Soviet Central Asia: A History

of Failure or of Success?]. *Acta Slavica Iaponica*, no. 29 (2011): 1–26. Cited in Keller, "Puzzle of Manual Harvest," 302.

– *Sovietskii kishlak: Mezhdu kolonializmom i modernizatsiei* [The Soviet *kishlak*: Between Colonialism and Modernization]. Moscow: NLO, 2015.

Abramson, David. "Engendering Citizenship in Postcommunist Uzbekistan." In *Post-Soviet Women Encountering Transition: Nation Building, Economic Survival, and Civic Activism*, edited by Kathleen Kuehnast and Carol Nechemias, 65–84. Baltimore, MD: Johns Hopkins University Press, 2004. Cited in Kandiyoti, "Politics of Gender," 609.

Abu-Lughod, Lila. "Do Muslim Women Really Need Saving? Anthropological Reflections on Cultural Relativism and Its Others." *American Anthropologist* 104, no. 3 (September 2002): 783–90. https://doi.org/10.1525/aa.2002.104 .3.783.

Ahmed, Leila. *Women and Gender in Islam: Historical Roots of a Modern Debate*. New Heaven, CT: Yale University Press, 1992.

Akiner, Shirin. "Between Tradition and Modernity: The Dilemma Facing Contemporary Central Asian Women." In *Post-Soviet Women: From the Baltic to Central Asia*, edited by Mary Buckley, 261–304. Cambridge: Cambridge University Press, 1997.

– "Islam, the State and Ethnicity in Central Asia in Historical Perspective." *Religion, State, and Society* 24, nos. 2/3 (1996): 91–132. https://doi.org/10 .1080/09637499608431733. Cited in Rasanayagam, *Islam in Post-Soviet Uzbekistan*.

Aminova, R.Kh. *The October Revolution and Women's Liberation in Uzbekistan*. Moscow: Nauka Publication House, Central Department of Oriental Literature, 1977.

Anderson, Barbara A. "The Life Course of Soviet Women Born 1905–1960." In *Politics, Work, and Daily Life in the USSR: A Survey of Former Soviet Citizens*, edited by James R. Millar, 203–40. Cambridge: Cambridge University Press, 1987.

Anderson, John. "Out of the Kitchen, Out of the Temple: Religion, Atheism and Women in the Soviet Union." In *Religious Policy in the Soviet Union*, edited by Sabrina Petra Ramet, 206–28. Cambridge: Cambridge University Press, 1993. Cited in Paert, "Demystifying the Heavens," 206.

Asozoda, Khudoinazar. *Dostoni zindagi* [Story of Life]. Dushanbe: Devashtich, 2006. Cited in Kalinovsky and Scarborough, "Oil Lamp and the Electric Light," 131.

Ata-Mirzayev, Ozod Baba-Mirzayevich, and Abdukhakim Abdukhamidovich Kayumov. "The Demography of Soviet Central Asia and Its Future Development." In Lewis, *Geographic Perspectives*, 211–21.

Attwood, Lynne. *Creating the New Soviet Woman: Women's Magazines as Engineers of Female Identity, 1922–53*. New York: St. Martin's Press, 1999.

Bacon, Elizabeth E. *Central Asians under Russian Rule: A Study in Culture Change*. Ithaca, NY: Cornell University Press, 1966.

Bennigsen, Alexandre. *Islam in the Soviet Union*. New York: Praeger, 1967.

Bennigsen, Alexandre, and Marie Broxup. *The Islamic Threat to the Soviet State*. London: Croom Helm, 1983.

Bennigsen, Alexandre, and S. Enders Wimbush. *Muslim National Communism in the Soviet Union: A Revolutionary Strategy for the Colonial World*. Chicago: University of Chicago Press, 1979.

– *Mystics and Commissars: Sufism in the Soviet Union*. Berkeley: University of California Press, 1986.

Bergne, Paul. *The Birth of Tajikistan: National Identity and the Origins of the Republic*. London: I.B. Tauris, 2007.

Bogumanova, Z.Z. "Pomoshch bratskikh respublik Tadzhikistanu v podgotovke kadrov vyshchei kvalaifikatsii (1959–1970 gg.)" [Assistance Offered to Tajikistan by Brother Republics in Preparing Cadres for Higher Qualifications (1959–70)]. *Izvestiia Akademii Nauk Tadzhikskoi SSR*, no. 1 (1974): 14. Cited in Kalinovsky, Laboratory, 56.

Bourdieu, Pierre. *Distinction: A Social Critique of the Judgment of Taste*. Translated by Richard Nice. Cambridge, MA: Harvard University Press, 1994. Cited in Dooley, "Selling Socialism," 412.

Bowen, R. John. *Muslims through Discourse: Religion and Ritual in Gayo Society*. Princeton, NJ: Princeton University Press, 1993. Cited in Rasanayagam, Islam in Post-Soviet Uzbekistan, 89.

Bridger, Susan. *Women in the Soviet Countryside: Women's Roles in Rural Development in the Soviet Union*. New York: Cambridge University Press, 1987.

Browning, Genia. "Soviet Politics – Where Are the Women?" In Holland, *Soviet Sisterhood*, 207–36.

– *Women and Politics in the USSR: Consciousness Raising and Soviet Women's Groups*. New York: St. Martin's Press, 1987. Cited in Corcoran-Nantes, *Lost Voices*, 176.

– "The Zhensovety Revisited." In *Perestroika and Soviet Women*, edited by Mary Buckley, 97–117. Cambridge: Cambridge University Press, 1992.

Buchli, Victor. *An Archaeology of Socialism*. Oxford: Berg, 1999.

Buckley, Mary. *Mobilizing Soviet Peasants: Heroines and Heroes of Stalin's Fields*. Lanham, MD: Rowman & Littlefield, 2006.

– "The Untold Story of the *Obshchestvennitsa* in the 1930s." In Ilič, *Women in the Stalin Era*, 151–72.

– *Women and Ideology in the Soviet Union*. New York: Harvester Wheatsheaf, 1989. Cited in Corcoran-Nantes, *Lost Voices*, 14, 50.

Chamberlin, William Henry. *Soviet Russia: A Living Record and a History*. Boston, MA: Little, Brown, 1933. Cited in Stites, Women's Liberation Movement, 340.

Charrad, Mounira. *States and Women's Rights: The Making of Postcolonial Tunisia, Algeria, and Morocco*. Berkeley: University of California Press, 2001.

– "Tunisia at the Forefront of the Arab World: Two Waves of Gender Legislation." In *Women in the Middle East and North Africa: Agents of Change*, edited by Fatima Sadiqi and Moha Ennaji, 105–13. New York: Routledge, 2011.

Chatterjee, Choi. *Celebrating Women: Gender, Festival Culture, and Bolshevik Ideology, 1910–1939*. Pittsburgh, PA: University of Pittsburgh Press, 2002.

– "Soviet Heroines and the Language of Modernity, 1930–39." In Ilič, *Women in the Stalin Era*, 49–68.

Chatterjee, Partha. *The Nation and Its Fragments: Colonial and Postcolonial Histories*. Princeton, NJ: Princeton University Press, 1993.

Clements, Barbara Evans. "The Utopianism of the Zhenotdel." *Slavic Review* 51, no. 3 (Autumn 1992): 485–96. https://doi.org/10.2307/2500056.

Cohn, Edward D. "Sex and the Married Communist: Family Troubles, Marital Infidelity, and Party Discipline in the Postwar USSR, 1945–64." *Russian Review* 68, no. 3 (July 2009): 429–50. https://doi.org/10.1111/j.1467-9434 .2009.00532.x.

Corcoran-Nantes, Yvonne. *Lost Voices: Central Asian Women Confronting Transition*. London: Zed Books, 2005.

Cowan, Ruth Schwarts. *More Work for Mother: The Ironies of Household Technology from the Open Hearth to the Microwave*. London: Basic Books, 1985.

Craumer, Peter R. "Agricultural Change, Labor Supply, and Rural Out-Migration in Soviet Central Asia." In Lewis, *Geographic Perspectives*, 132–74.

Cronin, Stephanie, ed. *Anti-veiling Campaigns in the Muslim World: Gender, Modernism and the Politics of Dress*. New York: Routledge, 2014.

– "Introduction: Coercion or Empowerment? Anti-veiling Campaigns: A Comparative Perspective." In Cronin, *Anti-veiling Campaigns*, 1–36.

Curtis, Glenn E., ed. *Tajikistan: A Country Study*. Washington, DC: GPO for the Library of Congress, 1996. https://countrystudies.us/tajikistan.

Davies, Robert William. *The Socialist Offensive: The Collectivization of Soviet Agriculture, 1929–1930*. Cambridge, MA: Harvard University Press, 1980.

DeHaan, Heather. "Engendering a People: Soviet Women and Socialist Rebirth in Russia." *Canadian Slavonic Papers* 41, nos. 3–4 (September–December 1999): 431–55. https://doi.org/10.1080/00085006.1999.11092228.

D'Encausse, Helene. *The Great Challenge: Nationalities and the Bolshevik State, 1917–1930*. New York: Holmes & Meier, 1992.

Dienes, Leslie. *Soviet Asia: Economic Development and National Policy Choices*. Boulder, CO: Westview Press, 1987. Cited in Patnaik, *Perestroika and Women Labour Force*, 87.

Direnberger, Lucia. "Representations of Armed Women in Soviet and Post
-Soviet Tajikistan: Describing and Restricting Women's Agency." *Journal of
Power Institutions in Post-Soviet Societies*, no. 17 (2016). https://doi.org/10
.4000/pipss.4249.

Dodge, Norton T. *Women in the Soviet Economy: Their Role in Economic,
Scientific, and Technical Development*. Baltimore, MD: John Hopkins Press,
1966.

Dooley, Amelia Kathryn. "Selling Socialism, Consuming Difference: Ethnicity
and Consumer Culture in Soviet Central Asia, 1945–1985." PhD diss.,
Harvard University, 2016.

Dudoignon, Stéphane A., and Christian Noack, eds. *Allah's Kolkhozes:
Migration, De-Stalinisation, Privatisation and the New Muslim
Congregations in the Soviet Realm (1950s–2000s)*. Berlin: Klaus Schwarz
Verlag, 2011.

Dunham, Vera S. *In Stalin's Time: Middleclass Values in Soviet Fiction*.
Cambridge: Cambridge University Press, 1976.

Dunn, Stephen Porter, and Ethel Dunn. *The Study of the Soviet Family in
the USSR and in the West*. Columbus, OH: American Association for the
Advancement of Slavic Studies, 1977.

During, Jean, and Sultonali Khudoberdiev. *La voix du chamane: Étude sur
Baxshi Tadjiks et Ouzbeks* [The Shaman's Voice: A Study of Bakshi Tajiks
and Uzbeks]. Paris: L'Harmattan-IFEAC, 2007. Cited in Tasar, Soviet and
Muslim, 21.

Ecevit, Yildiz. "Shop Floor Control: The Ideological Construction of Turkish
Women Factory Workers." In *Working Women: International Perspectives on
Labour and Gender Ideology*, edited by Nanneke Redclift and M. Thea Sinclair,
55–76. London: Routledge, 1991.

Eden, Jeff. *God Save the USSR: Soviet Muslims and the Second World War*. New
York: Oxford University Press, 2021.

Edgar, Adrienne. "Bolshevism, Patriarchy, and the Nation: The Soviet
'Emancipation' of Muslim Women in Pan-Islamic Perspective." *Slavic
Review* 65, no. 2 (Summer 2006): 252–72. https://doi.org/10.2307/4148592.

– *Intermarriage and the Friendship of Peoples: Ethnic Mixing in Soviet Central Asia*.
Ithaca, NY: Cornell University Press, 2021.

– "Nationality Policy and National Identity: The Turkmen Soviet Socialist
Republic, 1924–29." *Journal of Central Asian Studies* 1, no. 2 (Spring
/Summer 1997): 2–20. Cited in Edgar, "Bolshevism, Patriarchy, and the
Nation," 271.

– *Tribal Nation: The Making of Soviet Turkmenistan*. Princeton, NJ: Princeton
University Press, 2004.

Einhorn, Barbara. *Cinderella Goes to Market: Citizenship, Gender, and Women's
Movements in East Central Europe*. London: Verso, 1993.

El-Feki, Shereen. *Sex and the Citadel: Intimate Life in a Changing Arab World*. New York: Pantheon Books, 2013.

Eltahawy, Mona. *Headscarves and Hymens: Why the Middle East Needs a Sexual Revolution*. New York: Farrar, Straus and Giroux, 2015.

Epkenhans, Tim. *The Origins of the Civil War in Tajikistan: Nationalism, Islamism, and Violent Conflict in Post-Soviet Space*. Lanham, MD: Lexington Books, 2016.

Ergasheva, M. "Challenges for Women in a Changing Uzbekistan." Unpublished research paper, University of New York, 1997. Cited in Corcoran-Nantes, *Lost Voices*, 50.

– "Rural Central Asia and Women's Position." *IREX Papers*. Cited in Corcoran-Nantes, Lost Voices, 88.

Ersanli-Behar, Busra. *Iktidar ve Tarih: Turkiye'de "Resmi Tarih" Tezinin Olusumu (1929–1937)* [Power and History: The Formation of the "Official History" Thesis in Turkey]. Istanbul: AFA Yayınları, 1992. Cited in Khalid, "Backwardness," 249.

Faizulloev, Muhiddin. "Mahalla in Northern Tajikistan." In Roche, *Family in Central Asia*, 53–83.

Falkingham, Jane. "Women and Gender Relations in Tajikistan." Country Briefing Paper, Asi3an Development Bank, April 2000. https://www.adb.org/sites/default/files/institutional-document/32601/women-tajikistan.pdf.

Fathi, Habiba. *Femmes d'autorité dans l'Asie centrale contemporaine. Quête des ancêtres et recompositions identitaires dans l'islam postsoviétique* [Women in Authority in Contemporary Central Asia: The Quest for Ancestors and Recompositions of Identity in Post-Soviet Islam]. Paris: Maisonneuve & Larose, 2004. Cited in Tasar, *Soviet and Muslim*, 21.

– "Gender, Islam, and Social Change in Uzbekistan." *Central Asian Survey* 25, no. 3 (2006): 303–17. https://doi.org/10.1080/02634930601022575.

Filtzer, Donald. *Soviet Workers and De-Stalinization: The Consolidation of the Modern System of Soviet Production Relations, 1953–1964*. Cambridge: Cambridge University Press, 1992.

– "Women Workers in the Khrushchev Era." In Ilič, Reid, and Attwood, *Women in the Khrushchev Era*, 29–51.

Fitzpatrick, Sheila. "Middle-Class Values and Soviet Life in the 1930s." In *Soviet Society and Culture: Essays in Honor of Vera S. Dunham*, edited by Terry L. Thompson and Richard Sheldon, 20–38. Boulder, CO: Westview Press, 1988.

– *Stalin's Peasants: Resistance and Survival in the Russian Village after Collectivization*. New York: Oxford University Press, 1996.

Fleischmann, Ellen L. "The Other 'Awakening': The Emergence of Women's Movements in the Modern Middle East, 1900–1940." In *A Social History of Women and Gender in the Modern Middle East*, edited by Margaret L. Meriwether and Judith E. Tucker, 89–139. Boulder, CO: Westview Press, 1999.

Florin, Moritz. "The Many Ways of Being Soviet: Urban Elites, People's Friendship, and Ethnic Diversity in Postwar Soviet Frunze." *Ab Imperio*, no. 4 (2018): 147–70. https://doi.org/10.1353/imp.2018.0096.

Fuqua, Michelle. *The Politics of the Domestic Sphere: The Zhenotdely, Women's Liberation, and the Search for a Novyi Byt in Early Soviet Russia*. Seattle: University of Washington, Henry M. Jackson School of International Studies, 1996.

G.A. "Semia i brak v SSSR i v kapitalisticheskikh stranakh" [Marriage and the Family in the USSR and in Capitalist States]. *Sovietskaia iustitsiia*, no. 2 (1937): 29–33. Cited in Goldman, Women, the State and Revolution, 343.

Geiger, H. Grant. *The Family in Soviet Russia*. Cambridge, MA: Harvard University Press, 1968.

Gerstenzang, James, and Lisa Getter. "Laura Bush Addresses State of Afghan Women." *Los Angeles Times*, 18 November 2001. https://www.latimes.com /archives/la-xpm-2001-nov-18-mn-5602-story.html.

Ghodsee, Kristen. *Muslim Lives in Eastern Europe: Gender, Ethnicity, and the Transformation of Islam in Postsocialist Bulgaria*. Princeton, NJ: Princeton University Press, 2010.

– *Second World, Second Sex: Socialist Women's Activism and Global Solidarity during the Cold War*. Durham, NC: Duke University Press, 2019.

G'ilozquova, Yelena [Elena Glazkova]. "Ochilgan o'zbek xotin-qizlariga ko'makga" [Help for Uzbek Women Who Have Unveiled]. *Yangi yo'l*, no. 7 (1927): 5. Cited in Khalid, Making Uzbekistan, 358.

Goldman, Wendy Z. *Women at the Gates: Gender and Industry in Stalin's Russia*. Cambridge: Cambridge University Press, 2002.

– *Women, the State and Revolution: Soviet Family Policy and Social Life, 1917–1936*. Cambridge: Cambridge University Press, 1993.

Grehan, James. *Twilight of the Saints: Everyday Religion in Ottoman Syria and Palestine*. Oxford: Oxford University Press, 2014.

Grossman, Joan Delaney. "Khrushchev's Anti-religious Policy and the Campaign of 1954." *Soviet Studies* 24, no. 3 (January 1973): 374–86. https://doi.org/10.1080/09668137308410870.

Guboglo, Mikhail Nikolaevich. *Sovremennee ethnoiazykovye protsessy v SSSR: Osnovnye faktory i tendentsii razvitiia natsionalno-russkogo dvuiazychiia* [Contemporary Ethno-linguistic Processes in the USSR: Key Factors and Development Trends in Ethnic Russian Bilingualism]. Moscow: Izd-vo Nauka, 1984.

Hanson, Philip. *Advertising and Socialism: The Nature and Extent of Consumer Advertising in the Soviet Union, Poland, Hungary and Yugoslavia.*

Basingstoke: Palgrave Macmillan, 1974. Cited in Reid, "Women in the Home," 165.

Heer, David M., and Judith Bryden. "Family Allowances and Population Policy in the USSR." *Journal of Marriage and the Family* 28, no. 4 (1966): 514–19. Cited in Kandiyoti, "Politics of Gender," 607.

Heitlinger, Alena. *Women and State Socialism: Sex Inequality in the Soviet Union and Czechoslovakia*. Montreal: McGill-Queen's University Press, 1979.

Hellbeck, Jochen. *Revolution on My Mind: Writing a Diary under Stalin*. Cambridge, MA: Harvard University Press, 2006.

Heyat, Farideh. *Azeri Women in Transition: Women in Soviet and Post-Soviet Azerbaijan*. London: Routledge Curzon, 2002.

Hodnett, Grey. "Technology and Social Change in Soviet Central Asia: The Politics of Cotton Growing." In *Soviet Politics and Society in the 1970s*, edited by Henry W. Morton and Rudolf L. Tokes, 60–117. New York: Free Press, 1974.

Hoffmann, L. David. "Mothers in the Motherland: Stalinist Pronatalism in Its Pan-European Context." *Journal of Social History* 34, no. 1 (Autumn 2000): 35–54. https://doi.org/10.1353/jsh.2000.0108.

– *Stalinist Values: The Cultural Norms of Soviet Modernity, 1917–1941*. Ithaca, NY: Cornell University Press, 2003.

Holland, Barbara, ed. *Soviet Sisterhood*. Bloomington: Indiana University Press, 1985.

Humphrey, Caroline. *Karl Marx Collective: Economy, Society and Religion in a Siberian Collective Farm*. Cambridge: Cambridge University Press, 1983.

Igmen, Ali. *Speaking Soviet with an Accent: Culture and Power in Kyrgyzstan*. Pittsburgh, PA: University of Pittsburgh Press, 2012.

Ilbert, Ganna. *Klara Tsetkin*. Translated by A. Shtekli. Moscow, 1958. Cited in Stites, *Women's Liberation Movement*, 340.

Ilič, Melanie. Introduction to Ilič, *Women in the Stalin Era*, 1–8.

– "What Did Women Want? Khrushchev and the Revival of the *Zhensovety*." In *Soviet State and Society under Nikita Khrushchev*, edited by Melanie Ilič and Jeremy Smith, 104–21. London: Routledge, 2009.

– "Women in the Khrushchev Era: An Overview." In Ilič, Reid, and Attwood, *Women in the Khrushchev Era*, 5–28.

–, ed. *Women in the Stalin Era*. London: Palgrave Macmillan, 2001.

Ilič, Melanie, Susan E. Reid, and Lynne Attwood, eds. *Women in the Khrushchev Era*. London: Palgrave Macmillan, 2004.

Islamov, S. *Sem'ia i byt* [Family and Life]. Dushanbe: Donish, 1988. Cited in Tett. "Ambiguous Alliances," 65.

Jancar, Barbara Wolfe. *Women under Communism*. Baltimore, MD: Johns Hopkins University Press, 1978.

Jones, Ellen, and Fred Grupp. *Modernization, Value Change, and Fertility in the Soviet Union*. Cambridge: Cambridge University Press, 1987.

Joseph, Suad. "Brother/Sister Relationships: Connectivity, Love, and Power in the Reproduction of Patriarchy in Lebanon." *American Ethnologist* 21, no. 1 (February 1994): 50–73. https://doi.org/10.1525/ae.1994.21.1.02a00030.

Juviler, Peter H. "Women and Sex in Soviet Law." In *Women in Russia*, edited by Dorothy Atkinson, Alexander Dallin, and Gail Warshofsky Lapidus, 243–65. Stanford: Stanford University Press, 1977.

Kaiser, Robert J. "Social Mobilization in Soviet Central Asia." In Lewis, *Geographic Perspectives*, 251–77.

Kalinovsky, Artemy M. *Laboratory of Socialist Development: Cold War Politics and Decolonization in Soviet Tajikistan*. Ithaca, NY: Cornell University Press, 2016.

Kalinovsky, Artemy M., and Isaac Scarborough. "The Oil Lamp and the Electric Light: Progress, Time, and Nation in Central Asian Memoirs of the Soviet Era." *Kritika* 22, no. 1 (Winter 2021): 107–36. https://doi.org/10.1353/kri.2021.0004.

Kallander, Amy Aisen. *Tunisia's Modern Woman: Nation-Building and State Feminism in the Global 1960s*. Cambridge: University of Cambridge, 2021.

Kamp, Marianne. *The New Woman in Uzbekistan: Islam, Modernity, and Unveiling under Communism*. Seattle: University of Washington Press, 2006.

– "Unveiling Uzbek Women: Liberation, Representation and Discourse, 1906–1929." PhD diss., University of Chicago, 1998.

– "Women-Initiated Unveiling: State-Led Campaigns in Uzbekistan and Azerbaijan." In Cronin, *Anti-veiling Campaigns*, 205–28.

Kandiyoti, Deniz. "Bargaining with Patriarchy." *Gender & Society* 2, no. 3 (September 1988): 274–89. https://doi.org/10.1177/089124388002003004.

– "Emancipated but Unliberated? Reflections on the Turkish Case." *Feminist Studies* 13, no. 2 (Summer 1987): 317–38. https://doi.org/10.2307/3177804.

– "The Politics of Gender and the Soviet Paradox: Neither Colonized, nor Modern?" *Central Asian Survey* 26, no. 4 (2007): 601–23. https://doi.org/10.1080/02634930802018521.

– "Sex Roles and Social Change: A Comparative Appraisal of Turkey's Women." In *Women and National Development: The Complexities of Change*, edited by Wellesley Editorial Committee, 57–73. Chicago: University of Chicago Press, 1977.

– "Urban Change and Women's Roles in Turkey: An Overview and Evaluation." In *Sex Roles, Family and Community in Turkey*, edited by Çiğdem Kâğitçibaşi, 101–21. Bloomington: Indiana University Press, 1982.

– "Women and the Turkish State: Political Actors or Symbolic Pawns?" In *Women-Nation-State*, edited by Nira Yuval-Davis and Floya Anthias, 126–49. London: Palgrave, 1988. Cited in Khalid, *Making Uzbekistan*, 198.

–, ed. *Women, Islam and the State*. London: Macmillan, 1991.

Kasimov, Mazbut. "Nizoramo Zaripova: 'Ia proshu materei vospitat v detiakh trudoliubie i prilezhnost v uchebe'" [Nizoramo Zaripova: "I Ask Mothers to Educate Their Children to Be Industrious and Diligent in Their Studies"]. *Dialog.tj*, 13 March 2016. https://www.dialog.tj/news/nizoramo-zaripova -ya-proshu-materej-vospitat-v-detyakh-trudolyubie-i-prilezhnost-v-uchebe. Cited in Kalinovsky and Scarborough, "Oil Lamp and the Electric Light," 132.

Kassymbekova, Botakoz. *Despite Cultures: Early Soviet Rule in Tajikistan*. Pittsburgh, PA: University of Pittsburgh Press, 2016.

Keddie, Nikki R. *Modern Iran: Roots and Results of Revolution*. New Haven, CT: Yale University Press, 1990.

Keller, Shoshana. "The Puzzle of Manual Harvest in Uzbekistan: Economics, Status and Labour in the Khrushchev Era." *Central Asian Survey* 34, no. 3 (2015): 296–309. https://doi.org/10.1080/02634937.2015.1022037.

– *To Moscow, Not Mecca: The Soviet Campaign against Islam in Central Asia, 1917–1941*. Westport, CT: Praeger, 2001.

– "Trapped between State and Society: Women's Liberation and Islam in Soviet Uzbekistan, 1926–1941." *Journal of Women's History* 10, no. 1 (Spring 1998): 20–44. https://doi.org/10.1353/jowh.2010.0552.

Kelly, Catriona, and Vadim Volkov. "Directed Desires: *Kul'turnost'* and Consumption in Post-Revolutionary Russia." In *Constructing Russian Culture in the Age of Revolution: 1881–1940*, edited by Catriona Kelly and David Shepherd, 291–313. Oxford: Oxford University Press, 1998.

Khalid, Adeeb. "Backwardness and the Quest for Civilization: Early Soviet Central Asia in Comparative Perspective." *Slavic Review* 65 no. 2 (Summer 2006): 231–51. https://doi.org/10.2307/4148591.

– *Central Asia: A New History from the Imperial Conquests to the Present*. Princeton, NJ: Princeton University Press, 2021.

– *Islam after Communism: Religion and Politics in Central Asia*. Berkeley: University of California Press, 2007.

– *Making Uzbekistan: Nation, Empire, and Revolution in the Early USSR*. Ithaca, NY: Cornell University Press, 2015.

– *The Politics of Muslim Cultural Reform: Jadidism in Central Asia*. Berkeley: University of California Press, 1999.

– "A Secular Islam: Nation, State, and Religion in Uzbekistan." *International Journal of Middle East Studies* 35, no. 4 (November 2003): 573–98. https://doi.org/10.1017/s0020743803000242.

Khalikova, S.A. *Zhenshini sovietskogo Tadzhikistana* [The Women of Soviet Tajikistan]. Dushanbe: Donish, 1949.

Kisch, Egon Erwin, and Rita Reil. *Changing Asia*. New York: A.A. Knopf, 1935. Cited in Rakowska-Harmstone, Russia and Nationalism in Central Asia.

Kollontai, Alexandra. *Trud zhenshchiny v evoliutsii khoziaistva* [The Labour of Women in the Evolution of the Economy]. 2nd ed. Moscow, 1928. Cited in Hoffmann, "Mothers in the Motherland," 35.

Konchalovsky, Andrei, and Alexander Lipkov. *The Inner Circle: An Inside View of Soviet Life under Stalin*. Edited and translated by Jamey Gambrell. New York: Newmarket Press, 1991.

Kotkin, Stephen. *Magnetic Mountain: Stalinism as a Civilization*. Berkeley: University of California Press, 1995.

Krylova, Anna. *Soviet Women in Combat: A History of Violence on the Eastern Front*. Cambridge: Cambridge University Press, 2010.

– "Stalinist Identity from the Viewpoint of Gender: Rearing a Generation of Professionally Violent Women-Fighters in 1930s Stalinist Russia." *Gender & History* 16, no. 3 (November 2004): 626–53. https://doi.org/10.1111/j.0953-5233.2004.00359.x.

Lapidus, Gail Warshofsky. *Women in Soviet Society: Equality, Development and Social Change*. Berkeley: University of California Press, 1978.

– *Women, Work, and Family in the Soviet Union*. Armonk, NY: M.E. Sharpe, 1982.

Lewin, Moshe. *Russian Peasants and Soviet Power: A Study of Collectivization*. London: Allen & Unwin, 1968.

Lewis, Robert A., ed. *Geographic Perspectives on Soviet Central Asia*. New York: Routledge, 1992.

Louw, Maria Elisabeth. *Everyday Islam in Post-Soviet Central Asia*. London: Routledge, 2007. Cited in Rasanayagam, Islam in Post-Soviet Uzbekistan, 166.

Lubin, Nancy. *Labor and Nationality in Soviet Central Asia: An Uneasy Comprise*. London: Macmillan, 1984.

Madzhidov, R.M. *Osobennosti formirovaniia naucho-ateisticheskogo mirovozzreniia zhenshin* [Aspects of the Formation of a Scientific-Atheistic World View in Women]. Dushanbe: Donish, 1977.

Makhmudov, M.A. *Semeino-pravovye sredstva obespecheniia stabilnosti braka* [Family Law as a Means to Guarantee Marriage Stability]. Dushanbe: Donish, 1990. Cited in Tett, "Ambiguous Alliances," 111.

Manning, Roberta. "Women in the Soviet Countryside on the Eve of World War II, 1935–1940." In *Russian Peasant Women*, edited by Beatrice Farnsworth and Lynne Viola, 206–35. New York: Oxford University Press, 1992.

Martin, Terry. *The Affirmative Action Empire: Nations and Nationalism in the Soviet Union, 1923–1939*. Ithaca, NY: Cornell University Press, 2001.

Massell, Gregory J. *The Surrogate Proletariat: Moslem Women and Revolutionary Strategies in Soviet Central Asia, 1919–1929*. Princeton, NJ: Princeton University Press, 1974.

McAndrew, Maggie. "Soviet Women's Magazines." In Holland, *Soviet Sisterhood*, 78–115.

McAuley, Alastair. *Women's Work and Wages in the Soviet Union*. London: Allen & Unwin, 1981.

McBrien, Julie. *From Belonging to Belief: Modern Secularisms and the Construction of Religion in Kyrgyzstan*. Pittsburgh, PA: University of Pittsburgh Press, 2017.

Mernissi, Fatima. *Women's Rebellion and Islamic Memory*. Atlantic Highlands, NJ: Zed Books, 1996.

Michaels, Paula A. "Motherhood, Patriotism, and Ethnicity: Soviet Kazakhstan and the 1936 Abortion Ban." *Feminist Studies* 27, no. 2 (Summer 2001): 307–33. https://doi.org/10.2307/3178760.

Moghadam, Valentine M. *Modernizing Women: Gender and Social Change in the Middle East*. 2nd ed. Boulder, CO: Lynne Rienner, 2003.

Neary, Rebecca Balmas. "Mothering Socialist Society: The Wife-Activists' Movement and the Soviet Culture of Daily Life, 1934–41." *Russian Review* 58, no. 3 (July 1999): 396–412. https://doi.org/10.1111/0036-0341.00081.

Nikolaeva, K., and L. Karaseva. *Zhenshchina v boiakh za kommunizm* [Women in the Fight for Communism]. Moscow: Politizdat, 1940. Cited in Clements, "Utopianism of the Zhenotdel," 496.

Northrop, Douglas. "Subaltern Dialogues: Subversion and Resistance in Soviet Uzbek Family Law." *Slavic Review* 60, no. 1 (2001): 115–39. Cited in Kamp, New Woman in Uzbekistan, 72.

– *Veiled Empire: Gender and Power in Stalinist Central Asia*. Ithaca, NY: Cornell University Press, 2004. Cited in Corcoran-Nantes, *Lost Voices*, 42.

Nourzhanov, Kirill, and Christian Bleuer. *Tajikistan: A Political and Social History*. Canberra: ANUE Press, 2013.

Paert, Irina. "Demystifying the Heavens: Women, Religion and Khrushchev's Anti-religious Campaign, 1954–64." In Ilič, Reid, and Attwood, *Women in the Khrushchev Era*, 203–21.

Palvanova, Bibi. *Emantsipatsiia musulmanki: Opiat raskreposhcheniia zhenshchiny sovestkogo vostoka* [The Emancipation of Muslim Women: The Further Liberation of Women in the Soviet East]. Moscow: Nauka, 1982. Cited in Kamp, New Woman in Uzbekistan, 69.

Park, Alexander G. *Bolshevism in Turkestan, 1917–1927*. New York: Columbia University Press, 1957.

Patnaik, Ajay. *Perestroika and Women Labour Force in Soviet Central Asia*. New Delhi: New Literature, 1989.

– "Women in Uzbekistan." *Central Asian Review* 16, no. 1 (1968): 42. Cited in Patnaik, *Perestroika and Women Labour Force*, 43.

Peshkova, Svetlana. "Otinchalar in the Ferghana Valley: Islam, Gender and Power." PhD diss., Syracuse University, 2006.

Pipes, Richard. *The Formation of the Soviet Union: Communism and Nationalism, 1917–1923*. Cambridge, MA: Harvard University Press, 1964.

Pismannik, M.G. *Otnoshenie religii k zhenshchine* [The Attitude of Religion towards Women]. Moscow: Znanie, 1964. Cited in Paert, "Demystifying the Heavens," 216.

Poliakov, Sergei P. *Everyday Islam: Religion and Tradition in Rural Central Asia.* Edited by Martha Brill Olcott. New York: M.E. Sharpe, 1992.

Pomfret, Richard. "State-Directed Diffusion of Technology: The Mechanization of Cotton Harvesting in Soviet Central Asia." *Journal of Economic History* 62, no. 1 (2002): 170–88.

Pravda stavshaia legendoi [The Truth That Became a Legend]. Moscow, 1969. Cited in Stites, *Women's Liberation Movement*, 340.

Racioppi, Linda, and Katherine O'Sullivan See. "Organizing Women before and after the Fall: Women's Politics in the Soviet Union and Post-Soviet Russia." *Signs* 20, no. 4 (Summer 1995): 818–50. https://doi.org/10.1086 /495023. Cited in Corcoran-Nantes, *Lost Voices*, 14.

Rahim, Hosiyat. "Xotin-qizlar Bilim Yurtiga ta'rixi bir qarash" [One Historical Look at Educational Institutions for Women and Girls]. *Yangi Yo'l*, no. 10 (1926): 5–8. Cited in Kamp, New Woman in Uzbekistan, 69.

Rakowska-Harmstone, Teresa. *Russia and Nationalism in Central Asia: The Case of Tadzhikistan*. Baltimore, MD: Johns Hopkins Press, 1970.

Rasanayagam, Johan. *Islam in Post-Soviet Uzbekistan: The Morality of Experience.* Cambridge: Cambridge University Press, 2011.

Reid, Susan E. "All Stalin's Women: Gender and Power in Soviet Art of the 1930s." *Slavic Review* 57, no. 1 (Spring 1998): 133–73. https://doi.org/10 .2307/2502056.

– "Cold War in the Kitchen: Gender and the De-Stalinization of Consumer Taste in the Soviet Union under Khrushchev." *Slavic Review* 61, no. 2 (Summer 2002): 211–52.

– "Women in the Home." In Ilič, Reid, and Attwood, *Women in the Khrushchev Era*, 149–76.

Reikhel, M. "Voprosy semeinogo prava i proekt grazhdanskogo kodeksa SSSR" [Questions of Family Law and Draft Civil Code for the USSR]. *Problemy sotsialisticheskogo prava*, no. 2 (1939): 84–5. Cited in Goldman, Women, the State and Revolution, 343.

Roberts, Flora J. "Old Elites under Communism: Soviet Rule in Leninobod." PhD diss., University of Chicago, 2016.

Roche, Sophie, ed. *The Family in Central Asia: New Perspectives.* Berlin: Klaus Schwarz Verlag, 2017.

Ro'i, Yaacov. *Islam in the Soviet Union: From the Second World War to Gorbachev.* New York: Columbia University Press, 2000. Cited in Rasanayagam, *Islam in Post-Soviet Uzbekistan*, 91.

– "Secularism of Islam and the USSR's Muslim Areas." In *Muslim Eurasia: Conflicting Legacies*, edited by Yaacov Ro'i, 5–21. London: Frank Cass, 1995.

Rorlich, Azade-Ayse. "Islam and Atheism: Dynamic Tension in Soviet Central Asia in Soviet Central Asia." In *Soviet Central Asia: The Failed Transformation*, edited by William Fierman. Boulder, CO: Westview Press, 1991. Cited in Rasanayagam, *Islam in Post-Soviet Uzbekistan*, 81.

Rowland, Richard H. "Demographic Trends in Soviet Central Asia and Southern Kazakhstan." In Lewis, *Geographic Perspectives*, 222–48.

Roy, Olivier. *The New Central Asia: The Creation of Nations*. London: I.B. Tauris, 2000. Cited in Kandiyoti, "Politics of Gender," 608.

Rumer, Boris Z. *Soviet Central Asia: A Tragic Experiment*. Boston, MA: Unwin Hyman, 1989.

Ryndina, A.A., and V.V. Kopeiko. *Reshaet zhensoviet* [The *zhensoviet* Decides]. Moscow: Moskovskii rabochii, 1987.

Sacks, Michael Paul. *Work and Equality in Soviet Society: The Division of Labor by Age, Gender, and Nationality*. New York: Praeger, 1982.

– "Work Force Composition, Patriarchy, and Social Change." In Lewis, *Geographic Perspectives*, 181–205.

Sedghi, Hamideh. *Women and Politics in Iran: Veiling, Unveiling, and Reveiling*. Cambridge: Cambridge University Press, 2007.

Seniavskii, S.L. *Rost rabochego klassa SSSR (1951–1965)* [The Growth of the Working Class in the USSR (1951–65)]. Moscow, 1966. Cited in Filtzer, "Women Workers," 32.

Shahrani, M. Narif. "Islam and the Political Culture of 'Scientific Atheism' in Post-Soviet Central Asia: Future Predicaments." In *The Politics of Religion in Russia and the New States of Eurasia*, edited by Michael Bourdeaux, 273–92. New York: M.E. Sharpe, 1995. Cited in Rasanayagam, *Islam in Post-Soviet Uzbekistan*, 79.

Shoeberlein-Engel, John Samuel. "Identity in Central Asia: Construction and Contention in the Conceptions of 'Ozbek,' 'Tajik,' 'Muslim,' 'Samarquandi' and Other Groups." PhD diss., Harvard University, 1994.

Shulman, Elena. *Stalinism on the Frontier of Empire: Women and State Formation in the Soviet Far East*. Cambridge: Cambridge University Press, 2008.

Siegelbaum, Lewis. "The Double Burden." *Seventeen Moments in Soviet History*, [2012]. https://soviethistory.msu.edu/1968-2/the-double-burden/.

[Sredazburo, Zhenotdel]. *Besh yil* [Five Years]. Moscow, 1925. Cited in Khalid, Making Uzbekistan, 204.

Stalin, Iosif. *Dvenadtsatyi sezd RKP/b/. 17-25 aprelia 1923 goda. Stenograficheskii otchet* [The Twelfth Congress of the Russian Communist Party, 17–25 April 1923: Verbatim Report]. Moscow, 1968. Cited in Martin, *Affirmative Action Empire*, 12.

– *Marksizm i natsionalno-kolonialnyi vopros* [Marxism and the National-Colonial Question]. Moscow, 1934. Cited in Martin, Affirmative Action Empire, 12.
– *Tainy natsionalnoi politiki TsK RKP, Chetvertoe soveshchanie TsK RKP s otvetstvennymi rabotnikami natsionalnykh respublik i oblastei v g. Moskve, 9-12 iiunia 1923 g. Stenograficheskii otchet* [Secrets of the National Policy of the Central Committee of the Russian Communist Party: The Fourth Meeting of the Central Committee of the Russian Communist Party with Responsible Workers of the National Republics and *oblasti* in Moscow, 9–12 June 1923. Verbatim Report]. Moscow, 1992. Cited in Martin, *Affirmative Action Empire*, 12.

Stavrakis, Bette. "Women and the Communist Party in the Soviet Union, 1918–1935." PhD diss., Western Reserve University, 1961. Cited in Stites, Women's Liberation Movement, 340.

Stites, Richard. *The Women's Liberation Movement in Russia: Feminism, Nihilism, and Bolshevism, 1860–1930*. Princeton, NJ: Princeton University Press, 1978.

Stone, Andrew B. "'Overcoming Peasant Backwardness': The Khrushchev Antireligious Campaign and the Rural Soviet Union." *Russian Review* 67, no. 2 (April 2008): 296–320. https://doi.org/10.1111/j.1467-9434.2008.00485.x.

Stronski, Paul. *Tashkent: Forging a Soviet City, 1930–1966*. Pittsburgh, PA: University of Pittsburgh Press, 2010.

"Summary of XXI (Extraordinary) Party Congress." *Soviet Studies* 11, no. 1 (1959): 90. Cited in Reid, "Women in the Home," 165.

Taagepeva, Rein. "National Differences within Soviet Demographic Trends." *Soviet Studies* 20, no. 4 (1969): 478–89. Cited in Kandiyoti, "Politics of Gender," 607.

Tasar, Eren. *Soviet and Muslim: The Institutionalization of Islam in Central Asia, 1943–1991*. New York: Oxford University Press, 2017.
– "Soviet Policies toward Islam: Domestic and International Considerations." In *Religion and the Cold War: A Global Perspective*, edited by Philip E. Muehlenbeck, 158–81. Nashville, TN: Vanderbilt University Press, 2012.

Taubman, William. *Khrushchev: The Man and His Era*. New York: Norton, 2003.

Tekeli, Sirin, ed. *Women in Modern Turkish Society: A Reader*. London: Zed Books, 1995. Cited in Fleischmann, "Other Awakening," 120.

Tett, Gillian. "Ambiguous Alliances: Marriage and Identity in a Muslim Village in Soviet Tajikistan." PhD diss., University of Cambridge, 1996.
– "'Guardians of the Faith?': Gender and Religion in an (Ex) Soviet Tajik Village." In *Muslim Women's Choices: Religious Belief and Social Reality*, edited by Camillia Fawzi El-Solh and Judy Mabro, 128–51. London: Routledge, 1994.

Tignor, Robert. *Modernization and British Colonial Rule in Egypt, 1882–1914.* Princeton, NJ: Princeton University Press, 1966.

Timasheff, Nicholas S. *The Great Retreat: The Growth and Decline of Communism in Russia.* New York: E.P. Dutton, 1946.

Tokhtakhodjaeva, Marfua. *Between the Slogans of Communism and the Laws of Islam.* Translated by Sufian Aslam. Edited by Cassandra Balchin. Lahore, Pakistan: Shirkat Gah Women's Resource Centre, 1995.

Tokhtakhodjaeva, Marfua, and Elmira Turgumbekova. *The Daughters of Amazons: Voices from Central Asia.* Lahore, Pakistan: Shirkat Gah Women's Resource Centre, 1996.

Tolmacheva, Marina. "The Muslim Woman and Atheism in Soviet Central Asia." *Islamic Studies* 33, nos. 2/3 (Summer/Autumn 1994): 183–201.

– "The Muslim Woman in Soviet Central Asia." *Central Asian Survey* 12, no. 4 (1993): 531–48. https://doi.org/10.1080/02634939308400836.

"Urbanization." In *Tajikistan: A Country Study.* Washington, DC: Federal Research Division of the Library of Congress, 1996. http://www.country-data.com/cgi-bin/query/r-13623.html.

Volfson, S. "Semia v sotsialisticheskom gosudarstve" [The Family in the Socialist State]. *Problemy sotsialisticheskogo prava,* no. 6 (1939): 39, 43. Cited in Goldman, *Women, the State and Revolution,* 343.

Wheeler, Geoffrey. *The Modern History of Central Asia.* New York: Praeger, 1964.

White, Jenny B. "State Feminism, Modernization, and the Turkish Republican Woman." *NWSA Journal* 15, no. 3 (Autumn 2003): 145–59.

Whitney, Thomas P., ed. *Khrushchev Speaks: Selected Speeches, Articles, and Press Conferences, 1949–1961.* Ann Arbor: University of Michigan Press, 1963. Cited in Taubman, *Khrushchev,* 228–30.

Wilson, Elizabeth. *Women and the Welfare State.* London: Tavistock, 1977. Cited in Reid, "Women in the Home," 156.

Wood, Elizabeth A. *The Baba and the Comrade: Gender and Politics in Revolutionary Russia.* Bloomington: Indiana University Press, 2001. Cited in Ghodsee, *Second World, Second Sex,* 40.

Youseff, Nadia Haggag. *Women and Work in Developing Societies.* Berkeley: University of California Institute of International Studies, 1974.

Ziuzin, D. "Prichiny nizkoi mobilnosti korennogo naseleniia respublik Srednei Azii" [The Causes of the Low Mobility of the Indigenous Population of the Central Asian Republics]. *Sotsiologicheskie issledovaniia,* no. 1 (1983): 109–17. Cited in Ata-Mirzayev and Kayumov, "Demography of Soviet Central Asia," 244.

Index

Note: Italicized page numbers indicate illustrative material and photographs.

bride payments (*kalym / kiit*; *cont.*)
regime and, 4, 10; in Tajikistan, 130
Browning, Genia, 103, 115, 126
Buchli, Victor, 114
Buckley, Mary, 176n36
Bulgaria, 9, 154

censuses, 71
Chatterjee, Choi, 55
child marriage, 4, 10, 25, 29–30, 39,
64, 82–3, 130, 142
children: childcare, 83, 84, 115; cost
of raising, 70–1; education of, 92;
infant mortality rates, 70; labour of,
65, 76; names, 176n29
circumcision, 134
clan and kinship, 7, 68, 92
clothing: for athletics, 127; atlas
silk, 46; ironed shirts, 103; for
mourning, 186n74; policing of
choices, 154; scarves, 40, 100, 149;
shortness of shorts, 45; sleeveless,
46; Soviet influences on, 45; from
Tajik- to European-style, 3, 10,
100–1, 122; trousers, 46, 86; from
veils to headscarves, 149. *See also*
veil wearing and unveiling
collective farming: heroines of, 57;
labour conditions, 67; leadership,
59; men and, 60, 87, 135; private
plots for workers, 85; state's
creation of, 33, 48, 64; women's
work and, 42, 87–8, 151; workers'
documents, 67; *zhensoviety* and, 122
collectivity: agriculture and, 167n59;
countryside and, 11, 43, 64;
vs. individuality, 149; *mahalla*
communal divisions, 65
communism: indigenous peoples
and, 34; organizations, 32–3;
patriarchal practices and, 137;
propaganda, 26; vs. religion, 16;

Soviet press and, 18; against Soviet
reforms, 24
Communist Party Archive of the
Tajik Republic (Presidential
Archive), 17
consciousness-raising movements,
43–7
conservatism, 79
consumption habits, 123
cotton farming: children's
involvement in, 65, 74–6, 75,
76; export (of cotton), 170n17;
photographs of farmers, 44;
production expansion, 68;
production quotas, 44, 72; and
women's labour, 54, 55, 56, 57–8
countryside: activism in, 125–6;
clothing in, 123; development of (in
Tajikistan), 66; education in, 71–6;
labour revitalizing in, 138; Muslim
culture in, 132, 148; patriarchal
practices in, 58, 60; patriarchy in,
58, 59–60, 65; polygamy in, 58;
religious practices in, 135; Soviet
culture in, 113; Sovietization of,
113, 126. *See also* rural areas; rural
women and girls

dancing, 46
DeHaan, Heather, 165n15
dekulakization, 52, 167n57, 167n59
demographics, sources on, 18
diaries, 43
Dienes, Leslie, 170n17
divorce, 24, 26, 30, 37–9, 41
Dooley, Kathryn, 123
double burden, 15, 112, 120, 187n2
Dudoignon, Stephane A., 165n7
Dunham, Vera, 124
Dushanbe (Stalinabad): childcare
in, 84; education in, 95–6; ethnic
groups in, 112, 178n5; individuals

connected to, 147; industrialization
in, 64; jobs in, 88, 99, 128; life in,
12, 31; parades in, 50; population
of, 69, 73; rural parts of, 134;
Zaripova's life in, 20, 51; Zhenotdel
in, 29; *zhensoviety* and, 117. *See also*
Stalinabad

Ecevit, Yildiz, 159n54
education: birth rate and, 63; in
countryside, 71–6; dropout rates,
60–1; as ending inequality, 28;
free, 64; Khrushchev government
and, 122–3; mandated, 3, 7, 40; of
Muslim women, 10, 28, 42, 79–80;
orphanages and boarding schools,
92; public, 14; quality of, 64–5;
reforms, 14; shame and, 152; in
Tajikistan, 4, 10, 49, 60–1, 64, 71,
72–3, 87, 98; teachers, 72; in urban
areas, 81; of urban women, 152,
153; Zhenotdel and, 30
emancipation as term, 20
employment: of urban women, 94;
veil wearing and, 10, 138
entertainment, 127
Epkenhans, Tim, 17
Erkaeva, Aziza, 74, 80–1
Europeanization, 123

family: as bourgeois institution, 41;
indigenous, 78; laws regarding, 4,
32, 39; reforms related to, 4, 26, 37; in
rural Tajikistan, 70–1; social values
regarding, 47–8; structures, 47–8, 59,
63, 65, 70–1, 74, 83, 89, 92, 95
Family, Marriage, and Child Support
code, 37
farming. *See* collective farming;
cotton farming
femininity, 103, 108, 109
feminism, state, 6, 9–10, 16, 115

fertility, 47, 83
feudalism: abolition of, 8, 27;
feudal-boy traditions, 59, 61,
112, 122, 130, 136, 138, 139; and
marriage, 60; mentality, 141; Tajik
heritage and, 149
food shortages, 34
funerals, 142

Gafarova, M., 122, 147
Gafurov, Bobodzhon, 52
Gangelieva, Fazia, 76
gender: changing perceptions
of, 11, 42–3, 62; and education
segregation, 71; equality, 25–7, 38,
54, 84, 131; labour division and, 68;
literature on, 91; Marxist theory
and, 11; reforms, 7–8, 25–6, 88, 151;
roles, 5, 41, 43, 65, 74, 91, 105, 120,
124–5; in rural areas, 71; in Soviet
society, 90–1; state's agenda and,
11; urbanization and, 12–16
Ghodsee, Kristen, 9, 154
gorkom, 59, 60, 101, 106, 168n65
government work, 25, 49
Great Retreat, 41, 43, 164n3
Grehan, James, 133
Grupp, Fred, 13, 63, 84
Gufranova, Habiba, 93
Gufranova, H.G., 123–4

Halbaeva, H., 127
Hamraeva, B., 87–8
healing practices, 143–5, 184n24
Hellbeck, Jochen, 43
Heroine Mother title, 48, 125
heroines, 55–8
Hodnett, Grey, 171n18
Hoffmann, David, 165n16
holidays, 146
homes: cultural capital at, 40;
furnishings, 123–5; shortages of, 67